CHASING THE
DRAGON

CHASING THE DRAGON

DRAGON

HOW TO WIN THE WAR ON DRUGS

DAN ADDARIO

WITH **JON LAND** AND **LINDSAY PRESTON**

POST HILL PRESS

A POST HILL PRESS BOOK

Chasing the Dragon:
How to Win the War on Drugs
© 2019 by Dan Addario with Jon Land and Lindsay Preston
All Rights Reserved

ISBN: 978-1-64293-086-3
ISBN (eBook): 978-1-64293-087-0

Cover art by Cody Corcoran
Interior design and composition by Greg Johnson/Textbook Perfect

Post Hill Press
New York • Nashville
posthillpress.com

Published in the United States of America

For Joy, Daniel, Robert, and Mark
for all that came before
And my wife Donna for all that came after
And a special thanks to the brave agents who lost their lives
fighting this war they continue to wage

CONTENTS

"Selling my soul would be a lot easier if I could just find it."

—Nikki Sixx, *The Heroin Diaries: A Year In the Life of a Shattered Rock Star*

"We are losing the war on drugs."

—President George W. Bush, 2005

PROLOGUE

THE COBRA

The dope went out of Thailand in false tops of hats and false bottoms of suitcases. It went out stuffed in dolls of the children of our GIs taking their families home. It went out tucked into every conceivable cranny and orifice of the human body. It went out in coffins. In twenty three years as a federal narc, I'd seen some pretty mean tricks. But smuggling heroin into the United States in the bodies of GIs killed in Vietnam was the meanest.

I arrived in Bangkok in the autumn of 1974. My assignment was to somehow put my finger into the dike of the Golden Triangle and stop the flow of heroin into the States. I knew that the usual methods—smuggling dope home in furniture, cars, clothes, and kids' playthings—couldn't account for it. Something different was happening. Something horrific.

I first heard about the heroin caper as a rumor, picked up on the mean streets of New York by a Drug Enforcement Administration (DEA) tipster. In my business, you learn that the meaner the rumor, the more likely it's true. I didn't share this tip with the American

1

ambassador or the CIA station chief. I'd learned the best way to keep drug-busting secrets was to keep them from State and the Agency. When it came to stopping narcotics, they often had other—and, in their minds, higher—priorities. From my experience in narcotics enforcement, I can say that if it hadn't been for the CIA or State Department, or both, messing with our operations, we could have reduced by at least half the drugs that entered the US from Southeast Asia and South America.

And maybe if we'd done that, my son would still be alive today.

* * * * *

It was a hot July day in 1993, unusually warm for San Francisco, when I got the call that every parent fears.

"I'm calling for Dan Addario," greeted a female voice.

"Speaking."

"Are you the father of Daniel Addario?"

"Yes. Who is this?"

"The Coroner's Office, sir. I'm afraid I have some bad news."

The rest of her words remain a blur to this day, but not the message they carried: my thirty-four-year-old son had died of a drug overdose, specifically opiates. I remember my heart skipping a beat, then hammering against my rib cage. I remember losing my breath and feeling my stomach sink. I was lucky I was sitting down or I'm pretty sure I would've collapsed.

My son lived in a townhouse condo nestled in the Pleasant Hill suburb of San Francisco, not far away at all from my home in the city proper. This kind of thing wasn't supposed to happen in Pleasant Hill, where the fabric of the American Dream never frayed. My son had always been a good-looking kid; a strapping, athletic six foot two who was then working as a parking manager at Candlestick Park. He'd been talented enough in his younger years to try his hand at acting and scored a bit part in the classic Robert De Niro film *The Deer*

2

Hunter, set during the Vietnam War. I'd been in Vietnam myself two weeks before the country fell to oversee the exodus of my people out of there, right around the time that the film was set. I was a soldier, though I wasn't fighting a conventional war.

I was fighting the war on drugs.

I was retired from the DEA when that call came, just past sixty years old and fully ensconced in the world of San Francisco politics, an apt second act to a twenty-three-year career that had taken me all over the world, where I served on the front lines of a war I was convinced we could win, but never did. I was a decorated veteran of the Korean War, barely out of my teens, when I enrolled at the Philadelphia Police Academy, only to be plucked from my class prior to graduating and made part of an operation that resulted in one of the biggest drug busts in the city's history and launched my career.

In 1971, I was appointed the DEA's regional director for thirteen South American countries, a position from which I coordinated the capture and extradition of Auguste Ricord, the multimillionaire mastermind known to have imported more than 2.5 billion dollars' worth of heroin into the United States alone. Ricord was also famous for being the drug kingpin portrayed in the classic film *The French Connection*, who the hero, played by Gene Hackman, hadn't been able to catch.

In 1974, I became the DEA's regional director for the infamous Golden Triangle, the remote border region in Southeast Asia comprising Thailand, Laos, and Myanmar (formerly Burma). From that position, I helped wipe out a number of heroin labs hidden in the jungles of Thailand and coaxed the deadly Shan Army warlords to destroy the opium crops along the Thai-Burmese border. All this while busting a heroin pipeline that was smuggling vast quantities of heroin into the homeland in the corpses of GIs killed in the Vietnam War.

My success, though, was in spite of the US government, not because of it. Simply stated, we're losing a war we should be winning.

My son Daniel was a casualty of that war. You look at my background, my place on the front lines for a near quarter-century stint at the DEA, and you probably figure that I was the last person in the world likely to lose my own son to the scourge I'd spent the better part of my life fighting. Daniel and the rest of my family had been with me for a four-year stretch during my posting in Bangkok. He attended the International School there, where he excelled at both soccer and volleyball.

My career postings forced us to move a dozen times, no easy thing for any family. While we were in Bangkok in 1974, our black Lab named Smokey was sniffing around the garden when a cry rang out. By the time the gardener responded, a cobra the dog had flushed out of the low grass had strangled him to death. I wanted my family near me, and they wanted to be there, but how do you tell your kids their dog was killed by a snake, a cobra no less? It was just part of the culture shock that became part and parcel of the career I'd chosen.

Smokey's death to a coiling cobra made for an odd and tragic metaphor to Daniel's ultimate passing. His life had been choked off not by a snake but by the proverbial dragon he'd been chasing. I never had any clue, not even a hint or an inkling, that he was doing drugs, much less abusing opiates to such a level. The very thought was inconceivable, the nature of the tragedy exceeded only by its irony. But he'd chased the dragon until it finally killed him, snuffed out his life with all of the unfeeling cruelty of a snake snuffing out our dog's. And I've been chasing a different dragon ever since, a dragon emblematic of the scourge of drugs, particularly opiates, that's killing tens of thousands of people like my son every year.

In 2017 alone, 72,000 Americans lost their lives to overdoses, up 10,000 from the year before and virtually the same number as gun deaths and deaths resulting from car accidents *combined*. According to the website *Science Daily*, the cost of the opiate epidemic in 2016 was estimated to be 78.5 billion dollars in terms of all associated health care costs as well as lost productivity and expenses incurred by the judicial system. In some states—as diverse as Ohio, West Virginia, and New Hampshire—opiate addiction has reached epidemic proportions.

"More than 40 Americans die each day from overdoses involving prescription opioids. Families and communities continue to be devastated by the epidemic of prescription opioid overdoses," Centers for Disease Control and Prevention director Tom Frieden noted in the same article posted on *Science Daily*. "The rising cost of the epidemic is also a tremendous burden for the health care system."

That epidemic claimed the life of my son, but he didn't have to die, and neither did the 64,000 victims who fell in 2016 or the 54,000 lost in 2015 to the war on drugs. Because, contrary to popular belief, we *can* win the war, even though it often seems like we're doing everything we can to lose it. I know, because I've been there. I've sent letters to New Jersey Governor Chris Christie (head of the president's commission on opiate abuse), Attorney General Jeff Sessions, and President Donald Trump himself to advise them of my prescription for winning the war on drugs I've been fighting for over half a century. And I wasn't just a street cop busting a few kids for smoking weed. I was a diplomat and a narcotics attaché at the highest levels, assigned to the very front lines where the war on drugs had broken out. But I never got a real response from anybody, not even lip service in return.

I guess I shouldn't be surprised.

We keep fighting the same battles in the same places. A new administration comes in, makes some progress. Then another administration comes in and tries to reinvent the wheel that is the Drug Enforcement Administration, although the way it revolves is more like a door. Traction gets lost, as the DEA essentially is forced to start from scratch again. When I started, the Drug Enforcement Administration had only 260 agents. Today, the DEA has become this mammoth, labyrinthine organization with so many different layers and agendas that the right hand doesn't always know what the left is doing.

Who's out there to do something about curtailing the actions of pharmaceutical companies overproducing medication so it can be prescribed to people who don't need it? People who get hooked on painkillers often turn to heroin when their prescription spigot is turned off. And heroin, along with its sister drugs, is cheaper and more readily available than ever. Thanks in large part to terrorist activity, opium growing throughout the Middle East has reached record heights, adding to the shipments coming in from Mexico, Thailand, and Afghanistan to create a supply glut that further increases availability while lowering prices.

Like many who abuse drugs, particularly opiates, my son was leading a double life. He died of a lethal combination of cocaine and heroin, the kind of "speedball" that killed the actor John Belushi. Daniel was what's called a "functional" addict, never missing a single day of work. But the more drugs he did, the more he built up a tolerance to them. The more he grew tolerant, the more drugs he needed to ingest to get high until it killed him. Nobody forced Daniel to do it, nobody twisted his arm, and to this day I have no idea how he got hooked. The San Francisco police never found out where the drugs in his system came from or who had sold them to him. But I called in a few favors and Daniel's death went down as a heart attack to spare him the shame and embarrassment of the truth.

Plenty of those who attended his funeral knew that truth, their expressions uniformly blank. Many remained silent because they didn't know what to say, or were afraid to say the wrong thing. The fog was rolling in that day, and I don't remember what I was thinking as I knotted my tie and laced my shoes, probably because I was trying to figure out what else I could have done. And I can still see Daniel the way he looked at the viewing, a slight sewn smile stitched across his face, like he was about to awaken from a peaceful dream instead of paying the price for the nightmare that had consumed his life.

I wanted to reach out and touch him.

But I didn't.

I had this desire to reach out and jostle him, see if he might wake up.

I didn't do that either.

Daniel was anything but a stereotype, the last person you'd think would die of an overdose. And of the 72,000 people who died of opiate overdoses in 2017, plenty were just like my son. People living in great neighborhoods dotted with basketball hoops and BMWs in their driveways, parked alongside SUVs with third-row seating. Pack that vehicle with eight kids and chances are one of them will become addicted to opiates. Maybe he or she will overdose, and maybe he or she won't. Depends on the luck of the cards, I guess.

But here's something that doesn't depend on luck: we can win this war. I have solutions. I've seen what has worked in the past and what will work today. I've watched thirteen different attorneys general and six presidents claim they were going to do something about it, only to have nothing get done. You can't get a politician's attention unless you write a check for a hundred thousand dollars. Otherwise, you get a smile and some lip service. A warm handshake and a plastic photo-op smile. *Hey, we're building a wall,* some of them will say today, even though building a wall won't stop a single ounce of drugs from getting into the country.

Nothing I can do will bring my son back, but I can make it so no more families have to suffer the way I did. That's why I wrote this book. To chart a path forward through the minutia and politics toward devising a strategy to win this war instead of just pretending to try. Politicians and police like to proclaim we're already winning, but trust me when I tell you we're not. We're still chasing our tails.

Speaking of chasing, the origin of the slang phrase "chasing the dragon" actually springs from Hong Kong and refers to inhaling the vapor from a heated drug cocktail comprising morphine, heroin, opium, or oxycodone. The "chasing" occurs as the addict gingerly keeps the liquid moving in order to keep it from overheating and burning up too quickly, often on a heat-conducting material such as aluminum foil. The moving smoke is "chased" with a tube through which the user inhales. In more recent times, the phrase has come to be used as a metaphor for an addict's constant pursuit of the feelings of their first high. The "dragon," being mythical, represents a goal that can never be achieved, because it doesn't exist.

But I know how to catch the metaphorical dragon I've been chasing for the better part of my life, a dragon capable of snuffing out life with the ease of that cobra killing our dog in Thailand. And my task now, the reason I'm writing this book, is to get others to listen. Many of those others, like you maybe, have kids of their own, in which case they fear, more than anything, the kind of call I got on July 19, 1993. A disembodied voice you'll never hear again telling you something that's going to change your life forever.

I don't want you to get that call.

I don't want anyone to ever get that call again.

PART ONE

FROM ONE WAR TO ANOTHER

CHAPTER ONE

KOREA, 1953

Boom! Boom! Boom!

Smoke swallowed the sky. I stayed under cover until the thick black cloud began to dissipate. Even then, I could barely see past the dirt and debris that had kicked up from the C-4 packs that I had stuck to the bridge.

"Did the bridge fall, the whole thing?" Jonny, the young private, asked me, his eyes still closed tight.

"If you open your eyes you can see for yourself," I told him, coming out from behind the hill where we had taken cover.

The bridge had more than fallen; it had been blown to smithereens. I was proud of myself. I was getting really good at blowing up stuff. I should have been by then, given that I'd spent over a year serving in the 59th Bridge Company Combat Engineers. Our job was to build floating bridges for the US and South Korean troops to cross the Imjin River and then blow the bridges up before the enemy could follow.

As for when and if I got home from the war, well, I hadn't thought that far ahead yet. Maybe I'd go to college and become a lawyer or politician. My father was an important man in the West Philly area, and I always admired the clout he had in the city. If my father wanted something to happen, he made it happen. That's what I'd wanted to do before the war. But now I was already almost twenty-one years old. Most of the kids my age were finishing college, while I was running around a war zone blowing shit up.

"Nice job, Private First Class Addario," Corporal Andrews said after I'd escorted the private named Jonny to safety.

"Thank you, sir," I replied.

"That is how we do it, boys: get in, blow it up, and get out," Andrews said.

* * * * *

But blowing up bridges wasn't the only thing I did over there in Korea. My unit was assigned to a huge multinational encampment covering maybe a full square mile in the Panmunjeom region. Because of my engineering acumen, I was made acting sergeant in charge of communications. My job was to string wire all around the camp and rig it to an old-fashioned switchboard phone system that would allow the commander and the camp officers to be in constant communication with each other. The switchboard was just what you see in old movies, and the phones were of the crank variety. Hardly state of the art even by early 1950s standards, but it got the job done.

The biggest problem we faced in the camp were the minefields that ran along the single paved dirt road that connected to both Imjin and Seoul, which provided our supply line. We used to wear steel helmets that weighed over two pounds 24/7, and those minefields made driving anywhere a risky proposition at best. One day, a corporal named Will, who was our own version of Radar O'Reilly from the classic *M*A*S*H* television show, didn't make it back to camp in

Dan in uniform wearing an Australian hat borrowed from an Aussie soldier.

the old deuce-and-a-half supply truck he used to commandeer extra supplies for us at times, so we dispatched a search party. We found his truck off the road with its front end blown to bits, but no sign of him. The truck was smoking, so we rushed to off-load provisions like powdered milk, sugar, and coffee before it caught fire.

It turned out that Will had managed to score some cases of Budweiser on this trip—you just never knew what he was going to bring back when he set out on one of his supply runs. Some of the provisions were too damaged to salvage, but we managed to save the Budweiser. We even managed to find Will, who'd somehow wandered off. He was bloodied, dazed, and walking in the middle of the road, still carrying the shorn-off steering wheel like he was ready to pop it back into place. I don't think he had any idea where he was, but he must've had a pretty good idea of what had happened.

"Motherfucking gooks ain't gonna kill me!" he told us all. He recovered just fine and was back driving again within a week.

Besides the enemy and the minefields, the biggest problems we faced were the cold and challenges of procuring safe rations. We didn't have the right boots or clothing for the harsh winter, and, it turned out, the locals fertilized their fields with wheelbarrows of human manure, rendering local vegetables uneatable for us. We had to rely on C-rations, powdered eggs and milk, and whatever fresh vegetables Will could scrounge up from the nearest supply bases. We also couldn't drink the water without getting sick and had to make sure that any we swallowed, including what we filled our canteens with, had been purified first thanks to a small pill that made the water taste like iodine.

All told, I wasn't disappointed to see the war end on July 27, 1953. I'd spent eighteen months in Korea, at which point there was nowhere to go but home.

* * * * *

Philadelphia, Pennsylvania, Fall 1953

I was a first-generation Italian American, my grandfather having come to America via Ellis Island from Abruzzi, Italy. He'd been a barber in Rome, where he actually did the hair of any number of dignitaries attached to the Vatican; the pope was clearly not among them, since that would've made for a story to be repeated over and over again.

My grandparents had settled in the Center City section of Phila-delphia in a house big enough to put his barbershop on the first floor, with the family's living quarters occupying the second and third. I was born in that house, delivered by a midwife in 1929. It was a very nice neighborhood, located about a block from the train, and I often figured one must have been rumbling by the moment I was born, since I always took great comfort in that sound through the bulk of my childhood.

It was a different world back then. Multiple generations of a family lived close to each other, sometimes even in the same house. There was a real sense of community. Neighbors talked to each other, looked out for one another. We knew the beat cops by name and when there was a problem, like needing to do something about the bums gathering on the corner, you dealt with it together, as a neigh-borhood and a community. The drug problem didn't exist in those days; the close-knit nature of those neighborhoods precluded it. I can only imagine what the locals would've done to some pusher who set up shop on the corner. Based on the fact that the bums never returned after being shooed away, I can tell you it wouldn't have been pleasant.

I remember as a young boy walking up the stairs from my grand-father's barbershop into a combination living and dining room. A big open kitchen dominated our living space. I remember an old stove that was always warm and a coal shed in the backyard. In those days, we burned coal for heat. Hard to believe now, but back then that was about the only option. I can remember my grandmother outside tending to her tomatoes and herbs, while we shoveled heaps of the black coal shards into the wheelbarrows to ferry into the basement to supply our heat and hot water. I had a younger brother and sister and shared a room on the third floor with my Uncle Tony.

Sansom Street was mostly Irish, with a few African American families dotting the neighborhood, but we were the only Italians. In keeping with the Philly tradition, I played a lot of stickball, shot marbles, and tossed horseshoes. There was no television back then, so we had to find other ways to entertain ourselves, which almost always involved a bunch of kids. Most of us played sports, and my stickball prowess led me to give baseball a serious try, as the only Italian on a team sponsored by the Ancient Order of Hibernians, an Irish fraternal organization.

I attended a Catholic school where Italians were considered second-class citizens. The nuns there favored the Irish kids, one of whom was named McGinty—a real teacher's pet, even though he was a wiseass, a troublemaker, and a bully long before we even put a name to that sort of behavior. His older brother had become a monsignor and was made bishop a few years later, so I guess McGinty figured he had God on his side. And, boy, did he need Him one day when the nun left the room and he decided to lay into me one time too many. We got into a fistfight and ended up knocking over desks en route to me getting my licks in on him pretty good, all that pent-up anger that had built up finally spilling over. McGinty, true to form, went literally crying to the nuns. I was the one who ended up getting punished, but I didn't care. I had drawn my line in the sand, and McGinty never bothered me again. And, while I don't claim any linkage between this particular incident and my ultimately becoming a cop, it did feel good when my friends looked to me to protect them from the likes of McGinty and other bullies. I hated anyone who picked on somebody smaller than he was, and, when you think about it, maybe those bullies really did morph into the drug dealers I'd later spend a career fighting, since they too placed no value on the lives they ended up destroying.

I don't know if McGinty ever went into the service, but pretty much all my friends from West Philly did along with me, thanks to the draft. I was placed in combat infantry training at Fort Belvoir, Virginia, for three intense months, followed by two even more intense ones learning to be a combat engineer. The best lessons I learned in those days, though, were about people, thanks to getting to know fellow soldiers from all over the country. My life hadn't extended more than a few miles of West Philly at that point, and I'd never met anyone from the South, for example. These southerners proudly called themselves the East Coast Hillbillies and pretty much taught me everything I needed to know, skills that kept me alive and got me back home safely.

Once deployed, my team would be transported into combat-infested areas ahead of the infantry and had to seek cover over and over again when enemy shelling drew close. Our job was to build a bridge for the right troops to cross, not the wrong ones. So I became pretty much an expert on how to blow those bridges up, after our troops got across. We'd use this crude form of plastic explosive that looked and felt just like Silly Putty, which we'd wire under the corners of the bridge, sometimes with the enemy troops within earshot and even sight.

It was always left to me to be the last man across after I'd set the explosives and rigged the detonator. Sometimes I imagined I'd hear the boots of enemy soldiers clacking against the bridge plate directly over me. Sometimes they drew so close I could almost look them in the eye. Sometimes their gunfire sounded as the bridge blew. Kind of ironic when you think of it, given that years later I'd be the first through the door during drug busts—an eerie contrast with being the last man on the bridge.

Again, it was the interpersonal part of the experience that taught me the most. You work with the person on your left and your right, depending on them just like they depend on you, because in a combat zone, all you've got is each other. I can't even count how many times Chinese troops were shooting at us while we wired floating bridges across the Imjin River to blow. I remember a friend of mine named Ernie falling under one of our heavy transport vehicles when it over-turned, his legs crushed as bullets whizzed around him with a bunch of us trying to pull him free. We managed to save his life and he was medevacked out. It was the last time I saw him, though I heard later he'd gotten hooked on pain meds and never really got off them.

We'd go to Japan occasionally for R & R (rest and recuperation), which marked my first direct experience with heroin. I watched some of the soldiers I worked alongside chase that high and then bring the drugs back with them to our base to chase it some more. I guess it was how they dealt with the pressure of combat, getting zonked out of their minds, walking around like they didn't know where they were. Ours was a small unit, 158 servicemen. We were very mobile and would set up encampments at times when the enemy was no more than a half mile away. But you wouldn't know it from the behavior of those who'd been bitten by the heroin bug. They were so out of it. I remember one time, a private standing guard duty with a pair of cap pistols in his belt. He was so stoned out of his mind, he didn't think he needed his rifle, or maybe he'd forgotten where it was. Chasing the dragon had sucked the fight right out of him and all the others who'd chosen that path.

Speaking of fighting, my dad was a boxer. He won a ton of fights and the promoters wanted him to turn pro, but they couldn't sign him because he was under sixteen. So he went to school and became an electrical engineer. When I came back from the Korean War, I seemed destined to follow that same path. I apprenticed alongside him, learned skills like wiring and mechanical composition that way. I learned from watching, but it wasn't just trade skills my father taught me. I also learned how to get along with people, how to negotiate. He was a quiet man, but he could be tough when he needed to be and always got the job done, no matter what it was. He could estimate in his head the materials and manpower required to do a job, and I can't remember a single time he got things wrong.

One day I was out getting some work permits when a cop directing traffic waved to me and signaled me to stop. Turned out it was one of my old Catholic school friends, Jimmy Pierce.

"Pull that car over," Jimmy said, "I want to talk to you."

Then he abandoned his traffic duties to come up to my window.

"I thought that was you, Dan!" he greeted.

"Hey, Jimmy!" I beamed back. "I heard you joined the force."

He grinned. "Somebody had to keep the city safe while you were over there saving the world."

"The uniform suits you," I complimented.

"Hey, pal, it could suit you too."

"How's that?"

"What are you gonna do with your life?" he asked me, big hands laid on the roof of my car.

I told him I wasn't planning to stay in construction, that maybe I'd use the GI Bill to attend college.

"To study what?" Jimmy said.

"I don't know."

He nodded and took his hands from my roof. "Maybe I do."

Jimmy proceeded to explain that Philly's new mayor had brought a similarly new attitude to fighting crime in the city, starting with building a special force of incorruptible police officers. He had gotten approval for five hundred new hires. Jimmy explained that the money was good and that if I could handle getting shot at in combat situations, I could handle being a cop.

I decided to give it a try, starting with exams both written and physical, overseen by the Civil Service Commission. The written test proved a lot easier than I'd been expecting and, being in such great shape at the time, the physical endurance test of climbing walls and carrying dummies proved infinitely easier than helping an injured or shell-shocked fellow soldier avoid both bullets and capture. I finished number 365 out of 5,000 applicants, enough to earn my spot in the police academy on my own. But it didn't hurt that my dad was a ward leader in West Philly. Although he didn't exert any undue influence, he knew the right buttons to push and flesh to press, assuring that the spot I'd rightfully earned would be mine.

Even though my father was old school, he never let the fact that I'd decided against following in his footsteps bother him—at least, he didn't show it. Coming to America for the whole family had been all about chasing their dream, and he was content to have me now ready to chase mine.

Little did either of us know how quickly that dream would become a nightmare.

CHAPTER TWO

PHILADELPHIA, 1954

I was almost twenty-six when I entered the police academy, old by anybody's standards in comparison to the fresh-eyed kids, many of whom were still in their teens. Add to that my eighteen-month tour in Korea where I'd survived hostile fire on numerous occasions, and you might say I stood out.

And, man, you'd be right.

I don't want to use the phrase man among boys, but that's what I felt like. And I must've looked it too, based on the fact that a combination of my appearance and wartime experience attracted the attention of Lieutenant Tom McDermott. McDermott was an old-school Irish cop, white-haired and barrel-chested. A button-down kind of guy fond of fedora hats who I can never remember seeing, even once, without a jacket and tie on. McDermott was chief of the elite Special Crime Squad that handled vice, narcotics, burglaries, and robberies throughout Philly—pretty much the highest profile crimes, including those related to drugs, which McDermott was particularly determined to eradicate.

He may have been old school, but he saw drugs even back in 1954 for the scourge they already were and, even more, the drag on society they would eventually become if something wasn't done. And he was on the same page as Philadelphia's district attorney Sam Dash when it came to putting drug dealers away. Years later, Dash would go on to become a famous figure, familiar to all who dutifully followed the Watergate hearings on television, after he was named a Watergate prosecutor.

Chief McDermott had a daughter and a son who became a mailman, so I think to a great extent I was the son he wished he'd had. I wore my Korean experience on my face, kind of a hardened, world-weary look, and had let my coal-black hair grow out a bit longer than maybe I should have. In other words, I looked like a young musician grizzled by years on the road. I had dark skin and could have passed for Latino in appearance. Someone who could fit into the world of those the chief needed to infiltrate, the world of junkies, drug pushers, and distributors.

Like I said before, McDermott might've been old school but he pioneered the way drug cases are handled up until this day. In the chief's mind, it wasn't enough to take a couple pushers off the corner, because the next day two more would be there to take their place. And what good did arresting junkies do really, other than to pad the reports and take up another prison bed better utilized for a real criminal?

McDermott's plan was to start at the bottom of the food chain, with the junkies and street dealers, and work his way through the distribution and supply channels all the way up to the kingpins at the very top. Today that might draw a big fat *so what* from drug cops, but back then it was cutting edge. State of the art, as they say. The chief saw the war that was coming and wanted to win it while he still could, with me as one of his soldiers.

* * * * *

"Nice shooting, Addario," I heard a voice say behind me one morning when I was on the police academy shooting range.

I turned around quickly. I thought I was alone, just as I preferred to be when I came to the range for shooting practice. Standing before me was Chief McDermott. You didn't have to be a cop or a recruit to know who he was—all of Philadelphia knew Lieutenant Tom McDermott, an incorruptible cop who was our version of Eliot Ness from *The Untouchables.*

"I've been watching you, Dan," the chief said to me. "You got talent, kid, a real knack for this shit."

"Thank you, sir," I said, having no idea why the chief of the police department's crack Special Crime Squad was standing in front of a raw recruit with months of training yet to come.

"What do you know about dope?" McDermott asked me, getting to the point.

"Well, sir, to tell you the truth, not that much, outside of what I saw in the war."

I could almost see his ears perk up. "And what was that?"

"Men who got high and couldn't do their job or stand a post," I said, recalling that soldier who stood guard duty with a pair of cap pistols. "Never used it myself, sir, or even watched guys shooting up, but I do know the drugs followed plenty of men home."

The chief seemed satisfied with my answer. "Think you could handle dealing with a bunch of junkies?" he asked.

"If that's the job, I can handle it. You think I'm right for it, I'd jump in as soon as I'm out of the academy."

"Well, kid, you don't have to wait. We have an assignment we need you for now."

"As in…"

"As early as tomorrow. We need someone who's raw and young and ready to get his hands dirty. A new face not known on the streets the way junkies know every one of my men."

"I'm your man, Chief," I said, without any hesitation at all.

* * * * *

23

The next morning, instead of going down to the academy, I showed up at Chief McDermott's office located in an old police precinct at the intersection of 26th and York, in the heart of one of the city's prime African American neighborhoods, at six thirty sharp, a half hour before I'd been ordered to be there. I used the main entrance and was greeted by a desk sergeant standing behind a high desk, who informed me the chief's office had its own entrance in the rear of the historic building.

So I retraced my steps outside and walked around to the back. Climbing a flight of stairs brought me to Chief McDermott's second-floor office. A receptionist sat at a desk parked outside it. She was a middle-aged woman, with a stern face and broad shoulders. A squad room dedicated to the chief's elite crime-fighting squad was just down the hall, and I could hear the *clack-clack-clack* of cops typing out their reports on manual typewriters, hunting and pecking at the keys.

"Morning. I'm Dan Addario, and I'm reporting as ordered by Chief McDermott."

"He'll be in at seven. You can have a seat in the waiting area until he arrives," she said matter-of-factly.

I did what the woman told me. My leg was shaking a mile a minute. I had no idea what my assignment would be, but I was excited to be chosen for it. I busied myself by following the lines of cracked plaster and peeling paint, imagining the stories these walls might have to tell if they could talk. All the criminals who'd been brought up here to be placed in the single holding cell.

I never saw the chief enter the building, but at 6:55 sharp, I was called back into his office where the third man in the room was Chick Tyree, McDermott's right-hand man who I'd be reporting to once in the field as an undercover. These were heady, low-tech days for police officers, particularly undercovers, since we lacked cell phones, sophisticated surveillance equipment, and even the most rudimentary so-called "wire." Once on the streets, we were on our own, isolated on an island otherwise inhabited by the kind of lowlifes and criminals it was our job to put away.

"Welcome aboard, Dan," he greeted. "Ready to do a stint in lockup?"

I noticed a smirk stretched across his face that could be as warm as a priest's or as imposing as the devil's himself. "Uh, what?" I managed.

"Lockup," he repeated. "You're going undercover to find us a junkie we can use as a mark."

McDermott explained that my first job was to get close to someone in the holding cells, to figure out who was both a user and dealer. I was to make contact and turn that person into a CI (confidential informant), someone who could help us take down as many pushers as possible, as part of what was called "Operation Intake."

"Here, put these on," McDermott said, handing me a pair of tattered jeans and a T-shirt. "So you look the part," he added with a smile.

* * * * *

The chief had me handcuffed and two uniformed officers walked me to the lower level of city hall to where the lockup for suspects awaiting arraignment was located. As I took my perp walk, I began to get nervous. I had never seen a junkie before, let alone knew how to act like one. I swallowed hard as the bars came into sight. The cops uncuffed me and tossed me into the cell. There was no turning back now.

When Chief McDermott spirited me out of the police academy, I told my parents I had flunked out. I had no choice, given that nobody could know the truth of what I was doing. So for the next eighteen months, I had to live with the fact that they believed I was a failure. Having spent a stretch of similar length when I was in Korea, they remained as patient and loving as they could, but it was clear especially for my father that I had become a disappointment, a source of embarrassment.

If only they knew what I was really doing.... If only I could tell them the truth....

But I couldn't. It comes with the job.

The cell was packed, as many inmates standing as sitting. I tried counting them and came up with around thirty, many of whom were "fellow" junkies who were immediately recognizable from the hollow glint in their eyes, the way they scratched at themselves, and the shaking that accompanies even the first stages of withdrawal symptoms. There were so many in here on a daily basis, because back in those days Philly cops could pick up anybody they deemed so much as looked like a junkie. If a cursory inspection revealed track marks, no matter how old, that was cause enough for them to be held and put before a judge, which normally happened around nine o'clock in the morning but sometimes considerably later.

Of course, my biggest concern at this point was what if something happened to Chief McDermott? Imagine me trying to explain to the guards, or the judge, that I was working an operation for the chief when he was no longer around to confirm that fact.

Not everyone in the cell was a hard-core junkie, but you wouldn't know that from the overpowering stench of vomit and urine. There were also perps (perpetrators) who'd been arrested for lower-level drug offenses or some other nonviolent crime. I, though, took my cue from a few strung-out guys, because I needed to get close to one of them and gain his trust in order to use the lowest rung on the ladder to climb to the next. You had to get to them in order to get to their sources. And, since this was my first experience with confidential informants, I needed to pick one to turn here and now. The thing is, a cop is only as good as the informants he's nurtured and cultivated.

I slumped my head and shoulders and began to twitch ever so slightly, playing the part. A scraggly fellow in the back of the cell caught my eye. He was lying in his own vomit, obviously detoxing. I figured he would probably be rather malleable to my approaching him, if it meant release and access to heroin.

I approached slowly and took a seat next to my target. "You okay, man?" I asked.

I could tell that he wasn't sure what to make of me; that or he was still high and he couldn't get his eyes to focus.

I asked him again, "Hey, you okay?"

"I'm hurting," he said with a groan. "I need a fix."

"So do I," I said, trying to match the quake in his voice.

"I'm Petey," he said.

"Dan," I replied.

"If I make it out of here alive, Dan, I have a connection that can hook us up, like immediately."

"Oh man, could I use that," I followed, hiding my elation over the fact that Petey had just offered up the information that I needed. I was either really good at this shit or damn lucky.

Now, all I had to hope was that Petey didn't choke on his own vomit or have a seizure.

And Petey wasn't the only one in the cell in his condition. Heroin use had been on the rise, and for the first time it was trickling past the urban areas into mainstream culture. This kid had been an art student, once upon a time. He and his friends began experimenting with drugs—first it was pot, then he moved on to heroin. Once he got his hands on that he was hooked, and now here he was in lockup for the third time. I stared at poor Petey and his track marks. The guy had to be younger than my twenty-five years, but right now it didn't seem as if he'd last until he was thirty.

We were all marched down to be arraigned together, after which I left the building with Petey by my side. There were two cars waiting outside, with Chief McDermott in the backseat of one of them. Petey and I walked to the corner to grab a streetcar and that's when the chief's car pulled over alongside us.

"Get in, Petey," I said to him. "There's someone in the car who can help us."

He was so desperately in need of a fix, he'd do anything to the point where he practically jumped into the backseat to find McDermott waiting. Petey was like a limp noodle, so strung out his chin lopped against his chest.

"Hey, Petey," McDermott said, snapping his fingers to get him to lift his head back up.

Petey straightened and tried to focus on me and then McDermott, finally recognizing the chief from the many newspaper photos that had run of him.

"Dan?" he said, confused.

I nodded at him, knowing that McDermott had the lead here.

"How would you like to stay out of jail?" McDermott asked, not bothering to introduce himself because there was no need.

"I would, sir," Petey replied. "Very much."

"I can make that happen, but you're going to have to do us a favor," McDermott continued.

"Anything, I'll do anything," Petey said in desperation.

"Good. That's what we like to hear."

Nowadays, that whole scenario might seem like a cliché, but this was 1954, remember. As far as I know, Chief McDermott's Special Crime Squad was the first, the very first, in the entire country to run this kind of undercover drug operation, predating even the FBI's use of confidential informants to bring down the mob, which started in earnest in the 1960s.

Like I said before, prior to that point, narcotics squads would be satisfied arresting a single street dealer or junkie. Our strategy was to let it ride. We set up an elaborate system whereby we'd make the buys and learn the identities of the dealers and couriers, but not arrest them. Instead we'd climb the food chain, sometimes using the threat of prison to get them to turn and other times just cozying up and getting them to trust the undercover identities we were living under. Often it was both, taking our sources as far as they'd go before needing to lay the hammer down to get their full cooperation. There were no wires or electronic surveillance in those days, at least none that really worked, so we were left to our own devices and wits, knowing that when we walked into a precarious situation, nobody would be coming to break down the door if things went bad.

"We need you to make a buy for us," McDermott told him. "Score one for us and do what you want with the other. Just tell me what you need."

"About forty, fifty bucks," Petey stammered. "Heroin costs twenty a bag."

"So let's say fifty to be on the safe side," McDermott followed, handing me the cash.

From there, Petey brought me to a pool hall the police had long suspected was a haven for drug dealing, but we'd never been able to get anybody on the inside. The place was right out of *The Hustler* movie, with cigarette smoke wafting up toward the overheads spilling light downward over the tables. The crack of pool balls was constant, as were the comings and goings of various shady characters known to the city police to be involved in the drug trade.

Petey introduced me to his connection, a guy named Pat.

"Give me twenty bucks and I'll get you a bag," Pat pronounced.

I gave him forty to take care of Petey as well and off Pat went to make the buy. Since this was such a low-tech operation by today's standards, I had no way of alerting the detectives watching the pool hall who Pat was so they could tail him. Twenty minutes later, Pat came back with the heroin. He was reluctant to give it to me directly, since I was a stranger and all, so he gave it all to Petey to dispense and he passed it on to me—to be logged in later as evidence.

That was my first buy as an undercover fighting the war on drugs. The next time Pat left the pool hall to make a buy, detectives followed him into South Philly where he paid a visit to Harry Riccobene, a mobbed-up drug dealer no cop had ever been able to get near before. He was one of those guys who was like Teflon. But we didn't arrest him right away, because that would've stopped our undercover operation in its tracks. Instead we set up a system where we'd make the buys and tail the couriers higher and higher up the

Operation Intake undercover team with Dan pictured in the middle.

ladder, letting the process ride out. The more buys we made, the more solid our case became.

This was the first time in any city in the country a narcotics squad had gone at things with such an organized, disciplined, and far-reaching effort. Across the city, other officers worked other territories. Gil Dockery, for example, a short Irish guy you had to stretch to make him five-and-a-half feet tall, worked North Philly. Gil Hennigan and Bill Moore worked South Philly in the city's African American section. I kept to South Philly, which was still predominantly Italian. Chief McDermott even put four female officers undercover, another first at the time that caught the dealers totally off guard because they'd never expected a woman to be a cop, much less an undercover.

But things didn't always go smoothly. I was in the Chinatown district of downtown Philly making a buy, thanks to another informant

I'd turned named Ralph Toomey, a junkie musician. He set up a meet for us with a dealer there. The plain-front building with this solid steel door that must've weighed a ton turned out to be a Chinese gambling hall with all the gaming tables in the front and an opium den in the back where the drug deals went down. I had to front a hundred bucks, big money at the time, at the bar and was escorted back there.

"You wait here," our escort instructed.

And a few minutes later, the dealer comes in with the package of dope and gives it to me.

"You want to shoot up here?" he said expectantly, given that's what all the other junkies making buys were doing.

I couldn't blow my cover, but I also couldn't shoot up. The junkies weren't just sharing needles, they were passing them from one to another and dropping them on the dirty floor when they were finished, to be scooped up by the next shooter.

"Nah," I told the dealer, "it's for my girlfriend."

All this while my backup surveillance team was a couple blocks away eating Chinese food.

Along the way, we brought down some of the biggest drug dealers in Philadelphia, climbing the chain of command all the way to the top dogs. One time, the kingpin who ran the North Philly area, Tommy Jones, tried to run down my partner when we made the move to bust him. I fired at him from the rear as he tore away in his car and blew out his back window. I'd just missed blowing his head off too, which would've saved the country a ton of money prosecuting and jailing him, and nobody would've thought twice about it.

See, in those days, we were operating under a different set of rules. There was no reading of Miranda rights, no due process the way it's known today. A lot of cops back then carried throwaway guns or switchblades, just in case they needed to plant one near the body of a suspect they were forced to shoot so they'd appear to be armed. We could stop anyone we wanted in the city to check their arms for needle marks, a violation of something that was called "failure to

31

account for yourself." And, from our standpoint, the only accounting that mattered was how many pushers we took off the streets to disrupt the supply chain.

I worked undercover in Philly for eighteen months, some of the most rewarding of my life and career, and, man, did I learn a lot from the likes of Chief Tom McDermott. The mass raid that ended Operation Intake netted a staggering 103 arrests, virtually all of them resulting in jail time. The *Philadelphia Daily News* reported that "Operation Intake, designed to round up narcotics pushers, found police raiders banging on doors in pre-dawn hours." A later *Daily News* article chronicling the efforts of ten separate elite teams from the Special Crime Squad was headlined "Police Lauded for Dope Raids." Not to be outdone, on January 21, 1955, the *Philadelphia Inquirer* ran a story under the banner, "Four Rookies Pose as Addicts to Trap 68 Suspects in City-Wide Drug Raids."

The number of arrests varied by the day and article, from forty-six to seventy-one, because it was difficult in those days to collate all the information that was coming in machine gun fast. There was also the issue that a number of the 103 suspects arrested were actually confidential informants, swooped up in the raids to maintain their cover. Nobody likes a rat, and in those days of old-school Philly, rats were drowned before they could flee the sinking ship.

In the years to come, I'd apply the lessons I learned from that experience working under Chief McDermott to postings across the country and the world. The enemies and the bad guys changed, but the goal never did: reduce the supply of drugs through any means available.

In many respects, South Philly was a twenty-block microcosm of what I'd encounter for the next nearly half century. The places changed, the rules changed, the targets changed, but one constant remained:

Drugs and the lives they destroyed.

CHAPTER THREE

PHILADELPHIA, 1955

My reward for being a key cog in Operation Intake was a return to the police academy to finish my training and graduate a police officer. Strange putting it that way, given all I'd already been through. But rules are rules; I hadn't graduated yet and there was no getting around that, nor should there have been. I considered myself fortunate to have had so much on-the-job training, thanks to Tom McDermott, an experience I would put to great use in my career, both in Philly and beyond.

The chief was a special man in all respects, tough but fair. Working undercover meant a lot of time spent outside, especially on the surveillance side of things. There was a lot of dead time, and Philadelphia didn't exactly enjoy a tropical climate. So some guys who worked the streets found themselves looking for places to get warm, like ducking into a movie theater for an hour to take advantage of the climate-controlled environment. We'd come back at the end of our shifts on rainy days and McDermott would check our coats to make sure they were wet. And if they weren't, there'd be hell to pay because he'd know the wearer of that coat hadn't been doing his job.

You couldn't learn lessons like that at the academy. Such things came with experience, and I considered my own experience as having given me a leg up on the rest of my career. Of course, the real blessing here was that my reentry to the academy finally allowed me to tell my parents the truth of where I'd been, and what I'd been doing, for those eighteen months.

My parents, having seen the newspaper articles about the drug raids and all those arrests, and now hearing that I had played a big part in them—well, they were stunned to say the least.

"Oh my God," my mother said.

My father, not a man taken to displays of emotion, grabbed me and gave me a hug. "God bless," he said, elated. "That's great."

He was bursting with pride, especially given that he'd been under the impression I'd been screwing around for all those months. Hanging around with the guys, making nice with women, picking up odd jobs, maybe even messing around with mob wiseguys. I delivered the news inside the West Philly house we'd moved to from our Center City tenement. My father had slaved to put away the down payment, helped to a degree by the fact that during my tour in Korea, I'd had all of my meager paychecks sent home to put toward that down payment. I think that had really raised me in my father's esteem to a degree that was similarly lessened by the thought I might be a wayward loser. To hear I was anything but that was probably the best gift I could have ever given my whole family, even greater than that money that had helped us buy the house where I still lived.

Was it hard going back to the brass tacks and minutia of being a trainee again? Sure, it was. Those eighteen months undercover were like a drug in their own right, leaving me longing for my next fix, chasing a different kind of dragon. The experience, though, had also filled me with a deep appreciation of why I wanted to be a cop and, with only a few months to go, I put my nose to the grindstone, buckled down, and finished up in fine enough fashion to qualify for a return to Chief McDermott's what was now called Special Investigations Squad. The police commissioner was on a mission to take out the trash, and he had put together our special squad to get the job done. Nationwide, illegal drug distribution was being recognized for the major problem it was fast becoming. Narcotics officers were kicking ass and taking names, and I was thrilled to be involved in the journey to win a war we were just beginning to realize we were fighting.

I was working mainly nights, chasing dope at all of the local clubs in downtown Philly. I used what I had learned during Operation Intake and parlayed it into my modus operandi, turning the club scene on its back. The stalls of the bathrooms that were once littered with junkies were now the stuff of rumors and whispers of when a bust might be coming. We were a dream team of dope busters, a modern-day Untouchables, and no one was immune to our raids.

There was, for example, this hip jazz club in the heart of the city called the Town Hall. Some of the greatest musicians of our time played the small smoky bar where plenty of others had gotten their start. We'd gotten a report that the band members on stage were users and were sure to be carrying. For our squad, it was like shooting ducks in a barrel. The five of us brought several uniformed officers with us to block the doors. Once the exits were covered we took our positions, anxiously passing the last few moments before the raid, when I noticed something up on stage.

"Ray, are you seeing this? The lead singer is blind," I said to my partner, Ray Smith.

"Hell yeah, I'm seeing it. He must not realize that we can see his track marks from here," Smith replied, taking a long drag of his cigarette.

I shook my head. "Junkie or not, the guy can sing."

"So you wanna delay the raid until after the show?"

"How about until just after the set?" I said, only half-jokingly. "This guy is something special."

And he was. His soulful voice was magnified by the tic of how he moved his head in rhythm with the words, like he was playing to an audience only he could see. And he was belting out lyrics that stuck in my mind long after he sang them. I met his eyes through his sunglasses and I could swear, really swear, that he was looking at me too. I'd heard a lot of blues and jazz in my time, but I could listen to this guy all night and through the day tomorrow. I hated the thought of busting him, felt like I was breaking some unwritten law by what was about to go down. Sure, I had a job to do, but it seemed almost sacrilegious to put away a guy with that kind of talent.

Our plan was to grab the band members off stage mid-show. But there was a delay in getting the outside of the club secured, so we pushed the bust off even further. Ray Smith and I took seats among the rest of audience and watched the blind singer and piano player's performance a bit longer, and to this day I wonder if the delay wasn't due to distractions caused by the haunting melody of his voice. It turned out we waited until the next set was over and approached the stage as the band was taking a break.

Strangely, the sight of the uniformed and plainclothes cops rushing the stage didn't seem to rattle them at first, as if we were security or maybe there to get autographs. Either way, the illusion didn't last long.

"Sorry, folks," I said into the microphone. "Show's over."

And I really was sorry, which didn't stop the crowd from screaming, swearing, and yelling at us. Good thing they didn't start throwing bottles or we might've had a full-fledged riot on our hands. First thing I'd do if it came to that would be to get that blind singer off the stage to safety.

"Keep it up and you can come downtown too!" I yelled out, focusing on one especially rowdy customer.

He backed off and the rest of the crowd must've taken that as a cue, because they mellowed to a man and woman. It took the five of us and the uniformed cops to gather up all nine band members. I approached the lead singer, who seemed oblivious to what was transpiring, and gently tapped him on the shoulder.

"Sir, I'm Detective Dan Addario, Philadelphia PD. We're putting you and your band under arrest. Do you understand what is happening?" I asked, trying to be as courteous as possible under the circumstances.

"Just 'cause I'm blind doesn't mean that I don't see what is going on here," he replied.

"What's going on here is that you are being taken in on suspicion of drug possession and the use of illicit narcotics," I told him, stopping short of pointing to the track marks on his arms since he couldn't see me.

"Do what you gotta do, man."

And with that he laced his hands behind his back, waiting for the handcuffs to be slapped on.

"Raymond Charles," I said, "you are under arrest."

The next edition of the *Philadelphia Daily News* reported that "five members of the police commissioner's special squad proved today they are hip to jive. They cooled their heels and waited for the end of a performance before arresting a dance band and its blind leader on dope charges. Some 2,000 people were rocking and rolling to the music of Ray Charles and his band.... It was Charles' first band appearance in Philadelphia."

By the way, that article identified "Daniel Addavio" as one of the squad members.

"Going to the band stand," another *Daily News* article subsequently reported, "the raiders found a hypodermic needle, cotton and a spoon containing residue of what they suspected was heroin, near the Charles band's bass fiddle."

So we arrested none other than the great Ray Charles and his band, and I called Chief McDermott to give him the news.

"Chief, we arrested Ray Charles on the nightclub raid."

Ray Charles arraignment photo with Dan pictured from the side.

I heard him sigh on the other end of the line. "From the Perry Como show?" he said, the disbelief plain in his voice. "As in the Ray Charles Singers?"

"No, the other one," I corrected. "The rock guy."

The next day Ray Charles and his band went in front of Magistrate John A. Daly at the 12th and Pine Streets police station. The hearing room was jam-packed, thanks to a convoy of big-time lawyers who'd come down from New York with briefcases that might've been stuffed with cash, for all I knew and based on how things turned out.

"Mr. Charles," the magistrate asked Ray, "how do you explain the needle marks on your arm?"

"I've been getting anti-flu shots, sir."

John A. Daly nodded. "Well, that's good enough for me."

And with that, Magistrate Daly let the group go, much to our dismay and against the advice of Assistant District Attorney Lisa Aversa.

On November 26, 1955, the Philadelphia edition of the *Pittsburgh Courier* headlined a story on the case with "SYMPATHY FREES BLIND ORCHESTRA LEADER," adding in smaller letters, "Ray Charles Found 'Positive.'" A *Philadelphia Daily News* article similarly intoned in a headline that "JUDGE'S SYMPATHY FOR BLIND ORK LEADER SPARES DOPE RAP" in an article that also mentioned that it was the police surgeon who'd tested Ray positively for drugs.

Truth be told, I was kind of glad they'd let Ray go, but I resolved to stay in touch with him and do anything I could to help this incredible talent get himself clean. Otherwise, he probably wouldn't last another year, two at the most, and I didn't want to open the paper one morning and see his name in the obituary section. What a waste that would be; then again, what a waste all lives lost to the scourge of drugs were. Even back then, it wasn't just a job for me. I honestly believed in what I was doing and that I was performing a good turn by getting as many drugs off the street as I could so men like Ray Charles would stay clean.

Believe it or not, we stayed in touch over the years, but the lessons I'd hoped he'd learned from that night, sporadically anyway, went unheeded. As RecoverRanch.com has written of Charles:

As a young man performing on the piano in clubs, managers are said to have given him marijuana to help soothe performance anxieties. Marijuana then crossed over to heroin addiction as Charles became what is typically called today a "working addict"—someone who maintains employment while also enduring substance abuse addiction.

In his mid-thirties, Charles marked his third arrest for possessing heroin, although he had been using the drug for more than two decades. Attending a rehab facility in Los Angeles prevented the musician from spending time in jail for the arrest. In 1966, Charles completed a year on parole for drug violations, continuing to produce chart-topping hits. His career also included serving as a spokesperson for a major beverage company, global civil rights initiatives, invitations to presidential inaugurations and acting performances.

As is common with drug addictions among celebrities and non-celebrities, Ray Charles attended rehab centers more than once but continued to battle his heroin use. Heroin is among the most powerful drug addictions, requiring medically-supervised assistance to begin the detoxification process and treatments at a professional residential treatment center.

In the mid-1960s, Charles is said to have finally ended his addiction with heroin, but the legendary star is alleged to have been linked with a habitual use of alcohol. Portrayals of his life, including the movie "Ray," point to depression and struggles like poverty and family tragedy as precursors to his long-time drug addiction, which many say may have caused the star much more hardship than the loss of his sight.

Another website devoted to the price extracted by drug addiction, Heroin.net, openly theorized that heroin may have been the cause of Ray's ultimate death in 2004 at age seventy-three to liver disease that had been clearly exacerbated by his heroin use. Through the final years of his life, though, Ray would remain unapologetic about his addiction, something I found all too common among the users I busted over the years. When *Playboy* asked him, in 1970, how he started, he begged off the question. Asked if he might not be an influence to stop potential drug users, he replied: "Bullshit. Everybody's aware that cigarettes probably cause cancer, but how many people do you think would give them up just because Ray Charles stopped smoking?"

And, he continued, "I'm fed up with talking about that aspect of my life. Jesus Christ couldn't get me to say another word on the subject to anybody."

Several times when Ray returned to Philly to play that same Town Hall concert venue, he asked that I be the one to lead him off the stage after the show concluded, so I'd come on stage and serve as a kind of escort and bodyguard to keep Ray from getting mobbed by his fans. A few years later, after John F. Kennedy was assassinated, President Lyndon Johnson wanted Ray to sing the national anthem at his inauguration. Rumors of Ray's drug use had been circulating for a while by then so, knowing of my relationship with him, federal authorities asked me to check him out.

I met him backstage at Latin Casino, a club in Cherry Hill, New Jersey, and, sure enough, he remembered me very well. He had this big smile that was so warm and genuine and he flashed it at me as soon as we shook hands.

"How are you doing?" I asked him.

"I'm good."

And he looked good; he looked clean, in fact. I had caught the tail end of his performance before meeting him backstage and I can tell you that he sounded great, the best I'd ever heard him. That's what I reported back to the authorities at the Federal Bureau of Narcotics (FBN), and it was indeed Ray Charles who sang the national anthem at LBJ's inauguration. Without incident, I might add. In fact, he brought the house down on an otherwise solemn, somber occasion. I don't know if anyone has ever sung "The Star-Spangled Banner" better than Ray did that day.

* * * * *

Even though Ray and his bandmates were set free, our squad continued to hit every venue on the Philadelphia club scene. It was at this time that I realized that not everyone on the police force was on the up-and-up. Political favors and greasing palms came before the law. Not to me, though. I didn't care whose greasy palms were cut off; no one was getting away with shit on my watch.

Meanwhile, there was never a dull day working narcotics. There were more than enough junkies and dealers in the city to keep us busy 24/7. Some days we'd accomplish little more than catch a random junkie showing off his track marks; other days were more intense, with users doing their utmost to outsmart our unit. Those were the days that I loved the most, the ones defined by challenges.

* * * * *

The sun was beating through the police station windows, causing perspiration to fall from my brow onto the stack of papers on my desk. I wiped the sweat off the document, smearing the ink on a report we'd compiled from one of our informants that was the basis of our squad setting up a large raid. These suspects were not our typical run-of-the-mill junkies. The head of this organization was Dr. John P. Turner. We had gotten whispers that Dr. Turner was prescribing narcotics to the local junkies. This was something new for us. We were used to the dealers hanging out in the clubs or the streets, not the doctor's office. *If doctors were now dealers,* I wondered, *how could we trust anyone not to use and buy dope?* Anyone could be suspect or victim.

Ray Smith and I were poised to pose as junkies in dire need of a scrip. I was used to the undercover work, but fooling a doctor? I wasn't so sure he'd fall for it. Especially since Dr. Turner, now seventy years old, had spent more than twenty years as a police surgeon working closely with cops.

I was disgusted. Dr. Turner was a respected physician and served on the Board of Education. All I could do was hope that when we got to his office he would turn us down and that our informant had been misinformed. However, I had little hope because typically when there's stink there's shit. That said, interestingly enough, Turner wasn't dealing for the profits. According to what we'd been able to glean, he was providing narcotics prescriptions to junkies to get them off smack. Maybe he thought he was doing good, but that's not the way it turned out since the junkies he thought he was helping sold his prescription narcotics on the street and used the money to buy more heroin. We had enough probable cause to get a warrant that allowed Ray and I to go in undercover, and we were in the process of preparing.

Smith was in a long-sleeve shirt and a pair of tattered jeans. He was trying to look like a junkie, but not too much like a junkie. Back at squad headquarters he'd used a pen to put track marks on his arms.

"Ready to shoot up?" Smith had asked, coming at me with a red pen.

"Ready as I will ever be," I replied, pulling up my sleeve.

Smith put a few strategic dots in the crook of my arm. After I was penned, I went and changed into my undercover clothes and we headed off to Dr. Turner's office, taking our place in a waiting room packed with maybe a dozen junkies awaiting their turn. When mine finally came, Turner evaluated me in an exam room. He looked into my eyes and listened to my chest. He never asked to look at my arms as I was begging him for narcotics, and he happily wrote me a prescription. I met up with Smith after my appointment and it turned out he too had received a scrip for narcotics from Dr. Turner.

We had planned to return to Dr. Turner's a few weeks later. When we did he instantly wrote me another prescription, no questions asked. After nineteen prescriptions between Smith and I, we decided to take down the doctor in an arrest utterly without incident that was somewhat sad, given that Turner seemed to have no idea what his purportedly altruistic efforts had yielded, all the drugs they'd put on the streets toward no good end at all.

He ended up with probation but had to relinquish his medical license, a dishonor further magnified when he was questioned in a congressional hearing by Senator Herman Welker.

"This is one of the hardest hearings we have ever held," Senator Welker intoned, genuine regret evident in his voice. "It is not easy to interrogate you, a leader in the community in the twilight of your life."

"I thought it would be better to treat ambulatory drug addicts with drugs than have them go haywire because of a lack of these sedatives," Turner testified by way of explanation at the time, according to the *Philadelphia Inquirer*. "I have long been an advocate of the treatment of ambulatory drug cases. I've often felt that instead of convicting drug addicts and sending them to jail they should be receiving medical treatment. They will do anything to get money for dope. They will steal, they will kill and they are the biggest liars on earth."

* * * * *

Interestingly enough, Turner exemplifies two trends we see in the war on drugs today. On the plus side, more and more cities and states have established drug courts to reduce the levels of judicial backlog, decriminalize drug use, and reduce incarceration rates, while increasing treatment as a first resort instead of jail. As of 2016, according to the National Association of Drug Court Professionals (NADCP), the number of these courts had swelled to more than three thousand.

The US Department of Justice described drug courts this way in May 2017: "Drug courts are specialized court docket programs that target criminal defendants and offenders, juvenile offenders, and parents with pending child welfare cases who have alcohol and other drug dependency problems. Although drug courts vary in target populations and resources, programs are generally managed by a multidisciplinary team including judges, prosecutors, defense attorneys, community corrections, social workers, and treatment service professionals. Support from stakeholders representing law enforcement, the family, and the community is encouraged through participation in hearings, programming, and events like graduation."

Although opinions vary on the overall effectiveness of drug courts, DrugRehab.com stresses the stringent conditions subjects must accept toward ending up clean in the end.

"Drug courts comprise treatment, individual therapy, 12-step meetings, random urinalyses and court appearances," the website reports. "Many courts require participants to find a job or complete volunteer work while in treatment. Programs generally last between six months and one year. During this time, individuals undergo weekly drug testing and monitoring. They periodically appear before a judge who reviews their progress. Participants who follow rules and show improvements may receive incentives. But a judge may punish those who fail a drug test or refuse to fulfill program obligations."

On the other hand, Dr. Turner was similarly ahead of his time when it comes to an especially alarming trend: the overprescribing of narcotics by physicians. As Dr. Donald Teater, a medical advisor serving on the National Safety Council, reported to WebMD, "Opioids do not kill pain. They kill people. Doctors are well-intentioned and want to help their patients, but these findings are further proof that we need more education and training if we want to treat pain more effectively."

Of course, this more well-intentioned practice makes no mention of the far more malicious scourge of physicians who reap profits for their overprescribing, thanks to the deep pockets of the pharmaceutical industry.

* * * * *

Our squad's bust of Dr. Turner was followed by a succession of cases that fell more within the norm, like the dumpy third-floor apartment on North Marshall Street near Brown. The place was a mess and smelled like moldy cheese. I held my breath as I tossed the cushions off the small tan couch in the living room. We had a warrant to search the place but so far had found nothing.

I hit the bedroom closet next. I searched through the pockets of all the items hanging in there. On my second-to-last item, a long trench coat, I stuck my hands deep into the pocket. Jackpot! I pulled out an ounce and a half of black tar heroin.

"Found the dope," I yelled to Gil Hennigan, one of my partners. "And there's more. I know it," I added. "We gotta keep looking."

We continued to tear the house apart. Nothing. Everything was turned over, except a Bible that was sitting on the table. I picked up that Bible and could feel something inside. I opened it up. The pages had been carved out to make space for a large bag of heroin. A perfect way to smuggle drugs.

The suspects—nineteen-year-old William Harper, twenty-one-year-old Frances Reason, and twenty-nine-year-old Charles Jackson—were lined up against the wall in the living room. Ray Smith was watching them, paying attention mostly to Harper and Jackson since the woman was pregnant. When I held up the Bible to showcase what I'd uncovered, he turned away for just a moment, at which point the pregnant Frances took off into the kitchen.

"Get back here!" Smith hollered.

"Ahhhhh!" Frances screamed, rushing back out of the kitchen wielding a twelve-inch butcher knife. "I'm going to kill you all!"

She was headed straight for Smith. He could have drawn his service revolver and shot her, but the fact that she was pregnant froze him. Before he could react, Frances thrust the knife forward, burying the blade in his shoulder and upper chest, dangerously close to his heart. But then Hennigan slashed downward with his pistol, striking Frances in the back of the wrist with enough force to make her drop the weapon, after which he cuffed her to avoid any further entanglements.

I holstered the pistol that I'd managed to draw, also unable to shoot a pregnant woman. Then I rushed forward, took off my jacket, and wrapped it around Ray's shoulder as he fell to the floor.

"Stay with me, buddy," I said to him. "Stay with me!"

CHAPTER FOUR

PHILADELPHIA, 1956

It turned out that the trio of dealers had made a habit of using hollowed-out Bibles to move their product. In fact, Harper and Jackson were fond of wearing priest's collars with different-colored vestments out on the street, carrying these holy books stuffed with drugs under their arms and preaching just the kind of sermon their customers loved to hear. I encountered far bigger and more dangerous dealers over the years, but this took the cake when it came to creativity. Who'd ever suspect a priest, right? What cop would dare inspect a Bible?

The *Philadelphia Independent* ran a story under the headline "Amateur Dope Ring Hid 'Junk' in Bible." According to the police chemist, that junk, black tar heroin, was the strongest our department had ever seen. So not only was the opioid problem becoming more prevalent, it was also becoming deadlier.

Ray Smith, who the same *Independent* article reported had been "slashed in dope raid," ended up in surgery but emerged just fine. Frances Reason and her cohorts, meanwhile, found themselves a home in lockup for the next twenty years. Watching your partner get stabbed, wondering if he might bleed out while you're applying pressure to his wound, was scary, terrifying even, and sobering too. But it was also a risk every one of us took every day we went out on raids and worked drug cases.

Ray wore a white shirt and tie every day, but he wasn't afraid of kicking down doors and getting dirty. He was a great first partner. A down-home good guy, except every now and then he would go off the deep end. It was a department joke that "every full moon you have to watch Ray." Some guys said that the reason he went a little mad was because of the plate in his head he owed to a motorcycle accident. Either way, he was one of the best dope chasers I had ever met.

And this was a heck of a time to be in narcotics. Prior to the 1950s, the stance on illegal drug use and sales was pretty lax. In 1937, Congress passed the Marijuana Tax Act, somewhat of a catch-22. The law stated that distribution of marijuana would result in a one-dollar nuisance tax. Anyone distributing the drug was required to keep and submit a detailed account of transactions requiring buyer and seller. This backward law put distributors in a tight situation, because it was an action tantamount to confession. The fine wasn't worth the time of law enforcement officials to track down offenders.

In the 1940s, narcotics addiction in the United States had all but disappeared. This had almost nothing to do with laws or people and everything to do with the war. World War II had cut off nearly the entire supply chain of heroin and cocaine to the country. While the world was in disorder, the people of our country were staying away from drugs. When the war ended, the floodgates opened and people began using again.

Drug laws and enforcement was and still is controlled by the executive branch of the government. In late 1945, drug use escalated due in large part to a combination of a surplus of opium and the arrival of Demerol, a synthetic substitute for morphine, on the scene. Cocaine, after practically disappearing from the United States for fifteen years, was also starting to make inroads as a recreational drug thanks to a supply chain in Panama.

President Harry Truman took the issue seriously enough to prioritize an end to illegal drug use through stricter regulations. The new protocols, though, did little to stop the transporting of drugs, even when Truman added another piece of legislation called the Boggs Act of 1951. This amended the Narcotic Drugs Import and Export Act, which set mandatory sentences for drug convictions. With the law's passage, a first conviction for possession of marijuana set a mandatory minimum sentence of two to ten years, along with a fine of up to twenty thousand dollars.

It finally made sense for law enforcement to go after dope dealers, and business was booming, so to speak. A few years later, President Dwight Eisenhower decided to expand on Truman's efforts and signed the Narcotic Control Act of 1956, which increased sentences for any smuggling or sales violations. All discretion to suspend sentences or grant probation were ended, with the exception of first offenders convicted of possession only.

Little did I know how this experience would presage the efforts, or lack thereof, by other presidents in fighting the war on drugs. I should have learned then that wars were won from the top down, not the bottom up. But I wouldn't come fully to grips with that until my later experiences when the highest levels of our own government claimed to be dedicated to fighting a war they didn't really care about winning. Whatever I managed to achieve through my forty-year career was done almost exclusively in spite of Congress and the White House, not because of them.

As George Shultz and Pedro Aspe wrote on the opinion page of the *New York Times* on December 31, 2017:

> *"The war on drugs in the United States has been a failure that has ruined lives, filled prisons and cost a fortune. It started during the Nixon administration with the idea that, because drugs are bad for*

people, they should be difficult to obtain. As a result, it became a war on supply."

As first lady during the crack epidemic, Nancy Reagan tried to change this approach in the 1980s. But her "Just Say No" campaign to reduce demand received limited support.

Over the objections of the supply-focused bureaucracy, she told a United Nations audience on Oct. 25, 1988: "If we cannot stem the American demand for drugs, then there will be little hope of preventing foreign drug producers from fulfilling that demand. We will not get anywhere if we place a heavier burden of action on foreign governments than on America's own mayors, judges and legislators. You see, the cocaine cartel does not begin in Medellín, Colombia. It begins in the streets of New York, Miami, Los Angeles and every American city where crack is bought and sold."

Her warning was prescient, but not heeded. Studies show that the United States has among the highest rates of drug use in the world. But even as restricting supply has failed to curb abuse, aggressive policing has led to thousands of young drug users filling American prisons, where they learn how to become real criminals.

The prohibitions on drugs have also created perverse economic incentives that make combating drug producers and distributors extremely difficult. The high black-market price for illegal drugs has generated huge profits for the groups that produce and sell them, income that is invested in buying state-of-the-art weapons, hiring gangs to defend their trade, paying off public officials and making drugs easily available to children, to get them addicted.

Chief McDermott had been promoted to chief of county detectives, and the squad got a new commander who was his polar opposite, both corrupt and politically motivated. That, combined with the reputation I'd built thanks to Operation Intake, led the assistant to the city's police commissioner to bypass my new captain to give me my next assignment, which was to take down a private club in North

Philly that was a den for illegal gambling. It was a true Vegas of the East, crammed with craps tables, gambling wheels, blackjack, and other card tables. This generally high-end establishment also had a barbershop and massage parlor on the premises, making it a true gathering spot. The place never closed, staying open 24/7, and was owned by an underworld figure named Tommy Marino, better known as Tommy the Boot thanks to his penchant for kicking men he'd beaten in a fight when they were down.

The problem was that the club was located in the neighborhood of ward boss and head of the city council James H. Tate, who'd later go on to become mayor of the city of Philadelphia. But I was too young and in love with the job to realize I was being used and set up for political purposes, since no good could come out of a bust so riddled with political motivations and politicos themselves. To get the job done, I needed to return to my roots by infiltrating the club undercover, and it turned out I was friends with a car dealer who was a regular customer; more than friends actually, since I helped keep his son, a junkie, out of jail. That gave me a favor I could call in.

"What do you say?" I asked the car dealer, after I laid it all out for him.

"I can't do that," he said. "They'll kill me."

"You gotta get me in," I told him, my voice firm and the look in my eyes reminding the man that he owed me.

He nodded, shrugging. Turned out there was a group of car dealers coming into town and my friend had planned on taking them to the club to entertain them. He said if I pretended to be one of the car dealers, we could make this work. That provided me access to the club in order to see what I needed to see to coordinate the raid properly.

The place reeked of cigarette smoke and booze. I could hear the grinding spin of the roulette wheels and the clack of the dice landing on the numerous craps tables. In those days, no establishment in the city was permitted to serve alcohol after midnight. So my first order of business was to buy a drink from each of the servers behind the club's four bars. That provided sufficient probable cause to get the arrest warrants we needed to raid the club, the problem being I had to get in one more time in order to facilitate the raid itself.

After considerable protest, my friend the car dealer got me in again, and I gathered enough supplemental intelligence to net us the warrants we needed. The squad that would be accompanying me on the raid was handpicked by the commissioner from officers who, like me, remained untouched by the corruption that was running rampant through the department in those days. We couldn't afford any leaks, not with a man as powerful as James H. Tate about to go down, so instead of meeting in a squad room or some other facility, we met in the subway station at Broad and South Streets. These two-dozen or so officers had no idea what was about to go down, other than it was big. And we couldn't afford any additional time lag to give even a single one of them the opportunity to make a phone call and tip off Tate.

They didn't know where we were going until I told them to get in their squad cars and follow me. The convoy rode through downtown Philly in single file, six cars with four or five men in each of them. The raid team took their positions outside the club while, thanks to my friend the car dealer, I went inside. Finding everything in order, I used a pay phone to give the squad the go. They came in full blast, breaking down the doors and storming inside. We shut down the club, yanked the liquor license off the wall, and seized all the gambling equipment in perfectly professional fashion without a single patron getting hurt. All in all, a textbook operation.

But that didn't stop the political shit from hitting the fan. I didn't really realize anything was awry until I went to court for the arraignment, expecting all the boilerplate stuff. What I got was as far from that as I could possibly conceive. The judge was in deep with Tate and not about to cross the man earmarked to become the city's next mayor.

"Were you a member of the club?" he asked me from the bench.

"No, Your Honor."

"Then you shouldn't have been in the club in the first place."

My stomach sank, butterflies flapping around before the tension crushed them, the judge interrogating, and embarrassing, me rather than the perps. He had effectively put me on trial instead and dismissed the charges, throwing out every shred of evidence we'd collected. That was my first experience with how corruption works, what politics could do to people. The commissioner's office had purposely kept me in the dark about that end of things. I felt used and tossed away, a pawn in somebody else's chess game. I ended up getting bounced from the special squad and relegated to walking a beat in the boondocks. I went to Chief McDermott to see if there was anything he could do in his new position as chief of county detectives.

"Wish I could help," he told me. "But you're too hot for even me to touch, kid."

He went on to advise me to lay low and he'd see what he could do later. Given the fact that I'd landed such a prized posting because of Operation Intake and his efforts, I felt I'd let him down and resolved to do better. Guess I learned the hard way that politics and law enforcement might make strange bedfellows, but they go hand in hand. Little did I know at this point what an important lesson that was for me to learn, and how much I'd put it to use in the years that followed. And that new commander of mine, Clarence Ferguson, couldn't wait to throw me under the bus either.

"I can't control that fucking kid," he told anyone who'd listen, pinning the blame for the whole raid on me, as if it had been my idea.

Little did I know, too, how well Fergie was hooked politically. He knew how the game was played and preferred to align himself with the likes of James H. Tate, who'd used his station to protect gambling club owner Tommy Marino. But Fergie was savvy enough to cultivate a relationship with the likes of wealthy businessman and philanthropist Walter Annenberg as well. Annenberg owned the *Philadelphia Inquirer* at the time, and it was said that Fergie could make front page news by just going to the bathroom. The fix, as they say, was in, and that's what I fell victim to and what nearly cost me my career.

But here's the good news: it was during this period I met the first love of my life.

* * * * *

Her name, appropriately enough, was Joy. A friend of mine named George Kruger who worked for Philadelphia National Bank introduced us at a party in the upscale suburb of Collingswood, New Jersey. Joy had finished college a year before and was now working for the Philadelphia president of Babcock & Wilcox, a well-known electric company, and had working-class roots just like me. We talked a little bit, hit it off, and exchanged phone numbers. I called her the following week and we ended up going on a date to a nightclub in West Philly called Henney's that specialized in jazz, which, it turned out, we both really enjoyed.

It wasn't love at first sight, not like a thunderclap hit me or anything. But I knew Joy was the right girl for me and the first one I had a second date with in longer than I wanted to remember. Back in those days, families, and marriage itself, were different, because people and the world were different. My dad had met my mother while playing music, and I imagine their relationship was rooted in the same values that defined what I was building with Joy. Back then, there just came a time in your life where you felt the need, the obligation, to start a family.

Like I said, different times.

Of the many things I remember my grandfather telling me, one that stands out was, "When marrying, be careful if the woman comes from 'the Boot.'" The Boot was old-school slang for the Black Hand, or Mafia, since Italy is shaped like a boot, and my grandfather was the very definition of old school. He used to make wine in the basement of his barbershop, huge vats of varying kinds. The neighborhood mailman was an African American named Bailey, and everyone called him Mr. B. Every morning, when he stopped at the shop on his mail route, my grandfather gave him a glass of homemade Dago Red to help him get through his long day—except in winter when that was replaced by a sherry instead to help Mr. B. keep warm. We knew everybody by their first names, could name everyone who lived on my block and the ones on either side. We had a sense of real community, but you needed a family to be part of it. Here I was closing in on thirty and it felt like time for me to do that, just like it did for Joy.

Over the years, people have asked me a lot about how I could balance the kind of people I was trying to put away with being a husband and a father. I tell them the first thing was I never took the work home. I learned how to compartmentalize, be one person on the job and an entirely different one off it. The dad who watched his boys play soccer or baseball or basketball on Saturday wasn't the same man who'd busted a dozen drug dealers on Friday. I loved my work, but I wasn't about to let it consume me the way I had seen it do to other cops, especially undercovers. Serving in Korea in a position as front line as it gets helped me grow up fast and teach me how to manage my thinking. I think I was the same person laying explosives under a bridge as I was busting dealers and junkies in Philly. But when I came home from the war, I left all that behind me, just as I left the drug business behind me when I came home at night.

When I got home, Joy always asked me, "How was your day?" And not once did I respond with anything like "I had a bad day; I almost got shot." Even if it was the truth.

Maybe it was love; maybe it wasn't. Or maybe we just had a different definition of the word back then. We both called Frank Sinatra our favorite singer, and his song "I've Got a Crush on You" was our mutual favorite. We got married six months later and a couple years after that had the first of our three sons: Daniel, whom I was destined to lose thirty-four years later to the very scourge I'd dedicated my career to fighting.

* * * * *

"I can't control that fucking kid."

Captain Clarence "Fergie" Ferguson had always seemed like a quiet fellow. He was one of those guys that you never knew was in a room. He blended in to wherever and whatever he needed. Even so, he and his fedora hat, which he was never seen without, knew the streets, and he knew where all the bodies were buried. He understood the value of gossip and that somewhere inside the rumors lay the truth, so he followed the leads and he hit them hard. Fergie was ahead of his time as far as the drug business went.

Maybe so, but he was also old-school Philadelphia when it came to corruption and had set me up to take the fall in the drug raid that had only been ordered due to politically-charged internecine rivalries playing out in city hall. I had spent my whole life, other than Korea, in the city, enough not to be surprised. But I hadn't suspected anything like this was afoot prior to the raid and, even if I had, I still would've had to follow orders. Being the fall guy requires a push one way or another, and there was no shortage of hands to perform that task beyond Clarence Ferguson. He was just a small cog in the far bigger corrupt machine to which I fell victim.

Talk about deflating. Here I was, having made detective in the city's most elite police squad in record time, condemned to walking a beat in Philadelphia's hinterlands where a missing cat passed for a crime. I walked beat mostly on the overnight shift, no matter the weather. It's one thing when you're doing that as a cop looking to prevent crime, getting to know the people and serving as a deterrent to the bad elements to keep them from doing something that would lead me to arrest them. It was quite another thing when you could count the people you passed during your shift on one hand. Very boring stuff, totally isolated from real crime and real police work.

After six months, I finally got a call from my old friend Chief McDermott.

"Look," he said, "I can probably get you into the Highway Patrol. You game?"

"Oh, Chief, anything to get out of here."

"It's not just anything, Dan. It's the elite motorcycle division."

And *elite* was the right word indeed for this unit that had only a hundred members statewide. That extra two weeks of motorcycle training I did at the academy had qualified me, and it was something climbing on that bike in the trademark police leather jacket and boots. They used to send our unit into the highest-crime areas, wherever there'd been a rash of holdups or burglaries. Our job was to put the fear of God into criminals, supplement local efforts, and take no prisoners in the process.

I partnered up with one guy who used to take a nap on his bike while we were parked at an intersection, waiting to do traffic stops. Turned out he was quite the lady's man, with a thing for waitresses, and didn't get a lot of sleep plenty of nights.

One day he got off a pay phone, grinning, and said to me, "Gotta go lay some pipe."

He rides to North Philly, out of our patrol area, and next thing you know we get a call that he wrecked his bike and we need to get down there. A bunch of us headed over to North Philly and towed his bike back to our jurisdiction to keep him from getting suspended. This after we put him in a cab to get him home. I don't know who the woman was he'd been with, but I hope she was worth it.

The regular Philadelphia police cars were red with white letters, something like taxicabs. But our squad, when we weren't on motorcycles, drove black-and-white patrol cars, earning us the apt nickname "the Black and White Squad." We had a reputation. People knew if we got called in, there was going to be trouble. Criminals were always looking over their shoulders, telling their cohorts, "Whatever we do, we don't want to bring the Black and Whites in here." We were like the fabled Texas Rangers, except we rode in on bikes or squad cars instead of horses.

There was an area in North Philadelphia, around Columbia Avenue and Broad Street where Temple University was located, that had become a hotbed for drug activity. We'd storm into a bar and you'd hear the rattle of guns and knives being dropped to the floor amid the dime bags of heroin or baggies packed with weed. We'd come with a squad wagon, and the perps knew full well our intention was to load anybody we caught carrying drugs or weapons—next stop central booking. We came in our spiffy uniforms, Sam Browne gun belts lined with bullets, and shined-up boots that made us all seem two or three inches taller. You had to measure at least five feet ten inches to even get into the unit, so we were all pretty tall already. I guess our Black and White Squad was the ultimate deterrent against drugs and other crimes wherever we set up shop.

I'd been with the Highway Patrol for a little over a year when I got a call from Lieutenant Anthony Bonder in the police commissioner's office.

"The commissioner's setting up a special, dedicated narcotics squad," Bonder explained to me, referring to Howard Leary, who had an impeccable reputation for being incorruptible, "and he'd like you to come on board."

It turned out he and Leary both knew of my past exploits, including the circumstances that had led to my getting ostracized to walking a beat.

"I'm looking for people we can trust and can work together," Bonder told me. "We've heard a lot about you and the work you did undercover. We want you on the team."

The opportunity intrigued me, in large part because this squad would be dedicated to narcotics interdiction only. When I'd worked under Chief McDermott on the Special Investigations Squad, we covered all major crimes, not just drugs. So this was an opportunity to work only the part of the job I did the best and enjoyed the most, and I jumped at the chance, well before my new job gave me an opportunity to deliver some payback on my old friend Captain Ferguson.

Chief Tom McDermott presenting Dan with an award.

Al Perry and Big Butch Jones had also been plucked from the Highway Patrol's elite motorcycle division to join Bonder's squad, and we caught a case involving a run-down house just down the street from the headquarters of Fergie's squad at 26th and York. We'd been tipped off to some suspicious activity around the address in question. I made a buy that was enough to get us a warrant to raid a duplex. With the back door covered, we stormed in through the front and found a young family living on the first floor. But we hit pay dirt upstairs in the form of drug paraphernalia, scales, piles of cash, and a couple ounces of heroin. All in all, a really good bust, made even better by the fact that we'd made it literally a stone's throw away from Fergie's office.

"Look at this," I told a friend of mine who was the new director of one of the local TV channels. "We hit this joint maybe four doors down from Fergie's squad."

He ran with the story and so did another station, along with the *Philadelphia Inquirer* thanks to a reporter I knew there. Fergie, understandably, was furious. I heard from a couple of friends that he was screaming around the office, cursing up a storm over his perceived humiliation.

"What's next?" I'd been told he said. "They going to come in here and make a fucking case against us too?"

We worked a slew of cases, performed raids across the city, and pursued investigations up the food chain, from the street-level dealer all the way to the main supplier. We worked undercover, cultivated informants—pretty much everything I'd learned while working Operation Intake for eighteen months before I was even officially a cop.

Not long after the bust near Fergie's squad, Bonder called me into his office and told me the Federal Bureau of Narcotics (FBN), in the person of a federal district supervisor named Joe Bransky, needed some people from our narcotics squad who were current on the streets of Philadelphia. He knew of my work both undercover on the streets and from my days with Highway Patrol as one of the Black and Whites who struck fear into the hearts of local dealers and junkies. Bransky needed guys who knew the back roads and side alleys—where all the bodies were buried, so to speak.

We started our efforts there and expanded out, running cases outside the city in places like Chester, Pennsylvania, and Camden, New Jersey. I made a ton of buys, making good cases and also cultivating informants the FBN could make great use of down the road. I'd never given a lot of thought to the differences between working cases on the federal versus local level. But the gambling club incident that had nearly derailed my career had also educated me on the perils of working drug cases on the local level. We were always worried about arresting some judge's or politician's son and getting bounced, maybe put back in uniform and banished to walking a beat.

Sure, a local squad could get a lot of good done in a city like Philadelphia. But there were limitations. Drug dealing, to a great degree, is territorial: South Philly was run by the Italians, North Philly by African Americans, West Philly mostly by the Irish. The Latinos had begun to make inroads, meanwhile, around Gerard and Fairmont Avenues. But if you want to stop drugs, you have to interrupt the distribution channels. This was a war, right? And one of the first principles of war is to disrupt your enemy's supply lines. But there were jurisdictional issues involved in that, serious ones, on the local level. Fortunately, the Federal Bureau of Narcotics was looking for a few good men on more than just a part-time basis, one in particular:

Me.

PART TWO

A NEW BATTLEFIELD

CHAPTER FIVE

NEW YORK CITY, 1959

"How'd you like to be a fed full time?" Joe Bransky asked me after another of the busts I'd made while assigned to his Federal Bureau of Narcotics squad.

I didn't realize I'd been auditioning for a role that would define the next stage of my life while being detailed out to the FBN, but I jumped at the chance to be appointed there permanently.

"You'll have to take the civil service test in a year to make it official," Bransky continued. "Should just be a formality."

He sent a teletype to New York that I'd accepted and would be coming in. Wait, New York? I thought I'd be posted in Philly, then was informed I'd have to relocate to New York City. Given that I had a young family to tend to, I wasn't enamored with the move, but I was sure I could make it work and had Joy's support the whole way. She knew I was chasing my dream and wanted to do everything she could to help me catch it.

As the original forerunner of the Drug Enforcement Administration, the Federal Bureau of Narcotics was established in 1930 under the US Department of the Treasury and was intended to consolidate the roles of both the Federal Narcotics Control Board and the Narcotic Division, both of which had been established to enforce the provisions of the Harrison Narcotics Tax Act of 1914 and the Narcotic Drugs Import and Export Act of 1922.

The first commissioner of the FBN, Harry Anslinger, was appointed by Andrew Mellon, Herbert Hoover's secretary of the treasury. Under Anslinger's leadership, the FBN advocated for increased penalties for drug use and is credited with criminalizing marijuana (Marijuana Tax Act of 1937). Since the main focus of the FBN, however, was opium and heroin smuggling, the bureau had established offices in France, Italy, Turkey, Lebanon, Thailand, and other locations where narcotics smuggling was prevalent. The agents cooperated with local governments in intelligence gathering and were permitted to make undercover drug busts in conjunction with local officials where they operated.

I guess you could say this was a life-changing period, highlighted by raising my first son, Daniel Jr. It was the happiest time of my life. Dan was a happy kid with a head full of blond curly hair, just like his mother's. I was excited to be a father and was hoping to get as much time with him as possible. But life has a way of throwing curveballs at you, like that unexpected move to New York.

Just short of Daniel's second birthday, I was given a Schedule A appointment by Commissioner Harry Anslinger himself to join the FBN. Anslinger was allowed six appointments per year. That meant instead of going through intense screening and months of training to join the bureau, I was pushed right through. It was quite the honor, and I'd been recommended to the commissioner by the supervisor from the FBN who'd worked with us on several of our local cases.

I was sworn in by George H. Gaffney on Columbus Day of 1959. I was then assigned to Group One, one of ten separate squads operating out of the FBN's New York City offices located in a federal building dominated by a post office on the first floor. I had to move immediately. My heart sank. *What was I going to do with my burgeoning family?*

Joy told me to go on ahead to New York and she and Dan would stay in Philadelphia until I could find an apartment. They would move after I was settled. Moving to New York was one of the most exciting and heartrending things I had to do. I didn't want to miss a day of my son's life, but I knew what I was doing wasn't only bettering his life, but the world he would live in.

Jack Riley was the top Customs guy in New York and happened to have a spare bedroom in his apartment.

"Why don't you bunk with me until you get settled?" he offered.

I took Jack up on his offer and stayed with him for about a month while I looked for an apartment big enough to suit Joy and Daniel Jr. The room was small but clean. It was more than a fine enough place for me to lay my head at night. I was working long days, sometimes fourteen to sixteen hours, and I spent all of my free time trying to find a good home for my family.

Eventually, I found a duplex on Flatbush Avenue in Brooklyn big enough to allow my wife and infant son to move up from Philly. The owner of the duplex was an older man. He worked as a plumber and was handy to have around. He and his daughter lived on the top half of the duplex. Our half had two bedrooms, a full kitchen, and even a yard for Dan to go outside and play.

I went to Philly that weekend and packed up our place and brought Joy and Dan back to New York with me. It was a hectic time, but also a happy time. Joy and Dan settled in quickly and made the most of our New York life. And, I'll tell you, we made the most of my time off and our time together. We went to Broadway shows, including *Camelot* with the original cast that included Robert Goulet. We caught a show by Mel Tormé, saw Harry Belafonte at the Paramount, and took in the best talent the world had to offer at the Copacabana, the biggest supper club of them all. Looking back, so much of that stands out. I felt like a wide-eyed kid, enjoying the Big Apple for the first time. Sure, Philadelphia was a big city too, but it wasn't New York; nothing was.

When I arrived in the city, I had been assigned a new partner, Frank Waters, also known by his cover name, Frankie Black, which was what everyone called him. Frankie was crazy; that or he had a death wish, I never figured out which. Frankie always had to be the first guy through the door anywhere we were working on any bust. He wanted to be the guy that found the dope or the money. And because of his lack of regard for personal safety, he was typically the guy that found it, and he was quick to rub it in all our faces. Even so, he was a good guy. He was first-generation American, his Irish parents having gifted him a head of curly red hair and a face to match. His spirit matched his hair: fiery and out of control. He had been a college football player and was built like a fireplug. It was unwise to mess with Frankie Black when he was on a mission.

As plenty of bad guys would learn the hard way.

Our FBN office was located at 90 Church Street in the Financial District of Manhattan. It was a heck of a place to work during a heck of a time. The mob was a New York staple, and their drugs were taking over the city. These dope dealers were far more refined than most; they were sneaky and smart, and the big guys rarely dirtied their hands on the junk or the money, making it really hard for the FBN to pin anything on them directly.

In fact, we had one agent named Armando Mulgia, a stocky guy who was about forty, assigned to do nothing but attend funerals. See, when the heat got to be too much, mob guys were known to fake their own deaths up to and including the funerals. So Armando's job was to attend all these Italian funerals and make sure the corpse being viewed in the casket was, in fact, the right guy. Armando proved so adept at this role that he ended up doing the same thing at the funerals of Latino and even African American gangsters. He was always going to the chiropractor, thanks to a bad back we attributed to all the bending over he did to look into those caskets.

There were forty agents assigned to the New York office, ten agents to a squad. The FBN assigned each agent two major mob guys to follow. I was assigned John Ormento and Jose "Joe" Fernandez, a.k.a. Joe Bumfoot, because he walked with a limp. I had to write up a report on their movements, who they met with and what they did, and turn it in to headquarters each month. This was on top of all the other cases that were piling high on my desk.

I spent nights watching my perps drink and schmooze at the Copacabana. And while I would have liked to have been home with Joy and Dan, I did get to enjoy nightly performances by the likes of Frank Sinatra and Dean Martin. Actually, I missed having Joy with me during those shows, feeling almost guilty she wasn't there. Then again, I was working, not there to enjoy the music, and I did my best to make it up to her when I had time off.

It was over a thirty-minute commute to my office from Brooklyn, which felt more like three hours on the nights that I watched Fernandez and Ormento until two in the morning. On nights when I wasn't home to have dinner with Dan, I'd make sure to have breakfast with him the next day. One of my unwritten rules. He was such a happy boy, and so smart. I may have been biased, but he was the cutest baby I had ever seen. His curly blond hair mopped over his big blue eyes that sparkled with curiosity. I had dreams of him growing up in a drug-free world, which seemed like it just might be possible with all the drug laws and enforcement that President Eisenhower was putting in place. Ike had big visions that made sense, establishing the US Interdepartmental Committee on Narcotics and increasing rules and regulations for drug control being two prime examples.

As Federal Bureau of Narcotics agents, we typically hooked up with local and state police detectives to help gather and collate information and evidence, as well as cultivate informants. It was just as the FBN agents had done with me while I was working narcotics back in Philly under Lieutenant Bonder.

Frankie and I had found ourselves a pair of local New York City cops who were sharp and motivated to prove themselves. One fellow, Detective David, was an older guy. He had been on the force a long time and knew the ins and outs of the city. His partner, Detective Andrews, was a rookie but had a lot of grit and was able to turn a suspect into an informant faster than anyone I'd ever seen. He talked the talk, all right, but he also walked the walk, just like his partner.

One such informant was Marco. Marco was a user picked up by Andrews and David at a club one night, just a strung-out college kid really. He knew his life would be even worse, a lot worse, than it already was if he didn't cooperate. The mere thought of jail struck fear into the heart of such college boys, often leaving them teary-eyed in the interrogation room. They could be as easy to turn as steering wheels.

Marco told us that there was a big-time operation being run out on 150th Street in Spanish Harlem. He said that was where the good shit came from. He wasn't sure where the dope came from specifically, but he always met the courier at Arcoirish, a run-down corner bar.

So Frankie and I set up surveillance. We watched the cars coming and going. We figured out that the dope was coming out of an Angelet's Christian Book Store. The store sold stone statues of baby Jesus and Mother Mary and such; stuff that the Italian and Puerto Rican cultures ate up. It was a perfect cover, just like those perps dressed as priests who'd been selling dope out of hollowed-out Bibles back in Philly.

The Angelet brothers were no strangers to the FBN. They'd been on our watch list for quite some time but they, like the mob, knew never to touch the money or the drugs themselves. But Marco had a connection. He hooked me up with their courier, so we could do the kind of deal that would implicate them.

We met at the Arcoirish. I came with money, ready to do a buy. Marco came with me to help reassure the courier that I was on the up-and-up. This particular courier was a wiry, squirrelly Hispanic kid with bloodshot eyes and track marks. He was sketchy and having a hard time trusting me, which I took for typical junkie paranoia. They only trusted whoever could score them their next fix.

"Relax, man," I told him. "Relax."

His eyes ping-ponged off the walls. He was doing a terrible job of being inconspicuous. With a courier like this, it was surprising the Angelet brothers had managed to stay out of jail so long.

"I want to start dealing in Brooklyn," I said, cutting to the chase. "What can you do to hook me up?"

"I can get you an ounce of H," the guy told Marco, avoiding eye contact with me or Frank.

"How much?"

"Four hundred bucks. Cash up front."

I handed the courier the cash and he darted out the door. I wasn't worried. I knew he would be back, and if he wasn't I had a group of surveillance guys set up outside ready to grab him.

An hour later, the courier pushed his way through the door. My team outside had been able to follow him to the Angelets' store, but they never saw the Angelets touch the cash or dope; just the courier.

The courier handed Marco the heroin, who passed it to me. I thanked him and told him I would be back soon for more.

Over the next several weeks, we maintained surveillance on the store. We'd watch people go in who we were sure were buyers; we'd then follow them as far away from the store as we could before arresting them. Using the typical persuasive tools of the trade, dangling zero jail time in front of them as opposed to ten years behind bars, we'd convince them to turn on the Angelet brothers for a lesser sentence. Finally, after developing enough informants to build a strong case, we were able to get a warrant to stage a raid.

I had Marco call the courier and we set up a drop. This time the raid team was in place, ready and waiting to tear shit apart, when the courier stepped into the store. I gave him my four hundred dollars and it was go time!

Frankie was the first man into the store, the rest of us close behind him, our guns drawn as he yelled, "FBN! Hands up and nobody move!"

The courier dropped the money and fell to the floor crying—and he wasn't even a college kid! Without saying a word, he pointed to the back stairs.

Frankie, the team, and I stormed the upstairs apartment and there they were, the Angelet brothers. With glassine bags of heroin and piles of cash cluttering their desks and thirty guns pointed straight at them, they didn't even need to be told to put their hands in the air. They just froze and up their arms went, stretching for the ceiling.

Welcome to the Big Apple.

New York is also what I like to call the City of Temptation, to the point where I believe all narcotics officers should do a stretch there: survive that with your record intact and you can survive anywhere.

Frankie Black and I were working a case centered around a shop in Harlem being frequented by known dealers. We set up surveillance with a pair of NYPD detectives, busted one of the couriers, and broke him. Had him talking in five minutes. He told us about a big-time dealer operating out of this shop who was dealing in kilos. That was enough for the assistant US attorney for the area—none other than Charlie Rangel, who'd go on to a long and illustrious career as a congressman from that very district—to approve a warrant.

We busted in and found a guy in the front room wearing a white silk suit. He barely flinched when we broke down the door, not saying a word when we left a cop with him and proceeded to search the rest of the apartment. We didn't find a thing until one last door opened into a back room loaded with drug mixing and cutting tools, including scales, milk sugar (which was used to cut heroin), and Similac, the baby formula dealers also used to cut their final product. Last but not least we checked the closet, where we found two baskets loaded with a bushel of cash in each, maybe two hundred grand or so.

Well, the eyes of those detectives from the New York City narcotics squad practically bulged out of their heads. I could read their thoughts, and watched them doing simple division in their minds: four into two hundred thousand dollars, meaning that each of us could walk away with fifty grand.

"Ain't my money, ain't my junk," the kingpin in the white suit said, his eyes twinkling as he realized the same thing I did; his ticket out of this.

I could see where this was going. I knew those NYPD detectives wanted to make the money disappear and wouldn't take kindly to Frankie and me trying to stop them. Hell, maybe we'd even end up in a gunfight over this. So I immediately radioed the FBN squad for backup. Within minutes, six more of our agents were on the scene, forestalling what could have been a very nasty situation.

Lesson learned. We never worked with those two New York narcotics detectives again.

It was right around this time that one of our informants claimed he had an in with none other than Vito Genovese, one of the heads of the infamous Five Families and among the most powerful mob bosses in the country.

"I'm like a son to him."

"Son?" I challenged.

"Well, nephew," the informant, whose name was Hackey, conceded.

The opportunity to plant an agent inside a major crime family wasn't to be taken lightly. Our problem was the mob knew our guys so well you might've thought they had a baseball card-like collection of them taped to their walls. We brought in an undercover agent named Tony out of Chicago who the New York gangs didn't know, a wiseguy lookalike right out of central casting. We made sure he made the rounds to all the bars and clubs frequented by made guys, always in the company of our boy Hackey to establish his bona fides.

Finally, after a couple of months, the day came when Hackey brought him to the Italian Social Club to meet Vito Genovese himself, but on one condition:

"We don't talk drugs, nothing like that," Hackey insisted. "Nothing about crime. No business. I don't wanna get killed."

Tony and Hackey were drinking coffee at the social club when Genovese emerged from his private domain in the back.

"This is my good friend Tony from Chicago," Hackey said, by way of introduction.

Genovese gave Tony the once-over without shaking his hand, addressing Hackey. "How long you know him?"

"Long time. Ten, fifteen years maybe."

"When you know him twenty more years," Genovese said, "bring him back around."

Vito didn't really trust anyone who wasn't Italian. He may have liked Hackey, but Hackey wasn't Italian, so Vito didn't trust him. That's what made infiltrating the mob so difficult in those days. Underlings almost never got to meet the bosses and, if they weren't Italian, they were lucky to meet anyone at all. The mob wasn't stupid; they knew the right barriers to put up to keep us from getting to them.

A couple guys I did enjoy working with, however briefly, were New York City detectives Sonny Grosso and Eddie Egan, whose experiences were chronicled in the Academy Award-winning film *The French Connection* starring Gene Hackman, who played Popeye Doyle, who was really Egan. Although that film took a lot of liberties with the facts, one thing it did get right was that Grosso and Egan had caught wind of a huge heroin shipment coming into the Port of New York through Marseilles. At that point, they had no idea the French Connection itself was as huge as it actually was, an international drug cadre spearheaded by a man named Auguste Ricord, featured as the mastermind who gets away at the end of the Hackman film.

Grosso and Egan were media cops, on television and in the papers all the time, but they also knew how to work the streets. They might not have realized the extent of the network they'd uncovered at the time, but they found someone in Customs to keep them apprised of boat traffic to get a line on the incoming Marseilles shipment. I was

A still from the 1971 crime thriller film, The French Connection.

working Chinatown at the time, having been reassigned from Group One to Group Two of the FBN's New York squad. My partner Frankie Black was working the case with them for the FBN and called me when word of the shipment came down.

"We need somebody in Customs we can trust," he said. "Somebody who won't clip the case from us. Can you call Jack Riley?"

Frankie and the New York cops knew they'd otherwise have to go through the bureaucratic chain of command I could leapfrog thanks to my relationship with Jack. The problem then, as well as now to an extent, was that rival organizations were inherently competitive and territorial. Frankie was rightfully concerned that if he simply called Customs for help with the seizure, they'd end up inspecting every ship coming into port from Marseilles and make the bust themselves. Ego was a factor here, but it also looked good when your branch went before Congress to establish your next budget; the better you did, the more you got. And that meant sometimes you couldn't trust your so-called "friends" any more than your enemies. So I called Jack and got Frankie's team set up with a handpicked agent who'd help with the international aspects of the seizure.

In the classic film that chronicled these events, there's a federal agent character based on Frankie Black who gets into it several times with Popeye Doyle (again, Eddie Egan in real life). I seem to recall Popeye coming out on top of those skirmishes but in real life, the one time they really got into it, Frankie kicked the shit out of Eddie. He was tough as nails and crazy to boot.

Of course, I didn't realize at the time how much more intimately involved I'd later become with the network responsible for that shipment out of Marseilles and the whole French Connection. Auguste Ricord may have ultimately escaped Grosso and Egan's clutches, but a few years later he didn't escape mine.

By the way, being first through the door typically didn't work out that well for Frankie Black. Usually something went awry. Like when another informant told us that there was this heroin and cocaine operation being run out of a local furniture warehouse in the Flatbush area. We had nothing on the guy who owned the place. He wasn't on anyone's radar, until now.

Frankie and I sat surveillance for weeks on the store. Cars would come in from all across the Northeast. Whatever was going on inside there must've been worth a drive, with customers coming from as far as Pittsburgh and Connecticut. At that point, though, all we had was the word of a junkie and, maybe, people who really loved crappy furniture.

So we had our work cut out for us to convince a judge to issue a warrant. When someone from out of state came in to what we suspected was a drug buy, we'd follow them, almost back to their hometown, and then arrest them. First, it was a young couple from Connecticut, a couple of yuppies with a taste for cocaine. We arrested them and they sang like birds. Then there was a guy from Jersey and another guy from Philly. Users are much easier to turn than dealers.

All of them stated that they were indeed buying drugs from the furniture store and signed affidavits to that effect. That was all we needed for our warrant.

It was a hot night in August 1960 when we decided to raid the furniture store. We went in with a large team, made up of local police and FBN agents. Again, Frankie had to be at the point of the spear. We rushed in and we saw nothing at first. Then a Hispanic man came running toward us, screaming in Spanish. Now, how it was that no one on our team knew how to speak Spanish is beyond me. We had to rely on my tenth-grade Spanish education for communication at that point. Not good.

"Pollo peligroso en el sotano!" he yelled, *"Pollo peligroso en el sotano!"*

"What the fuck is he saying?" Frankie shouted.

All I had made out was "chicken" and "basement." But I thought it was best for Frankie to learn a little lesson.

"He said the drugs are in the basement," I told Frankie.

"I got it!" Frankie said, kicking down the basement door.

He ran down the steps. Then the screaming started. And the clucking. Then the gunshot. Then feathers flew by the door.

The entire team erupted in laughter.

Frankie emerged from the basement, unharmed. I couldn't say as much for the chicken.

"You fucking asshole!" he said.

Apparently, not only were the perps running drugs out of the warehouse, they also held cockfighting events.

Frankie began cutting open the furniture and we eventually found a dozen pounds of heroin and cocaine layered amidst the stuffing in the chairs, sofas, and bedding.

I would have thought that after being attacked by a vicious cock that Frankie may have learned his lesson.

Uh-uh.

We were back in Harlem, one side of which at the time was called Black Harlem to differentiate it from Spanish Harlem. There was a ten-story tenement apartment where word was someone was moving a shitload of heroin. We set up a series of undercover buys that both my colleagues and I executed to perfection. The only problem was, at no point did the dealers ever have us come up to the apartment, because the deals were always done out back. So we had no idea what apartment in the building the drugs were coming out of.

We began doing surveillance from the rooftop across the street. After several long nights freezing our asses off in the New York winter, we finally figured that the apartment was on the sixth floor. We did our best to identify the apartment number from the position of the exterior window, but we wouldn't know if we were right until we were inside.

The team headed across the street to the target building. Agents were going to storm the apartment; with a peephole and a steel door, though, they were worried about dealers escaping through the fire escape. That was when Frankie came up with an idea that would not only trap them but also make him number one on the scene. The plan was for us to lower Frankie down off the roof, positioning him to bust through their window at the same time the raid team burst through the door.

It sounded insane, but so insane we figured it just might work. There we were, lowering Frankie down off the roof of a ten-story building as if he were rapelling down a mountain. The raid team got in place at the door we thought belonged to the suspects and, with a loud crash, Frankie burst through their window to find ten dealers cooking heroin! A lady was strung out on the couch, her baby in the crib near the window now splattered with shards of glass.

The raid team burst through the door right on schedule…except it was the wrong door! We had miscalculated the floor numbers, so the raid team ended up in the home of an elderly lady, while Frankie was in the home of ten big-time dealers and their guns.

The men drew their guns on Frankie. The rest of the team was already on their way, but Frankie was going to be turned into Swiss cheese before that. So he did the only thing he could think of:

He yanked the baby from its crib and a put a gun to its head.

"Drop your weapons or I'll shoot the kid!" Frankie cried out.

We couldn't believe it. He had taken a *baby* hostage! Crazy, beyond crazy. But it worked; the dealers dropped their guns.

The strung-out mother began to plead for the life of her baby, which was never actually in danger, although she couldn't have known that from Frankie's demeanor. The team broke through the door in the next moment and only then did he put the baby down.

"Kid needs his diaper changed," Frankie told the mother.

CHAPTER SIX

PHILADELPHIA, 1961

After a year and a half of surveilling Fernandez and Ormento, the US Attorney's Office for the Southern District of New York had enough to get warrants on over eighty members of the New York mob, my guys included. I was there when the lot of them was arraigned in court and spent several days testifying in front of the grand jury. Fernandez and Ormento, along with almost all of their cronies, were put away for life in what was then one of the largest and most successful mob arrests in history.

I'd spent two years in New York, and near the end of 1961 we headed back to Philadelphia, proving that the old adage "you can't go home again" isn't always true.

Literally, as it turned out. Our family was growing. Joy had given birth to our middle son, Bobby, and was now pregnant with our third. We had joined Springfield Country Club, where Daniel Jr. spent every summer day in the pool. He was on the swim team and was quick as hell in the water. I started to get involved with more things with my boys, learned everything I could about swimming, and became the coach of Dan's team. He was breaking records, records that stood long past Dan's short life.

I can visualize his bedroom even today, a kid's room likely neater than most, but with the typical posters hanging from the wall and various awards battling for space atop his desk and shelves, proudly on display. As a boy ages into a young man, the wall hangings change, the number of trophies grows, the jeans left spread out on the bed picking up one size and then another. That boy's interests may change, but not his heart. And the fact that we'd later lose Daniel to the very scourge I've spent my life fighting reinforced the conviction I learned the all-too-hard way:

It really can happen to anyone.

And it was happening to plenty on the streets of Philadelphia. More people were willing to smoke dope than they were to shoot up, which gave rise to marijuana becoming more and more popular. That meant all of a sudden we were chasing a different drug, as well as different suppliers and dealers.

I had gotten word that a large shipment of marijuana was going to be coming in via the Railway Express from Los Angeles. My informant didn't have any names or many specifics, only a date: September 11, 1963.

"A whole shitload of dope" was how he put it. "That's what's coming in."

Obviously, that wasn't much to go on. But experience had taught me that most informants tend to have their finger on the pulse of the supply chain, even if they can't fully articulate every link of it. It didn't take much for me to put a team together, even with the minimal amount of information that I had. My people took me at my word, because they knew I'd been spot-on when it came to sniffing out dope time and time again. This was just a different kind of dope than what we were used to chasing.

My partner, Laforest Russel, was quick to follow my lead. He had come from the Secret Service and was used to being given directions. A far cry from my last partner, Laforest was soft spoken, kept to himself, and never went after the glory of the bust. He was content with doing his job, which he did quite well, but he never mingled or hung out with the rest of the guys. In my two years as his partner, I had yet to find out anything personal about him other than he had no wife or kids—that was it, nothing more. Even so, I knew he had my back. He would die to protect his partner, just like he would his protectee; the Secret Service had taught him well indeed, and he was a perfect fit to be my partner.

Russel and I pulled together a very large surveillance team so we could cover both the entire North Philadelphia railway station and the primary suspect's home simultaneously, no small feat with just two days' notice, but we pulled it off. We had the place surrounded. We placed agents and officers in plainclothes around the station. Without having a firm time for the dope's arrival, we started our watch at five in the morning, and things begin to quickly drag. Surveillance was nothing new for us, of course; it was part of the job. That said, normally we have a lot more intelligence to go on, and the lack of that intelligence here left us unsure of what and who exactly we were on the lookout for. There were several suspicious individuals, but nothing was panning out. I was getting worried that maybe, this time, my intelligence was bad.

Ugghhhhhh…

I had an entire team of agents on this, no manpower or expense spared, and it was going south right before my eyes. I was going to hear it from Sam Levine, the district supervisor. He hadn't been too keen to begin with about me pulling all these guys into the field. The scope of the operation I'd assembled had gone so far as to get Levine out of his office and into the North Philadelphia train station with us. A rare feat indeed, given that he never came out from behind his desk. The guy couldn't arrest anyone if his life depended on it. He was a pipe-smoking pseudo intellectual who'd shown up only to analyze everything I did wrong, which was plenty right then.

Then I got the word from the surveillance team at the suspect's house that the shipment of drugs had shown up there, having been transported by car instead of train. I acted fast and moved the agents with me at the station to join the rest of the team surveilling the house. And, sure enough, my guys there had Ided the perps carrying duffel bags full of drugs into a tenement house in the center of the city that reminded me of the house where I'd grown up.

Russel took one team to the back of the house, leaving me the front. The plan was for me to wait until he was safely positioned before launching an assault from both sides at once. Then I heard dogs barking and shots fired, and I led my team across the street, no longer with a reason to wait.

"I got you covered!" I heard a voice say softly in my ear and swung to find a television news reporter and cameraman right on my ass.

He meant they had me covered with the camera, not guns, having somehow caught wind of the bust and wanting to cover it live.

"Stay the fuck back!" I ordered him and resumed my advance, ultimately crashing through the front door when two more shots rang out amid more barking and growling.

Bang! Bang!

An agent next to me named Steve Giorgio, a former priest who'd traded his vestments for a gun, jumped into my arms. I mean, literally jumped into my arms.

"Jesus Christ, what are you doing?" I snapped at him, not struck at all by the irony as I lowered him back to the floor.

It turned out one of the dogs, rottweilers, had lunged at Russel and he had no choice but to shoot it. Meanwhile, before our suspects could run, my team had them boxed in and surrounded. They were Esteban Cardovex, his wife Georgina, and Armando Enriques. Georgina broke into tears as we opened the bag they'd been trying to hide and placed her in cuffs.

We had seized over four hundred pounds of marijuana, along with a stash of uncut heroin, valued at two hundred thousand dollars, making it the largest seizure in our history.

How large?

Dan inspecting a marijuana plant with Bill Jennings, director of the Pennsylvania Narcotics Unit.

This shipment was easily enough to supply the entire city of Philadelphia, Delaware, and South Jersey for months.

Atlantic City, 1964

The ringing of the phone startled me from a restless sleep. In the gloom of the darkened bedroom I could just make out the clock on the nightstand: 3:00 a.m. This had to be the call I'd been waiting for with the news that would commit us to action.

I'd had a small undercover army out on the streets of Atlantic City for weeks. My agents were working at over a half a dozen clubs trying to dredge up info on what was rumored to be a huge drug operation involving a major pharmacy in town. The problem was, this was way outside of my usual stomping grounds as chief investigator for the Federal Bureau of Narcotics based in Philadelphia.

I knew almost no one in Atlantic City but had heard rumblings that the Atlantic City Police Department, particularly the vice squad, was riddled with corruption. That meant, as far as the drug bust was concerned, we weren't going to be able to rely on the locals for any assistance or backup. It had actually been Atlantic City's elected sheriff, Gerard Gormley, who called in the FBN, because he couldn't trust the vice cops to follow up on the intelligence his deputies were providing. Paramount among their conclusions was that the cops charged with keeping order on the streets were part of the problem, not the solution.

The summer of 1964 federal narcotics probe into corruption in Atlantic City was under my command. In that capacity, I had placed six undercover agents working as bartenders, cab drivers, and waiters at various Atlantic City venues. In August, I received that early morning telephone call from one of my informants in the city, saying he wanted me to meet him immediately at the Long Port Inn. The inn was located in Margate, New Jersey, a safe place for us to rendezvous. It was impossible to meet in Atlantic City proper thanks to our corruption probe of the police department, particularly the Vice Narcotics Squad. The cops had the resort town wired, and we didn't dare risk the sanctity of our intelligence.

I took the drive from Philadelphia down to Black Horse Pike, arriving at the Long Port Inn about two o'clock Friday afternoon. Given that the inn's restaurant catered to the Philadelphia Ivy League crowd, I was dressed in a white short-sleeve shirt, khaki pants, and white tennis shoes. I parked my government undercover vehicle, a 1958 white Caddy, in the inn's lot. The place was packed. Wall-to-wall people, most of whom had taken the afternoon off. But I managed to spot my man waiting in a booth located near the rear. My informant, Patty Demarco, was an otherwise nondescript guy, forty years old with black hair, dark complexion, and a busted-up nose from his days as a professional prizefighter.

I ordered two vodka tonics and started right in with Patty, avoiding the typical small talk.

"I think I got something," he told me. "A lead on a group that's ripped off several drugstores in Atlantic City."

I nodded, waiting for Patty to continue.

"Word on the street is that the group wants to unload a suitcase full of heroin and cocaine and other pills they got from the drugstore."

Patty proceeded to explain that he had met a guy by the name of Donovan who wanted twenty thousand dollars for the entire load. I told him to tell Donovan he had a buyer from Philadelphia who was interested. Then I instructed Patty to go to his New Jersey apartment and wait for my call before finalizing the arrangements. I had to discuss this plan with Atlantic City Sheriff Gormley, who was working closely with the FBN on the corruption investigation.

Patty left the inn, after which I drove straight to the Gormley funeral parlor located in downtown Atlantic City. Appropriately enough, we used the sheriff's family business as a safe house; several of my undercover agents slept in the funeral parlor rooms normally used for viewing, hopefully not a harbinger of things to come. You can call overnighting within steps of corpses and caskets above and beyond the call of duty.

Sheriff Gormley was waiting in the parking lot when I got there, having just arrived himself. He was a grizzled, hardened sort. Fifty-eight years old, a true warhorse as well as war veteran and political animal, having been elected sheriff for six consecutive terms. He wielded genuine power throughout the state of New Jersey, and his most trusted deputy, Joe Jacobi, had accompanied him to the family funeral parlor.

I filled the sheriff in on my conversation with Patty and the drugstore caper, and he was elated by the prospects of making such a bust.

"I've got thirty men assigned to the drugstores round the clock trying to catch these bastards," he said, barely able to restrain his excitement. "This is a hell of a break. Let's set this thing up!"

As in immediately.

I placed a call to Patty and instructed him to call Donovan to set up a meet in the next several hours. Patty called me back at the funeral parlor to say that Donovan had agreed to meet us behind the train station in Atlantic City at seven o'clock sharp that night. It would be left to Sheriff Gormley to make plans for the surveillance of my undercover meet with Donovan, using his best and most trusted guys.

Patty met the surveillance team at the Gormley funeral parlor, where we made plans for the rendezvous with Donovan at the train station. Patty explained to the team that Donovan was a high-strung sort: nervous, suspicious, and very dangerous, which made for a really bad combination when it comes to a drug deal.

"Another nice day in Atlantic City," I said to myself.

But we were a go. Sheriff Gormley had six undercover radio cars and motorcycles covering the train station. He also had several undercover officers working the inside to make sure all the bases were covered. I was carrying a .25-caliber Beretta automatic concealed in my sock. Patty and I climbed into my Caddy and drove to the train station, then parked in the front to await Donovan's arrival.

"There he is," Perry said fifteen minutes later, gesturing toward a figure crossing the street.

The figure was built like a gorilla, maybe thirty years old, with black hair, black shirt, black pants. Donovan stopped in front of the station, surveying the scene. Patty got out of the car and walked over to him. Donovan spoke briefly to Patty and then walked around to the rear of the station as planned, while Patty returned to my car.

I thought to myself that if I had to shoot this gorilla, my small-caliber shells probably wouldn't even hurt him, just make him mad. The guy made me wish I had come packing a magnum.

"We're supposed to meet him in the back of the train station by the old section of unused tracks," Patty told me through the open driver's side window.

We drove around to the old section of the tracks and waited. A few minutes later, Donovan appeared from nowhere and tapped on the window. He was carrying a large suitcase. I opened the door and he seated himself in the front seat alongside me, Patty having moved to the back seat. Patty introduced me to Donovan as the buyer.

"This is Rico from Philadelphia," he said casually.

We talked for a few minutes about people that Donovan had done business with in Philadelphia. He was satisfied that I was legit, relaxing and losing the hard-edged stare that had looked painted on his face. Then he laid the brown leather suitcase on the front seat between us and opened it. Loaded inside were bottles of cocaine, heroin, Demerol, bennies, and various other forms of drugs. Over a hundred bottles and vials in total, a big-time haul.

"Rico, you satisfied?" Donovan asked.

"I am. But I don't have the money. It's stashed. I don't carry that kind of bread with me on the first deal."

This was the most precarious moment of any drug bust, that interlude between nailing the suspect and the takedown itself. I started looking around for Sheriff Gormley's surveillance team to signal them to make the bust. Only I didn't see anyone anywhere in the area. Several long moments passed with the evidence still sitting beside me. I tried to stall but I could tell Donovan was getting anxious, suspicious even. Guys like this don't live in a world that encourages trust; they're like tightly wound springs ready to pop at any moment.

Where the fuck was the arresting team?

Donovan pulled a .45 automatic from under his shirt and pointed it at me. "If you're a cop, if you set me up, you're dead, motherfucker."

The hair on the back of my neck was standing up. "I'm no cop. Do I look like a cop to you?"

I figured if I pulled out the little .25 automatic and started shooting we were all dead, but I wasn't seeing a lot of options at the moment. Then I spotted Gormley's arrest team.

Finally....

But flashing the signal to them now, given Donovan's heightened state of agitation, might well lead to the shootout I was determined to avoid. I thought fast.

"The money's stashed at the Greyhound bus terminal," I said. "In a locker."

Donovan calmed down immediately, nodding stiffly. "Meet me back here with the money." Then he fixed his empty, dark eyes that looked like a shark's on the back seat. "Patty, if this guy's a cop, you're both dead motherfuckers."

Donovan climbed out of the car and walked into the darkness of the early night.

"Let's get the fuck out of here," Patty stammered, visibly shaken.

I drove straight to the Gormley funeral parlor, the hair on my neck still standing on end.

"That crazy bastard was going to kill us," Patty resumed.

I entered the parlor and laid out where we stood to the sheriff, Patty none too happy over the prospects of having to see Donovan again.

"I ain't going back to this crazy guy!" he insisted. "No way, no how!"

I was pretty much of the same mind. "I'm not going to let that guy get in the car with me, even if he has ten million bucks' worth of dope, not carrying only this peashooter," I said, adding, "You can take this Beretta and stick it."

"How about we make a trade?" the sheriff offered, taking the .357 Magnum from his holster. "That make you feel better?"

"Oh yeah," I said, testing the pistol's familiar weight. "You bet it does."

"You won't need it, Dan. We've got to change that meet to out on the street, more open, or arrest him before he gets into your car. I won't let him in the car with that gun. No case is worth anybody getting killed."

Gormley informed us that his surveillance team had followed Donovan from the train station to an apartment house in the inlet section of Atlantic City. He didn't have the suitcase with him when he entered the apartment house.

"I think he must've stashed the drugs at a locker located in the train station. That's where surveillance made him."

Gormley went on to tell me that his team was currently watching the apartment house.

"If things go bad," I said, "I could use a flash roll big enough to hold this guy off. Keep him from drawing."

The sheriff provided me the flash roll I was referring to, basically 10K in bills that looks like 20K. The plan was to stake out the lockers at the train station and try to arrest Donovan pulling the drugs from the locker before he even got to my car.

"Sounds good," I said.

Patty and I returned to the station, me now with a .357 Magnum stuck in my belt that I had no intention of actually using. No way was I going to let this wacko in the car, even if I had to make the arrest on the street myself. I had Patty sit in the back seat of the car with the flash roll in an attaché case, while I stood outside. What could go wrong?

Plenty, as things turned out.

A short time later, one of Gormley's undercover officers riding a bicycle yelled to me that they didn't know where Donovan was. They'd lost him.

Shit! Now I was worried.

Patty wanted out of the car, wanted to run now. Before he could try, Donovan appeared wearing a white shirt, white pants, dyed gray hair, and glasses. Completely different than before, a whole new man.

"You bring the bread?" he asked me.

I told Patty to open the attaché case, and he did with his hands shaking.

Donovan looked at the money and said, "Wait here."

He turned and walked back toward the train station. I spotted Gormley himself seated at the bench in the lockers area, waiting for the Donovan who'd shown up before, not this one. I chanced a dash inside, grabbed the sheriff, and told him that Donovan had changed his appearance and was already over by the lockers.

The sheriff and I walked over behind him, close enough to touch him as he was opening the locker. We nodded at each other.

I pulled out the .357 Magnum and stuck it in Donovan's ear. "Federal agent!" I cried out loud enough for the whole station to hear.

Gormley pulled out a sawed-off shotgun from under a newspaper he was holding and stuck the barrel in Donovan's gut. I removed the fully loaded .45 from Donovan's waistband and cuffed him. A search of the locker he'd been about to open revealed the suitcase packed with narcotics.

Donovan looked at me and smiled thinly. "You are one hell of an actor. You got me.... Guess I'll be seeing you around."

Maybe, but not until he got out from a ten-year stretch in a federal pen.

Getting back to Philly after all that seemed like a vacation, but not for long. I got a call from Shane Kramer, chief of criminal investigations for the US attorney's office under Drew O'Keefe, telling me he'd just gotten off the phone with my friend Sheriff Gormley. Their conversation, initiated by Gormley, had centered around police corruption in Atlantic City that had begun to rear its ugly head in the Donovan case. Gormley could no longer work with the Atlantic City vice squad that handled narcotics and wanted the Federal Bureau of Narcotics to get involved and rectify things. As a local guy and elected official, there was only so much he could do on his own.

Around that same time, we got word that Attorney General Bobby Kennedy was coming into town. The late president's brother already knew all about the police corruption running rampant in Atlantic City and had decided it was time to do something about it, put the pedal to the metal. With that priority in mind, Kramer was assembling a task force that included Customs, the FBI, the US attorney's office and, now, the FBN.

Bobby knew a turf war had erupted over who was going to control organized crime in New Jersey, exacerbating the situation. Angelo Bruno, head of the Mafia in Philadelphia, also ran Jersey. But he was an old-school guy prone to erring on the diplomatic side, which had run him afoul of the young hotheads who wanted to do things their way. So General Kennedy was up to speed on the landscape and addressed all of us by our first names as he asked for our reports and our opinions from the various perspectives we represented.

Finally, he got to me, having educated himself on my background undercover and the recent Donovan bust.

"Tell me what's going on in Atlantic City, Dan."

"We got a handle on things. Couple of solid informants keeping us in the know."

"I want those crooked cops put away. Think you can handle that?"

"Yes, sir. You bet."

I got in touch immediately with my old friend Sheriff Gormley at his family funeral parlor and he laid it all out for me. It turned out that the corrupt cops Bobby Kennedy was after were making buys from dealers they'd later arrest, confiscating their stashes in the process. They'd turn in the heroin for evidence, but only after cutting it with milk sugar and baby's Similac, keeping half the pure heroin for themselves to sell on the street through dealers they'd turned for their own ends.

It shouldn't have been difficult, given that this was such a poorly kept secret from those in the know. And there was no reason not to have people in the know because these corrupt cops believed themselves immune to prosecution. They figured that, as cops, nobody would ever dare cross them, and they were right about their fellow Atlantic City brothers in blue. But that said nothing for the FBN and Sheriff Gormley, and I wanted to give Bobby Kennedy good reason for calling me by my first name.

Working side by side with Gormley, my strategy was to put my informants on the street to buy up as many drugs as they could, looking for a match with the dope the corrupt cops were putting back onto the street. They'd cut it so much, it was identifiable thanks to the fact it retained only 3 or 4 percent pure heroin, according to the qualitative analysis done by police chemists we employed. That, and getting a few of the dealers to turn on their police suppliers, was enough to get us indictments on enough members of the vice squad to lead to wholesale changes at the Atlantic City Police Department from top to bottom. The chief and squad captain both retired, having escaped direct implication. It was a psychological thing because they had no idea who was ratting out who, so they quit. We may not have put them in jail, but we got them out of the department and off the streets, thanks to the work of a federal grand jury.

One person who didn't escape was my informant Patty Demarco. He was a long-haul truck driver and what I call a functional heroin addict. He never led me down a wrong road, and the information he'd provided over the years had helped land us Donovan as well as these corrupt cops. But the dirty cops learned his identity as a confidential informant thanks to none other than Donovan himself, who was still smarting over being put away on the drugstore bust. They fed him a Hot Shot, a lethal combination of heroin and cocaine. They killed him. I could never prove it, but I knew one of those dirty cops was behind his murder, and that haunts me to this day. I'd lost not just my informant, but also my friend.

The cops tried to infiltrate Gormley's squad with a sheriff's deputy they'd managed to turn because of his weakness for prostitutes at the Harlem Club, where Sammy Davis Jr. used to play and which was owned by none other than Atlantic City's vice squad captain. But Gormley found out through my squad that this was happening and he fired the deputy before any damage could be done. He ran a tight ship, and I'll never forget our meetings with his family's funeral parlor as a backdrop.

Police corruption was something I came up against again and again, both at home and abroad. It even allegedly haunted the career of Eddie Egan, the real Popeye Doyle of *French Connection* fame. As the *New York Times* reported in his obituary, "After *The French Connection*, Detective Egan asked to retire. Instead, he was accused of withholding drugs and of failing to appear in court when he was scheduled to testify. He was dismissed from the Police Department. Mr. Egan denied the charges and his dismissal was reversed in court. He was allowed to retire and receive his pension."

Later, Mayor David Dinkins established the Mollen Commission to do a deeper dive into the levels and root causes of police corruption in New York City, more or less typical for big cities across the country through the '80s and '90s (including Miami, thanks to the infamous "Miami River Murders," just to name another). According to a 2013 Bowling Green State University study entitled "A Study of Drug-Related Police Corruption," after two years of investigation and hearings, the commission found in part:

> *Whereas previous scandals usually arose within the context of payoffs tied to gambling or prostitution rackets, the Commission described how the burgeoning narcotics trade had become the source for more "aggressive, extortionate, and often violent" corruption that "parallel[ed] the violent world of drug trafficking.... The distinction between the criminal and the corrupt cop has disappeared. Corrupt cops no longer merely use their authority to exact payoffs; they now actively engage in criminal activity." The Commission highlighted the role of cocaine and crack markets that afforded opportunities to use illegal drugs as well as engage in acts of perjury, burglary,*

robbery, and the brutalization of citizens involved in the drug trade. The corruption scandals of the 1980s and 1990s also illustrate how drug-related corruption contributes to the overall production of misconduct and other forms of police deviance, at least in the composition that existed in several big-city police departments during that period. These investigations revealed how drug corruption tends to spawn impropriety and in some cases violent crimes perpetrated by police, a phenomenon the Commission referred to as the new "patterns" of modern police corruption.

The bottom line when it comes to police corruption is that too many of the soldiers charged with fighting the war on drugs are actually profiteering from it. The problem persists to this day, particularly overseas, and winning the war on drugs starts with eliminating corruption that still riddles law enforcement and lessens the effectiveness of the vast majority of cops who want to do the right thing. Penetrating that Blue Wall, getting good cops to give up bad ones, is a heavy lift, and more lives are lost every day because they're in business with the dealers they should be putting away.

I'd experience this to the nth degree later in my career when I was in South America and the Golden Triangle, to the point where I'm often reminded of the great scene in another classic film, *Chinatown*, where Faye Dunaway's Evelyn Mulwray asks Jack Nicholson's Jake Gittes why he left his police job in Chinatown.

"You can't always tell what's going on there," he replies.

But that never stopped me from trying.

CHAPTER SEVEN

PHILADELPHIA, 1966

M y part in the war on drugs continued for a new branch that had formed under the auspices of the Food and Drug Administration. The Bureau of Drug Abuse Control (BDAC) was created to deal with newer scourges, specifically LSD, along with barbiturates and amphetamines, which I was placed in charge of. The FBN, meanwhile, continued to work opium, cocaine, and heroin.

All this reconfiguration was both the cause and effect of the political and internecine struggles waged by rival agencies that shouldn't have been rivals at all. There were a lot of ongoing conflicts and turf wars between Customs on the one hand, BDAC on another, and FBN on a third. Eventually this would lead to all the organizations being placed under the single umbrella of the Drug Enforcement Administration. At its heart, though, these petty squabbles and battles became another impediment to winning the war on drugs. Imagine waging a global war in which the army, navy, air force, and marines are fighting each other instead of the enemy. That was the net effect of what we were facing in the '60s as rival groups staked out their claims to territory and, at times, refused to work with each other or did so under duress. And, like the scourge of political corruption, it continued to fester and expand through the bulk of my tenure fighting this particular war on the front lines, hindering my efforts at every turn.

An August 1989 *Los Angeles Times* report headlined "Interagency Rivalries Said to Hinder Drug Fight" summarized a testy Senate Judiciary Committee hearing on the subject this way:

> *A former cocaine trafficker and money launderer, describing how one federal law enforcement agency questioned him about information he already had given another, testified Thursday that interagency rivalries are crippling the nation's anti-drug efforts.*
>
> *Max Mermelstein told the Senate Judiciary Committee that the Drug Enforcement Administration questioned him about certain drug activities 10 months ago, unaware that he had provided the same information to the FBI three years earlier.*
>
> *"The FBI won't tell the DEA, the DEA won't tell the FBI and nobody wants to talk to Customs," said Mermelstein, who was convicted in 1986 on drug charges and served two years in federal prison. "Everyone has his own budget priorities."*

For my part, I was determined to keep any jurisdictional squabbles from hindering the efforts of my BDAC squad, which comprised both Federal Bureau of Narcotics and Customs agents. Our initial focus was on drugstores, specifically pharmacies suspected of illegally dispensing barbiturates and amphetamines. One of my informants I called Charlie the Rat was a paregoric addict. Paregoric was a kind of tincture infused with minor opiate derivatives once used on infants during the teething phase. Charlie the Rat was a long way from that but, understandably, nobody played the role of an addict better because he was a real one. So, in cooperation with Bill Jennings, who was in charge of the Pennsylvania State Narcotics Bureau, we started targeting drugstores with Charlie playing the role of the stooge trying to buy illicit drugs kept behind the pharmacy counters.

One of these was Pastor's Pharmacy, owned and operated by the man who'd given his name to his business, Edward Pastor. They were selling drugs like crazy, supplying long-haul truckers with amphetamines, maybe or maybe not on behalf of the Teamsters Union. Charlie the Rat made the buys, enough to get us a warrant so we could raid the place. A reporter for the *Philadelphia Inquirer* got wind of what we were up to and I promised him access to the actual raid in return for him not running the story early, which would've blown our bust. We arrested Pastor; we had him dead to rights, thanks to all those bulk sales he was making, and I figured he'd be going away for a long time.

"Federal agents under Addario," the *Inquirer* reported in the exclusive I'd given them, "arrested Pastor when it was charged he participated in the sale of 43,000 amphetamine tablets to undercover agents. At the time, Addario accused Pastor of being in business to sell the illegal 'pep pills' to long-haul truckers in Teamsters Union Local 513."

The article went on to report that we had "seized more than 500,000 amphetamine and barbiturate tablets and 20 gallons of a liquid drug when a Federal audit disclosed bookkeeping inaccuracies."

The *Evening Bulletin* covered the same story under the headline "Druggist, Union Organizer Seized by Narcotics Agents." But Pastor wasn't done yet, and neither were we. My squad raided the drugstore for the third time in three months in June 1967 and arrested Edward Pastor's wife Thelma "after a State audit showed 'very large shortages' of some narcotics and unexplainable oversupply of others," according to the *Philadelphia Inquirer*. The Pastors, I guess, were one big happy family.

But I was soon to learn that a different kind of family was coming after me.

Not long after both Pastors made bail, the Newark office of the FBI got word from an informant that Angelo Bruno, crime boss of Philadelphia and thus New Jersey too, had put out a hit on me. Newark contacted BDAC's New York office, which got me on the phone and told me to hang tight—they were sending eight men, who soon arrived in Havertown where I lived with my family, armed to the teeth and loaded for bear. They hustled Joy and the kids to a hotel out by the airport, leaving two agents with them while the other six stayed with me and set up shop in our home to provide protection 24/7. Was the Newark informant's information accurate? Did Bruno really put a hit out on me? Well, we had this German shepherd named Blitz, a great dog. He died the day before my protection showed up, poisoned to death. So, yes, the intelligence was solid and it indeed appeared that one of the most powerful crime bosses in the country wanted me dead.

As bad as anybody putting a hit out on me, this was worse, because Angelo Bruno was a very powerful man whose orders were always obeyed. The kind of guy who, when he put a hit out on you, it was time to start planning your funeral. Bruno had been born in Sicily, the son of a grocer who grew to become a close associate of powerful New York crime family boss Carlo Gambino. He earned his nickname "the Gentle Don" after refusing to kill rival mobster Antonio Pollina when the two were both up to succeed Joe Ida as boss of the Philadelphia family in 1959. Over the next twenty years, Bruno managed to stay under the radar in a fashion hardly in keeping with other dons of the time. He avoided the intense law enforcement and media scrutiny that plagued his contemporaries, along with lengthy prison terms, in large part by not allowing his family to get mixed up in narcotics trafficking. Angelo was old school, preferring bookmaking and loan-sharking to keep his hold on power. But he did allow other gangs to distribute their heroin in Philly in exchange for a share of the profits, which kept his top people happy enough to accept the status quo and not attempt to wage war within the family.

His reign lasted two decades, brought to an end not by drugs but by gambling. Since New Jersey was part of Bruno's territory, he inherited all the potential profits that could be squeezed out of the lucrative Atlantic City gambling industry. The Five Families wanted a piece of the action but, under arcane Mafia edicts, they couldn't move in without Bruno's permission. Wanting to keep the peace, the Gentle Don, as he was still known, elected to open the casinos up to them in exchange for a cut of their profits. But his underlings in Philly were considerably less than enamored with the deal, setting the wheels in motion for his assassination on March 21, 1980.

Like I said, though, back in the early '60s when Bruno wanted you dead, it was time to go shopping for a coffin. I knew that doing nothing was not an option. I couldn't hide or leave town, and a six-man protective detail wasn't going to hang with me forever. I had to act, but how?

It was no surprise to anyone that the mob had certain cops in their pockets. The top mobsters were smart, living by the credo that you keep your enemies close, and that worked in a town like Philly, which then had the third largest police force in the country. That many cops meant a lot of opportunities for a few to turn dirty and be steered by corruption. And I was hardly the most loved guy to those in the Philadelphia Police Department, given that I maintained a zero-tolerance attitude when it came to things like those New York detectives who wanted to pocket a dealer's heroin and cash for themselves. I still had a modicum of clout, however, and now was the time to use it, since I wasn't keen on sitting on my hands while my six bodyguards went to the mattresses, as they say in gangster speak. So I made a call to Police Commissioner Frank Rizzo, who would later go on to serve as Philadelphia mayor from 1972 to 1980, one of the most colorful characters to ever serve the city.

"I need a favor," I said to Rizzo, and proceeded to fill him in on my predicament.

"You're a dead man walking," he said.

"Tell me something I don't know. Can you get me in with Bruno?"

They were both South Philly guys, reason enough for me to figure Rizzo might be able to do something, and intervene. He had a lieutenant who was tracking Bruno's every single move and was able to

Dan pictured with Tom McDermott and Frank Rizzo at an International Chiefs of Police meeting in the early '60s.

set up a meet with him. We drove out to this modest row house in South Philly at 8th and Snyder, indistinguishable from the others on the block, where Bruno lived like he was no different from anybody else in the neighborhood. I was in a car with two of the agents and Rizzo's man Lieutenant Zarelli, the other four agents in a trail car immediately behind us.

101

All of a sudden, a Chevy sedan pulls up next to us and these two mobbed-up Italian guys with shoulders busting out of their suits climb out ahead of a smallish figure wearing a fedora who was maybe five foot eight if you stretched him.

Angelo Bruno.

He climbed into the back seat of the car I was in, pushing the FBI agents across the bench seat. Next to me in the front seat, Zarelli turned his gaze on Bruno, then gestured toward me.

"You know this man?"

"Never saw him before."

Zarelli nodded. "This is Dan Addario. He's a federal agent and you put a contract out on him."

"Absolutely not. Who the fuck's using my name?"

Zarelli didn't answer the question. "We arrested one of your top drug earners, Angelo: Pastor. We figured he was the one who put the hit out."

"No way! I look like I'm crazy enough to kill a federal agent? You think that's how I stayed in this business so long?"

He shook his head, turned toward me, and laid a beefy hand on my shoulder. "*Paisan*," he said, "you're going to live a long and prosperous life."

Then he climbed out of our car and back into his.

We never did figure out who actually ordered the hit, although some suspected the Teamsters were behind it since they were protecting Pastor and the other pharmacy owners we'd taken down. Whatever the case, after that one and only meeting Angelo Bruno must've made the contract go away, but not before the *Philadelphia Inquirer* headlined a story with "Gangsters Offering $5000 for Slaying of Top U.S. Drug Agent."

And I was about to make some new enemies, the kind I could've done without on both sides of the law.

CHAPTER EIGHT

DETROIT, 1968

My move from Philadelphia to Detroit coincided with the birth of the Bureau of Narcotics and Dangerous Drugs, yet another attempt by the government to deal with the internecine struggles roiling agencies, in this case namely BDAC and FBN. Another example of how even fifty-plus years ago, the war on drugs was plagued by politics and jurisdictional infighting.

Hey, weren't we all supposed to be on the same side?

I was to become deputy regional director in Detroit, but not before the office threw me a great going-away party at Frank Polumbo's nightclub in South Philly. Frank Rizzo was there, along with a whole bunch of politicians. I couldn't believe it when my former captain Clarence "Fergie" Ferguson entered and made a beeline toward me. He couldn't have been nicer or more reverent of my service, apparently having forgotten that in another life, he'd set me up to take the fall for the raid on that gambling hall in the ward of James H. Tate. Fergie was somehow very friendly with Jimmy Durante, then still a major act on the entertainment circuit. Whenever Jimmy was playing in town, Fergie assigned a couple detectives to take him around. He was playing Polumbo's the following night, so Fergie took the opportunity to bring Jimmy to my party.

"Dan," he said to me as the night wore on, "you know Jimmy's got a birthday coming up. He's playing the Copa that night in New York. Everyone's going to be there, even Sinatra. The place is going to be packed."

I nodded, waiting for the other shoe to drop. And then it did.

"You got some solid contacts in New York, right? Because some of the boys want to come up and celebrate."

I nodded again, now much better versed at playing this kind of game. Fergie was a chameleon who could change shades at will. From my current position, he knew I could do a lot of harm to him if I wanted to, so he made nice. Thanks to the politics of this game, I'd learned to keep my enemies close. The more I could do for a guy like Fergie now, the more I could call upon for later.

"Let me see what I can do," I told Fergie.

Turned out I was able to do a lot, managing to get a table held for Fergie and ten of his men that night at the Copa, mixing with all manner of mob guys and movie stars. Durante noticed Fergie during his first set and came straight over to the table as soon as he was done, making Fergie feel like a star in his own right. The whole group ended up upstairs after the show in Jimmy's private suite of rooms.

With each new presidential administration comes change. They all have to make some sort of mark on history. In 1968, Lyndon B. Johnson decided that his mark on the war on drugs was going to be that merger of the Federal Bureau of Narcotics and the Bureau of Drug Abuse Control into the Bureau of Narcotics and Dangerous Drugs. And, while it was a step forward for progress, it came from a dirty place—corruption. The FBN in New York had been a hotbed of dealers, gamblers, and hustlers. After watching over the organization in that city, I knew how easy it was for a bribe to be too tempting. Many a good agent was enticed to do things that weren't kosher.

From the going away party held at Palumbo's just prior to Dan's reassignment from Philadelphia to Detroit. Dan and Joy are standing.

This proclivity was typified by a gambling squad set up by the chief of the criminal division for the US Attorney's Office for the Southern District. One night an agent from that squad got drunk and lost, literally lost, his government car. The police returned it, but not before finding ten thousand dollars in the trunk. The agent claimed his father ran a used car lot and had given him the money to hold because the banks were closed. Another agent was making deposits into a bank account kept under the radar by the fact none of the transactions were large enough to attract federal attention. But the bank noticed and notified the office. Turned out the guy owned three houses, expensive cars, and a Rolex watch—all, purportedly, on an agent's modest salary.

Too many agents attached to this squad were getting rich off graft. They drove expensive cars or had second homes on the beach.

This happened on the watch of the squad's number two man, Pat Malone. Once the criminal division learned what was happening, the squad was dismantled and agents were quietly farmed out to less than desirable posts in the hope they would quit, since the results of the investigation were just too messy to disclose. In Malone's case, that was Detroit, the same city I was headed for. He was made regional director, which meant he was now running the show. As for me, I was told to pack my bags and be the man behind Malone, the deputy regional director of Detroit, which also covered Ohio and Kentucky.

Talk about your hostile work environment! Malone figured I'd been sent to Detroit to spy on him and get him off the job. Not the case at all, of course, but the tension between us was palpable, only increasing as I plunged myself into my new job, making him look all the worse by comparison. I didn't care. I had a job to do, and nothing was going to stop me from doing it.

To make matters worse, when I got up to Detroit, I discovered that the atmosphere in the office was hostile, untrusting, and a bit paranoid. Most of the agents had never been out of Detroit and were angry by the merger that brought new people onto their turf, stepping on their toes.

After being in the office for only a few days, it was obvious that their toes needed stepping on. The agents didn't seem to know how to run a viable undercover operation. They had no knowledge of how to deal with true intel, much less cultivate and oversee confidential informants. I put in a request to get support from agents I knew I could trust and depend on. Eventually, four guys I had worked with in Philadelphia were moved to Detroit. I could now actually get shit done, whether Malone liked it or not.

I had other matters to take care of that were beyond my duties as an agent. My family was still back in Philly. The older the kids got, the harder it was to move them. I had made my move in April, the boys still with three months left of school, and there was no way I was going to upset their worlds that way. So Joy and the kids remained in Philly until the school year ended. In July, the boys said tearful goodbyes to lots of good friends and moved to Bloomfield, Michigan, a quaint midwestern town outside of Detroit.

I was so happy to be reunited with my family, but I was so busy that I barely had time to be with them. I was trying to whip this new office into shape while still keeping one eye on Malone and one on the target that was painted on my back.

That said, the agents that I had imported were adjusting well in Detroit. Within a few months, they had established informants and were making buys and doing deals. But those deals, more than anything else, uncovered yet more layers of corruption.

"Boss," the agent who'd been one of my top guys back in Philadelphia greeted me one day, walking into my office with a bundle in his hands.

He opened it up and dropped a brick of heroin on my desk.

"What's this?" I asked.

"This is the shit we are seeing. It all seems to be the same," he said.

"Where is it coming from?" I asked.

"Chicago. Gotta be a big organization."

"Do you need a crew bigger than the four of you?" I asked, hoping that he would be able to make it work.

"We can't pull this off by ourselves. No way," he told me. "Not just the four of us and cover all the bases to make a bust this big."

That was going to be a problem. The rest of the agents in Detroit had no experience busting narcotics. They went after pot dealers. Easy prey. Heroin was a totally different game. I knew the entire team needed to be trained.

I explained to Malone what we needed to do. He wasn't hearing it and wouldn't even entertain a conversation about it. But I'd been sent in to troubleshoot the office, not to be pushed around by this asshole. Malone never realized that I was there to help things run more smoothly. He was convinced I was placed there by the BNDD to catch him currying favor and courting corruption. I could have cared less what the fuck the guy was doing as long as he wasn't interfering with the true nature of my mission. And now he was.

I decided that I was going to do it my way and take Malone out of the loop.

My Philly guys and I began to train the Detroit-born agents. Slowly, I began to see the office take working form. Malone backed off and stayed out of it, realizing that he wasn't going to push me around; in fact, I was the one pushing him. He finally decided to quit, as the BNDD had hoped, and I was made the regional director in the midst of this investigation of all that heroin coming out of Chicago.

With Malone no longer around to impede me, I was able to make even greater strides. Chicago wasn't in our jurisdiction, which meant we'd be working cooperatively with the BNDD office there to take down this latest new scourge—literally, as it turned out, since the first thing our intelligence indicated was that the black tar heroin was coming in from Mexico. The normal supply line into Chicago came in through Marseilles by way of New York. And that meant we were facing a new enemy and a new challenge. But the Chicago office put their guys on the streets and cultivated informants, and we were able to flush out the network bringing the black tar heroin to the streets as a result.

I raise this also because it was symbolic of a sea change in the way intra-agency investigations were handled. This case was emblematic of the centralization that resulted from the creation of the BNDD. The mindset in years past had been to fight over who got credit for the bust and got to write up the arrest reports and do the perp walk. That encouraged fractionalization and a refusal of one office to share information with another out of fear that their work would be usurped. The old breed of agents and supervisors were creatures bred from that culture. But BNDD had been created to change all that in the person of agents like me who'd built our careers on the streets in operations that required trust and cooperation with various law enforcement entities, including the courts.

Just as I had gotten the Detroit office running smoothly, a different kind of shit hit the fan. Out in Los Angeles, the twenty-year-old daughter of famed Hollywood personality Art Linkletter, Diane, jumped out the window of her sixth-floor apartment at the Shoreham Towers in West Hollywood. And she wasn't alone. The number of suicides on the West Coast showed a huge spike, with the Golden Gate Bridge and high buildings becoming popular places from which to jump. The government credited this mass increase in suicide, especially in San Francisco, to one thing:

LSD.

I sat at my desk in Detroit shaking my head at the news that Art Linkletter's young daughter had killed herself. What was it going to take for people to realize that drugs kill? Just then, my phone rang.

"Addario?" a voice greeted.

"Yes?"

"This is Nelson, Nelson B. Coon from BNDD headquarters."

"What can I do for you, Nelson?" I asked one of the BNDD's assistant directors, who was in charge of personnel.

"Have you read this shit about Linkletter?" he asked, his voice radiating anger.

"I have," I said. "It's a damn shame."

"It is." A long pause followed. "You up for another move, Dan? Because I need you in San Francisco. You did the job in Detroit and now I need you there. I need you to shut this LSD craze down before anybody else jumps out of a building."

CHAPTER NINE

SAN FRANCISCO, 1969

"Yes, sir. Thank you," I said to Coon, biting my tongue. Because I wasn't really appreciative. Although I welcomed the praise and faith, I didn't welcome the move. We'd been in Detroit less than two years. My family was just starting to get settled and my boys were making friends. Now, I was uprooting them again. Oftentimes I had to remind myself that there was a greater good, and I was saving the world for my boys so that they would not fall victim to the virulent disease of addiction.

I had to leave my family yet again. Dan was in junior high, Bob in middle school, and my youngest son Mark in elementary. They had to finish out the year, which meant I was going to again be separated from Joy and my boys for several months once more. I think they were getting used to it, but I certainly wasn't. Even so, I had to put that to the side and tackle what was in front of me.

The San Francisco office consisted of San Francisco, Sacramento, Marin County, and San Jose. This was the largest office I had ever run, consisting of over two hundred agents, together with a hundred-person

Pictured from left: Mark, Bobby, Dan, younger Dan, younger Dan's girlfriend.

support staff. Luckily, it was running smoothly. This time, I wasn't coming in to fix the office but to help control the issues outside.

After visiting all four offices and having discussions with the respective Agents in Charge, I realized that no one was educated enough to deal with the LSD craze. I had a briefing with the top honchos at the BNDD. I told them that I needed to have a task force that understood LSD to come in and educate my agents appropriately.

Busting dealers and users is not equal across substances. Marijuana is the easiest to bust because it's large and gives off a distinctive odor: easy pickings. Heroin and cocaine, although odorless, are still bulky and, therefore, easy to spot. Plus, heroin addicts wear their addiction on their sleeve—literally.

LSD was a whole different monster. It was small; thousands of hits could be carried in a pocket. They were printed on small postage stamps, inconspicuous to the untrained eye. Most unassuming individuals would think a dealer just really liked to send mail. As well, this synthetic material was not being run over borders through the kind of networks I'd dealt with in the past. It was manufactured right here in the United States, which made distribution quick and easy.

The task force from headquarters trained my agents in all four of the locations that fell under my jurisdiction. Once my agents were skilled up, they were ready to hit the streets, starting with the most infamous streets of them all: Haight-Ashbury, the mecca of LSD. The place was crawling with drugs and hippies. While agents working out of the San Francisco office were wandering the Haight, other agents from Marin and Berkeley were gathering intelligence in their back-yards. All were doing a series of buys without ever making a bust. We had to start from scratch and lay the groundwork to fully understand this new group of users, employing all the lessons I'd learned in my first post under Chief McDermott.

Eventually, my agents ingratiated themselves with the LSD community and infiltrated the Haight-Ashbury scene. Starting at the bottom and climbing the food chain to flush out the big-time dealers who went by clever nicknames and decorated their "acid stamps" with colorful designs like the sun and smiley faces. Call them the precursor to emojis.

At the same time, school ended and Joy and the boys were able to move to California. I had bought a house for my family, without Joy even seeing it. It was a beautiful ranch home in Orinda, over-looking a country club that we'd eventually join. The boys quickly made themselves at home in California. They joined sports teams, made friends, and of course were loving the sun. Having them with me lifted my spirits and, for a change, there wouldn't be any harsh winters to deal with.

As time passed, we began identifying the labs in Marin and San Francisco that were making LSD. We slowly started to pick them off one by one. While my guys were in the field, I was now spending most of my days on television. It was a far cry from drug busting, sure, but worthwhile given that the misconceptions running rampant about LSD contributed greatly to the explosion of the drug's popularity.

Eventually, we figured out the identity of the ringleader behind the entire viral nature of the drug. Never before had an entire craze been laid at the feet of a single individual, until now:

Timothy Leary.

Leary was the guru of LSD and far from the kind of gangster or drug runner I was used to and experienced at dealing with. Leary was a clinical psychologist and writer at Harvard University. He had conducted research at Harvard using LSD and psilocybin in 1960–1962, back when both substances were legal. His study was questioned because he was personally using the psychotropics during the course of his work and pressured several of his students to join him. Despite his critics, Leary strongly believed that LSD had a therapeutic use in psychiatry. He even claimed that the drug could reverse homosexuality. He eventually joined the counterculture that worshiped and followed him. President Richard Nixon declared Leary "the most dangerous man in America," and he became my new target. Not a typical drug kingpin in any way, shape, or form, but nonetheless guilty of inflicting incredible damage on society.

I met Leary for an informal interview in Berkeley—informal because we still lacked probable cause to get a warrant. He was doing drop in, drop out kind of stuff, never hanging around anywhere long enough for us to nail him on felony drug charges. I found Leary to be pleasant and likable, as charming as he was charismatic. But interviewing him was like talking into a dead phone. He gave me nothing worthwhile I could act on, paying me lip service and seeming to enjoy the fact that I couldn't nail him for all I knew he was involved in. He'd already been arrested once in 1965 but skated on all charges, and that episode seemed to have only hardened his approach to law enforcement in the ensuing three or so years. He was going to be a tough nut to crack, and I'd have to find another means to crack him.

My LSD task force started focusing its efforts elsewhere to stem the tide of this particular epidemic. Timothy Leary may have been the guru of LSD, but he was by far not the largest producer and distributor of the drug. That honor would go to Augustus Owsley Stanley. Stanley was a clandestine chemist and a sound engineer for the Grateful Dead. By the time I hit the scene, Stanley had produced almost five million doses of LSD, the largest amount by any individual.

In late 1967, Stanley's La Espiral, Orinda lab had been raided by police; he was found in possession of 350,000 doses of LSD. His defense was that the illegal substances were for personal use, but he was found guilty and sentenced to three years in prison. After he was released, Stanley resumed working for the Grateful Dead as their live sound engineer, with my office's task force hot on his trail again. In the wake of the band's show one night, nineteen members of the Grateful Dead and crew were arrested for possession of a variety of drugs.

Under questioning, Stanley gave up Leary, implicating him in the existence and operation of no less than a dozen additional LSD labs. An arrest warrant was finally issued. But Leary must've gotten tipped off, because he'd fled by the time we arrived to arrest him. We finally got him when he was found hiding in the Midwest. On January 21, 1970, Leary received a ten-year sentence for his 1968 offense, with another ten added later for that prior arrest in 1965 that was reinstated, for a total of twenty years to be served consecutively.

Many called him a counterculture folk hero. For me, he was just another drug pusher.

While in San Francisco, my middle son Bobby's tennis game really bloomed. He made the Junior Davis Cup team and was tutored by Rod Laver, the world's top-ranked professional player at the time. Dan was swimming and playing water polo and baseball. Young Mark discovered T-ball and sports in general, in between wandering off and disappearing for hours at a time, a penchant that would be cause for considerable anxiety a few years later.

As for me, part of the job was ingratiating myself into the San Francisco political scene, cultivating relationships and trust with the officials I needed to have on my side, in gatherings at Lorenzo Petroni's famed North Beach Restaurant. All manner of politicians, from San Francisco mayor George Moscone to Willie Brown to Jerry Brown and Nancy Pelosi. Bill Newsom, a judge and father of Gavin, the recently elected lieutenant governor of California, was one of the first to champion my efforts. I was in high cotton, mixing and mingling with the likes of Gordon Getty of the Getty oil dynasty and Quentin Kopp, a future candidate for mayor. I also became very good friends with newspaper reporter Paul Avery, who'd later become famous for his work on the Zodiac murder spree case. (His character was played by Robert Downey Jr. in the David Fincher film.) There was Herb Caen, a Pulitzer Prize–winning columnist, who used to pop into the restaurant all the time. And Warren Hinckle, Hunter Thompson's writing partner who was married to John Cheever's daughter and wrote for both the *San Francisco Examiner* and the *Chronicle*.

Learning how to cultivate the media was a crucial tool in the war on drugs, when so many believed that people were free to manage their lives however they chose. In response to that, it was important to get the word out there that every dollar the so-called "casual" drug user spent on the street got funneled into the next buy on the part of his dealer, pusher, supplier, and so on, all the way up the chain of command. When it comes to drugs, there's no such thing as a victimless crime.

I enjoyed some lighter moments in my San Francisco posting as well. I had the pleasure of getting to know Paul Frees, a voice actor famous for doing the voices of commercial characters like the Jolly Green Giant and the Pillsbury Doughboy. In those days, nobody was more famous for that kind of work than Paul and the great Mel Blanc, who voiced Bugs Bunny and many more cartoon characters. Frees had his own honorary badge from the sheriff of Marin Country and did ride-alongs with the sheriff's people and the state narcotics guys. Call it the privilege of fame.

Anyway, Paul was flying east one day, sitting next to Elvis Presley on the plane. They started talking and showing off their respective badges. Presley, a police buff himself, flashed his Memphis police badge, but Paul trumped that by showing the King his federal narcotics badge. It happened that Presley had a White House visit with President Nixon scheduled soon after and, while there, told Nixon he wanted a badge like that too. So the president called the BNDD and told them to issue Elvis a badge that he was proud of flashing in numerous photos right up until his death.

I also had the opportunity occasionally to drive luxury cars that had been confiscated during asset seizures as part of our drug busts. My neighbors didn't really know what I did or who I was until the drug arrests started piling up. I drove a Jaguar, a Corvette, and a Bentley for an entire month. The Bentley was a right-drive car, meaning I had to negotiate the often perilous streets of San Francisco from a totally different perspective. Challenging, but worth it for that brief stretch.

And I attended to business other than drugs in San Francisco as well. I walked into my office early one morning to find a dapper man reading a newspaper, his feet propped up on my desk.

As I entered, he stood up and said, "I'm Jim Browning. You must be Dan Addario. Pleased to meet you."

His voice was polite, and he seemed to have no regard for the fact that he was sitting in another man's office.

"What are you doing in my office?" I asked.

"Waiting for you, of course," he laughed. "I apologize if I was being presumptuous."

I nodded at him, attempting to indicate that he was.

"I'm the US attorney for California. I've been meaning to stop by."

Jim Browning would go on to prosecute and imprison Patty Hearst. However, I could tell he was well on his way to becoming a legend even at that time. Something about his demeanor, the no-nonsense way in which he carried himself.

"What can I do for you?" I asked.

"Heroin," he said, his brow furrowing.

"Pardon?"

Brown explained to me that his office was seeing a new type of heroin in town, something that they had never seen before. The number of overdoses was also rising.

"I know you guys are busy with this LSD stuff, but I can't have this new shit coming in and killing my people. Can you get on this?"

Heroin was my specialty. I assured him we would figure out where the stuff was coming from and do everything we could to snuff out the problem.

I sent out an intelligence group to comb the streets. It didn't take them long to find out that the shit was coming in from the Latino section of town, known as the Mission District. We began the usual intelligence and infiltration process, finally making a buy of this new dope.

My agent brought it back and dropped it on my desk, "Sir, take a look at this shit."

I picked up the bag and recognized it immediately from both Philadelphia and Detroit: black tar heroin, only thicker and stickier.

"Let's get this to the chemist," I said. "See exactly what we're dealing with here."

The chemist's analysis indeed found this to be an especially potent form of black tar heroin, consistent with samples originating in Mexico. This was the first time anyone in the BNDD had seen heroin coming up from Mexico. However, I wasn't surprised. The opium and heroin epidemic was like putting out a brush fire; every time we shut one down, a new one opened right up. As far as Mexico's role in the epidemic, the roots date back to the 1870s or so and the explosion of Chinese immigration. Those Chinese brought stores of poppy seeds across the world with them and found the Mexican climate to be ideal for growing the flowers that would ultimately sprout heroin.

And now black tar heroin.

A few weeks after that first brick was dropped on my desk, Browning was in my office again to greet me when I arrived. This time, he was at least considerate enough to bring a cup of coffee.

"Hey, Jim," I said, sipping the coffee he had brought me. "We haven't had any luck finding the source in Mexico yet. It's crazy down there right now. Cartels are popping up left and right. No one wants to speak."

"I'm not here about that," he said. "I need to drop another problem in your lap: right here, on Alcatraz."

I cinched my brow: What could be happening on Alcatraz? President Kennedy had closed the prison several years ago and it had been abandoned ever since.

"Indians," Browning said, taking a sip of his coffee, like I should understand.

"Excuse me?" I said.

"American Indians, they over took the island."

"Why?" I asked.

"I don't know. But I want you to find out. I need them to get off the island peacefully. Quietly," he said, his voice low.

"You realize this isn't our specialty."

"I know. But I trust you. And I trust you to do it right and without making headlines. Can you please just let me know what you find out?"

"I'll send some guys out to do some digging," I told him.

"Thank you," he said, and extended his hand.

Browning had come to me because he'd heard about the hard sources I'd managed to cultivate in the drug world, and he figured I might be able to put those to use in this Alcatraz takeover. He needed to know exactly what was happening on the island, and what might be about to, in order to properly devise a diplomatic solution. I put an agent of mine named George Heard, who'd played professional football for the Philadelphia Eagles, on the case because he was expert at working sources on Fisherman's Wharf, and those people might have a line on what was happening on Alcatraz.

George and his partner scouted around, talking to sources in search of the intelligence we sought. Sure enough, he was able to learn from a boat captain who'd ferried supplies to the area that we were dealing with between thirty and forty Indians. Another of George's sources indicated those Indians were heavily armed with some serious firepower. Federal marshals, I'd later learn, had been ready to storm the island when Browning came to me. The Indians were serious and weren't leaving that island without a fight.

With that intelligence in his pocket, Browning was able to forestall an armed raid by US marshals and, ultimately after several more months, to negotiate a diplomatic solution to the crisis that ended in June 1971with only fifteen stubborn stalwarts being taken into custody. While Browning wasn't about to simply yield the island, the armed assault that may have been in the initial planning stages never happened, avoiding what would have almost certainly been a bloodbath.

Little did I know that this particular incident was preparing me for the next challenge of my career in my first foreign posting.

South America, 1970

I'd gotten a reputation as a troubleshooter, someone who could clean up a lot of shit once dispatched to hostile environments.

Like South America.

South America, of course, promised to be far different from Atlantic City, Detroit, or San Francisco. BNDD deputy directors John Finlator and Nelson B. Coon, well-established guys at headquarters in Washington, had recommended me for the job, and BNDD chief John Ingersoll signed off without question in the hope that the reorganization I was a part of could stem the rising tide of drugs flooding north into the United States. As part of that reorganization, instead of having one office for three countries, there would now be one attached to the embassies in every single South American nation with which we enjoyed diplomatic relations. Up until that point, that region had been lumped in with Mexico. Going forward, the BNDD separated out Mexico and named me regional director for the remaining thirteen countries.

Before I could simply head south with passport in hand, I had to endure a background check where the only family member or acquaintance who escaped an interview was our dog Smokey, and I can't even be totally sure about that, since he wasn't talking. As that process was transpiring, I underwent diplomatic training on all levels—from the various embassy posts I'd be intermingling with on a daily basis, to the proper protocol to follow at a cocktail party or dinner. I had to be briefed on all military efforts ongoing in the region and all the American businesses, like IBM, operating down there. It was a laborious process and one that left me with a keen appreciation for the depth and importance of foreign service.

Once cleared, having passed so called State Department "Charm School" with flying colors, my first task would be to check out the area and see what I needed to get things up to snuff and set the new standard that Ingersoll and company had in mind. On my first trip, I was joined by the director himself and Mexico's regional director, infamous former Maricopa County, Arizona, sheriff Joe Arpaio, who, until my assignment, had been responsible for the rest of the region I was now taking over.

The three of us boarded a plane out of Washington and headed to Panama, where I first met Manuel Noriega, then a colonel in military intelligence and already one of the most powerful men in the country. We hit it off from our first meeting. He'd done his homework on me and seemed to relish the fact that, like him, I'd come up from working the streets, a fellow police officer. There was an authoritative aura about him, a sense of power and control. A guy, in short, you wanted in your corner who could help you get a lot of things done. We had started our trip in Panama because the previous agents assigned there had been thrown out of the country for committing diplomatic violations, and we needed Noriega's okay to bring down replacements.

"How do I know these will be any different, any better?" asked the man I was ready to put my money on for the future.

"Because you have my word," I told him.

"That's good enough for me," Noriega smiled.

PART THREE

OPERATION SPRINGBOARD

CHAPTER TEN

BUENOS AIRES, ARGENTINA, 1971

The drug business doesn't operate on a straight line. Instead, the product follows a circuitous, often serpentine route from crop to lab to the streets. And the most elaborate of these routes, under the direction of the world's most infamous network, originated in the Golden Triangle of Southeast Asia. But that's not necessarily where you need to go to stem the flow of drugs into the United States, thanks to the way the drugs actually work their way in.

That's how my next stop after San Francisco, and first international posting, came about in Buenos Aires as the regional director for the entire South American continent.

Numerous couriers arrested by narcotics agents had revealed that one single ring in particular had smuggled a thousand pounds of pure heroin into the United States, equal to 10 to 20 percent of the country's annual consumption. The dope, according to our intelligence, may have originated in Hong Kong, but both Hong Kong and Southeast Asian heroin was actually being smuggled across the Pacific into Chile, while European heroin smuggled across the

A freighter ordered by Dan to be searched when it arrived at a Buenos Aires port.

Atlantic into Argentina ended up in Paraguay before being shipped to the United States.

Argentina and Paraguay had long been popular refuges for Marseille gangsters wanted in France for serious crimes. The most prominent of these was Auguste Joseph Ricord, a Marseille-born gangster who worked with the Gestapo during World War II. Using a variety of means ranging from private aircraft to hollowed-out artifacts and antiques, Ricord was believed to have smuggled thousands of kilos of heroin into the United States from Argentina and Paraguay through the network he commanded. Although law enforcement officials had always assumed that Ricord and his associates were being supplied from Marseille, current reports of shipments from Hong Kong and Southeast Asia to Paraguay raised the possibility that their sources had shifted to Asia and the Golden Triangle in recent years. The most unholy of unholy alliances.

My orders came straight from the Oval Office: President Nixon wanted Ricord badly. In the later 1960s, drug trafficking to the United States had been temporarily disrupted by the "French Connection" made famous by those New York detectives, Eddie Egan and Sonny Grosso, with whom I'd worked when I was detailed to the Federal Bureau of Narcotics in New York. That case had netted the biggest street seizure in drug enforcement history. Hundreds of dealers on both sides of the Atlantic had been rounded up, but narcotics agents and Interpol had failed to capture the key players. Many, including the ringleader Ricord, fled to South America. By the time I arrived on the scene, Ricord was the acknowledged kingpin of the entire South American drug network, moving unprecedented and ever-increasing volumes of heroin that dwarfed the twenty-five million dollars captured in the French Connection case, and were estimated to be in the area of 2.5 billion dollars annually.

My job was to pick up where Eddie Egan and Sonny Grosso had left off, by nailing Auguste Ricord and shutting down his network. I'd be working out of Buenos Aires, where I had built a strong team of agents who helped bring me close to key cogs in Ricord's network we'd managed to identify and eventually get to know up close and personal.

On my first official day on the job, building security buzzed me as I was brushing my teeth. I spat out a mouthful of Colgate and answered the phone cautiously. The caution was for no other reason than my Spanish was basic, to say the least.

"Como estas?"

I was also never sure whether the Argentinian guard would speak English or Spanish. Today it was English, in which he informed me that "John" was on the way up to my apartment.

I didn't bother to look at my watch—it would read a few minutes before 9:00 a.m. The man I knew as "John" was always on time. You could wind your watch by him. At most, it would take him a couple of minutes to ride the elevator up seven flights. I'd been working with him on all the prep work that preceded my formally assuming the post behind a desk at the US Embassy and had yet to see him slip up on even the minutest detail. The spook, as I liked to call him, had spent fifteen years in South America, first with the CIA and then the Bureau of Narcotics and Dangerous Drugs. BNDD had been right on target when they assigned him to be my liaison.

The doorbell rang and I opened the door, keeping most of my body behind the steel-reinforced door. It wasn't much protection, but it blocked from sight my free hand, which rested on the Walther tucked into the back of my pants. John stood quietly in the hallway. His glassy blue eyes made one last sweep up and down the corridor, then locked for a second on my face. Just as quickly his gaze darted beyond my shoulder, checking to see if I had any other visitors. Not a nervous habit for someone as seasoned as John; it was a professional one.

"Hi, come in," I greeted, and gestured his gaunt figure inside.

"Good morning," he said in his flat, even voice as he stepped through the door.

With his characteristic tiptoe walk, the ex-spook wandered around the living room in a seemingly random fashion. I watched John for a few seconds, his eyes studying the room as if expecting something awry, ever vigilant and alert. The normalcy of the morning was gone. I could feel a rigidity beginning to work its ways in between my shoulders. Meetings with John tended to have that effect on me, and it would be a few minutes anyway before he finished his once-over.

Leaving John to that task, I went back to completing my own morning rituals, knowing exactly how much time I had to complete them. John was a frequent visitor and by now I was used to his routine. I knew that he would walk over every inch of the apartment before uttering a word beyond his initial greeting. Even though the embassy electronics crew regularly debugged my house, he never failed to case the five rooms himself. I knew even without watching that John would be peering out the window from the sides, checking the lampshades, unscrewing the light bulbs, taking apart the phone, running his hands methodically down the sides of the furniture, under the bed, behind the pictures on the wall, and opening up the electrical outlets.

Finally, he came into the bathroom, satisfied that all was well.

"A place is only as clean as the last person in it," he proclaimed to me, repeating the same language he always used.

I looked at John's reflection in the mirror. His gray-brown hair was cropped close to his skull like a helmet. He had sunken eyes, and hollow cheeks dominated his sallow complexion that touched his face with the subtle shadings of gray wallpaper. While John could have passed for a young Boris Karloff, I could have stood in easily for Robert De Niro. A trim five ten, I was well groomed with shiny black hair, dark eyes, and the Italian features that had made me stand out all my life. The common denominators between John and I were that we were both very good at what we did, and we had a mutual admiration for each other, along with a common cause:

Eliminating the supply chain of drugs coming into the States from South America.

"Good morning to you too, John. Ready for the beach? Where's your surfboard, *paisan*?" I said with a smile.

I wiped my hands and face and walked out into the spacious master bedroom, John nipping at my heels. Bright morning sunlight swept in from the half-opened drapes, warming the room in a golden glow. It was mid-March in Buenos Aires, the beginning of autumn. The well-furnished bedroom was tastefully painted in tones of blue and cream, the carpet a plush blue. A pair of comfortable armchairs and a small couch with matching end tables and a portable color television set were artfully arranged in one corner of the large room. A full-size built-in closet covered the length of one side of the bedroom wall. The rank of regional director of BNDD's South American operation had won me this luxurious setting. It was one of the best apartments in Buenos Aires that the US Embassy had rented and furnished for its personnel. The perk was lost on me;

to me, it was just a place to hang my hat until my Joy and the boys joined me after school was out in three months, at which point we'd relocate to something more appropriate for a family. I smiled as I considered how my family's coming arrival might greatly complicate John's reconnaissance of the apartment. I could picture him going through the toy chest and dissecting a suspicious-looking Godzilla for possible bugs.

My dinner suit was laid out neatly on the king-size bed. John eyed it approvingly before gliding noiselessly over to the window.

"The emperor's new clothes," I commented wryly, and opened the closet door to get my wool jacket.

"Just don't get it stained," advised John. "The rental place will charge you extra."

I'd forgotten to pack my evening clothes, and my secretary at the embassy had ordered a tux delivered to me that morning. It was all very efficient and orderly. So, in this case, I guess bureaucracy did have its usefulness.

I smiled at John. "Don't worry. I'll be doubly careful. If someone spills anything on me at the party tonight, I'll report them to the ambassador to avoid taking the heat."

This would be my first social event since being officially posted as a narcotics attaché in Buenos Aires, a formal black-tie cocktail party arranged by the embassy in my honor that evening. I'd met some of the local officials on my earlier trips to Buenos Aires before officially taking up my duties. John had already briefed me about intelligence sources on the continent, people who'd helped with CIA capers in the past and who could be trusted in the future, which meant now. John definitely knew how to find and keep good help.

"The party tonight isn't just for fun, Dan," he warned, his face not moving a muscle, like it was frozen in place. "You need to work it, work the room."

I laughed. "Don't worry. I wouldn't dream of having fun at my own party."

I had learned quickly that drug busting down here was largely conducted over imported scotch and hors d'oeuvres, especially at the start. It was a far cry from my first job as an undercover cop in Philly where my usual MO was fake track marks and a night in the tank with the junkies.

I tucked my jacket over my arm and picked up my attaché case. "Time for a cup of coffee?"

"Just enough," John replied.

We adjourned to the living room. I poured coffee and John settled down opposite me, opting for the darkest part of the room farthest from the windows, which spanned two sides of the walls. I didn't worry much about potential snipers or surveillance and, anyway, the warm sun and the view were difficult to resist. The apartment was perched in a quiet residential neighborhood on Avenida Charcas. Beyond Charcas was a partial view of sprawling downtown Buenos Aires, where steel and glass office buildings rose on Avenida Florida. On a sunny day, I could stick my head out the window and get a spectacular view of the ships cruising through the harbor of Rio de la Plata.

Buenos Aires, next to Mexico City and São Paulo, was the largest city in South America, as cosmopolitan as any major city in the world. Of the roughly twenty million people in Argentina, eight million of them lived and worked there. It was a lush city that lived for the present, since there was so little left of the original sixteenth-century colony that had been founded there. An increasing number of skyscrapers kept sprouting in the downtown area. The theaters, museums, hotels, and shops were large, luxurious, and modern. Buenos Aires's high society was low key, old world, and decidedly elegant. Part of it retained the pervading tradition of old-world Castellón Spain. The other included a large, thriving European community, a community reeking of old money and breeding.

I opened my briefcase. Inside were folders of intelligence files filled with copies of the latest reports and briefings. My case also held a stack of three-by-five index cards rubber-banded together. The cards were my miniature dossiers, notes scribbled in my own shorthand. Decipherable only to me, the index cards were my bible, each one containing a verse all its own.

As I pulled out the cards for review, I asked John, "How long is the trip going to take?"

"Twenty or twenty-five minutes, if we don't get stuck in traffic. They're expecting us," John answered, and lit up a Marlboro.

I was in the process of trying to quit smoking, which meant the sight of someone else smoking was like dangling a chocolate bar in front of a kid. I finally pried my eyes off the cigarette and concentrated on the business at hand.

"Do I have anything to worry about?" I asked, referring to my morning meeting.

"No. These boys are pros. They won't cross us."

Although nothing new was being discussed, I wanted to clear away any mental cobwebs before the morning's appointment with the Brothers. I could feel the tension seeping into me. The meeting had not been far from my mind since I had authorized John to set it up. The night before, alone in the apartment, he had read through and reviewed the files he'd compiled on the Brothers. Not all his information was declassified, or Company originated. And I hadn't made it this far chasing drugs by relying solely on other people's sources. At some point, I had to do my business up close and personal, face-to-face.

"I want to look into their faces, listen to them talk, see how they act," I told John. "If I can trust them, we'll make this happen. I know these guys come highly recommended, but I want to check them out firsthand before we begin any fucking around."

The Brothers had been recommended to me by John, and I knew John well enough by now to trust his judgment. That said, I'd also survived about twenty years of undercover police work and drug enforcement by trusting my own instincts. The Brothers were locals who'd worked with John before on Company assignments. Locals were employed primarily on locate and monitor jobs (as in "eavesdrop and tail his ass") or locate and kidnap (as in "pump him for info, then dump him at a local police station"). A few, however, were locate and lose scenarios, which was *get out of him what you can and make him disappear afterward.* The Brothers were experts in all three categories, especially the final one. They knew how to perform services in such a way that the US government had plausible deniability about their actions should questions arise at a later date.

"Are these guys as bad ass as everyone says?" I asked.

"More," John answered solemnly. "They have the nose of a blood-hound, the cunningness of a panther, and the jaws of a shark."

I laughed. "Fucking A.... Can we control them?" I asked, not realizing at the time how prophetic my question would turn out to be.

John drew a deep drag of his cigarette. "They're good friends of mine," he replied quietly yet firmly, dismissive of caution and concern.

He might've waved the white flag with the Brothers, but their rep-utation for violence, and playing both sides, raised a red one with me.

"We can use them as far as this operation goes," John continued. "They've got the setup and the associations to ferret out Ricord even if he's hiding in the sewers. The Brothers have incredible contacts at all levels of society throughout South America, from the street punks of Asunción to the elites of Buenos Aires. Besides, you and I already know Ricord is in Paraguay."

I smiled. But the gesture lacked in any genuine humor.

"The bastard's in Paraguay, all right. He lost his CIA trackers in Panama, and again in Colombia. Paraguay is ideal for him, especially with his connections there. Something's going down in Asunción, John. I've got this fucking bad feeling in my guts. I want to know what the hell is going on down there. If your boys, the Brothers, can get to Ricord, and we can trust them, I want them on it."

John nodded, cigarette dangling from the corner of his mouth. "What about Frank?" he asked. "You already sent him to Asunción."

Before I came to Buenos Aires, I'd unofficially dispatched my assis-tant deputy Frank Chiccilo to the Paraguayan capital as a follow-up on the status of the Ricord case with Raymond Ylitalo, the US ambassador to Paraguay.

"The same shit," I told John. "They claim they want to cooperate with the US government, but what's the difference, since there's no extradition treaty between the United States and Paraguay. Ylitalo swears he is doing everything he can to pressure the Paraguayans and recommends we coordinate all matters with his chief counsel." I paused, adding, "Bullshit."

"Probably," John agreed, not one to mince words either.

My lips twitched. "I need someone in Paraguay I can trust. Ylitalo's no good; neither is Frank. I need someone 'unofficial.' If the ambassador finds out, I'll be persona non grata with a heel mark on my ass. Screw it. It's the only way I know to get the information I need. But before I make a play for Ricord, I've got to know what the game is."

I never doubted my own ability to arrange for the extradition of Ricord to stand trial in the States. Some might have questioned me being selected as regional director for all of South America, since my base of operations had always been stateside. But I could give anyone a thorough rundown of the drug traffic in every major city in the United States. And for those cities I knew firsthand—Philly, New York, Detroit, and San Francisco—I could even pinpoint the street corners, bars, movie theaters, and park benches where someone could score. (The wares moved at some park benches were priced based on the time of day.) In some parks, the territory was divided according to a "dealers' code," and each drug was dealt near a different tree: the buyer only had to line up at the coke tree, the heroin tree, the pot or hash tree, or the psychedelic tree, and his drug of choice was sure to be available. It was kind of like standing in a dinner buffet line, and I knew the prices, the sellers, and their suppliers. I had an index card file filled with the names of domestic drug traffickers, but I was the first to admit that until several months ago, I lacked comparable intelligence on the foreign players I'd now be confronting.

After I was promoted to the South American post, I applied a singular intensity and tenacity in beefing up areas of my own ignorance and augmenting my intelligence files with every resource available. There weren't many things that daunted me. As far as I was concerned, in leaving my BNDD post in San Francisco, I wasn't losing a city, I was gaining a continent; it just had more hiding places and more corrupt people in high places. And the prevailing political currents, coupled with my knowledge of undercover investigations, made me instantly suspicious of how Ricord was being handled in Paraguay. Despite the reassurances of the Paraguayan government, as well as my own people, I had a sense that there were considerable powers that didn't want to see him captured and handed over to US custody.

"How's the Watchmaker doing on putting the heat on Ylitalo?" I asked John.

The Watchmaker, a.k.a. John Ingersoll, had been appointed by Attorney General Ramsey Clark to head the BNDD. A former police chief of Oakland, California, and, before that, an Oakland police officer, Ingersoll was my immediate superior to whom I reported directly. At this point, President Nixon was fed up with what he viewed as bureaucrats unwilling to get their hands dirty to bring in Ricord. Nixon didn't want cowboys so much as a new attitude by federal law enforcement to do what was necessary to bring a foreign national to justice. That may seem like old hat now, but back then we were making up the rules as we went along and writing the book for how to run a drug operation from page one that others would be reading for a long time to come.

For instance, at one point in our pursuit of Ricord, we got word through an informant of the Argentinian police's normally reliable Captain Rojas that a huge shipment consisting of twenty kilos of heroin, shipped into Buenos Aires from Marseille, would be making its way to the United States on a freighter carrying tons of Argentina fish that would be on ice for the journey. The shipment, bound for New York after a stop in São Paulo, Brazil, was emblematic of the

Ricord group's efforts to find another means, and route, to get their heroin into the United States. Customs had done a pretty good job of interdicting their efforts on ships coming in from Europe. Accordingly, this shipment originating in Buenos Aires marked the potential beginnings of a whole new conduit system, which made it doubly important for us to stop the process in its tracks at the very outset.

At this point, the second-guessers and naysayers back home had a field day questioning the wisdom of staging such a massive operation riddled with logistics that were challenging at best. We knew, for example, that to find those twenty kilos of heroin we'd likely have to off-load the ship's entire stores of iced-down fish. That promised to be a huge undertaking, given the men and equipment required to pull it off. It was my call, and I gave the order to go for it as soon as the ship docked in São Paulo, coordinating the operation with my people in Brazil along with the federal authorities there.

I saw pictures of these cranes that looked like iron dinosaurs lifting the massive pallets now dripping plumes of water from the melting ice off the ship. Man, was my ass on the line! And if it turned out my decision based on what I'd been told was proven wrong, Ingersoll and plenty of others would want to forget my name as soon as they could.

Finally, a call came in that the drugs had indeed been found. The officials on scene feared they might have to begin slicing open all those frozen fish themselves when they found the tightly wrapped bags of heroin mixed in amidst the ice.

I breathed easier, but not too easy, because the scope of what we were facing indicated the degree of sophistication and resources with which Ricord's network operated, the expansive reach of their tentacles. They presented formidable challenges to us every step of the way, challenges never faced in the battle against narcotics that required us to respond on the fly in ways we never had before.

"Ingersoll's working on it," John said, in answer to my question about how the head of the BNDD was doing in pressuring

Ambassador Ylitalo in Paraguay. "But it's easier to pressure you than a US ambassador."

I shrugged. "If it's a low priority to Ylitalo, that's his problem. It's bad enough that I keep bumping into Customs officials everywhere I turn. These guys are so fucking uncoordinated, just like our illustrious policy makers. Every time a new president or congressman gets elected, a new subcommittee on an old subcommittee appears and there's a new set of guidelines. What was the last memorandum?"

"Number two-zero-two-three-nine-eight."

"Shit. Is that right? I think I must've been in diapers when that came out."

I laughed, and John managed a smile. It spoke much about our frustration, along with the frustration of others in a high enough position to witness the legislative wheels continuing to grind exceedingly slow. The BNDD spent more money and manpower organizing itself, I felt, and adjusting to the political ripples and infighting among the various drug enforcement agencies, it was a wonder there was any left over to mount operations like the one that had just netted us twenty million dollars' worth of heroin.

"Can Ingersoll get me more men down here?" I asked. "Do you know we've got just one guy in Colombia, and his last report was nine months ago?"

The fact that we had only one agent stationed amidst such a rising hotbed of drug activity was typical of the challenges we faced down here, confronting a problem that had been approached in sporadic fashion up until now. We were fighting a new war on new territory and had yet to get the lay of the land and put a face to both the enemy and the challenges we were confronting. We needed a unified effort, not a scattershot one, and to a large extent that was the nature of my mission as regional director.

"That's Raul Caeser," John said, referring to that single operative we had active in Colombia. "He's native."

"Tell Ingersoll I need more men," I said. "Later, let's go over the names you gave me, okay?"

I put away my index cards and finished my coffee. "You ready?" I asked.

John nodded.

I tucked my Walther securely into one of the upper flaps inside my attaché case. "Then let's go meet the Brothers."

As we left the apartment, the uniformed doorman who was polishing the brass railings on the glass door smiled and greeted me. Outside, a cool breeze dispersed some of the heat and humidity already permeating the air.

I was wearing my brown light woolen suit with an official white shirt, a dark brown vest, and a matching silk tie. I had a keen eye for lines, colors, and style, and most would say I carried myself with a sense of arrogance. I simply called it walking—speaking of which, John walked slightly behind me and faded unnoticed into the sidewalk. Today he was wearing his wash-and-wear gray suit. Tomorrow would be the blue polyester. The day after, the gray one again. He was nothing if not predictable.

We walked briskly over to Avenida Florida and hailed a taxi. I had an embassy car but didn't want to use it this morning. We had barely settled into the cramped back seat of the battered Fiat when the cabbie screeched away and pulled into traffic to a chorus of honking horns. Good thing that John and I were both slender; as it was, we were literally sitting on top of each other in the cab's cramped confines.

"Twenty-three Avenida Sarmiento," John directed the driver, the address being two blocks away from the actual meeting place, in keeping with his security protocol.

The scrawny middle-aged cabbie glared at us in the rearview mirror before hunching over the steering wheel with the fixed countenance of a demolition derby driver.

As we bounced through tiny little neighborhoods en route to downtown Buenos Aires, the right of way belonged to whoever reached the intersection first or turned a corner faster. The taxi roller-coasted up and down over holes where cobblestone used to be. We found ourselves clutching the sides of the doors just to remain upright. My head thumped against the rooftop as I caught a glimpse of the dashboard. The speedometer read a sedate forty kilometers an hour. More like ninety kilometers, I thought, cursing silently as I was nearly crushed by John, who bounced onto my lap as the cabbie swerved to avoid being sideswiped. The scrawny driver stuck his head out the window, eyes glaring at the other driver as they raced on, neck and neck.

"Carajo! Hijo de puta!"

I was relieved to see the older section of the city give way to the newer neighborhoods near General Paz Avenue, the belt highway that marked the city limit and the area where the Brothers lived. Clean and unobtrusive, the streets were dominated by modern brick buildings, playgrounds filled with children, and stores. It was the kind of unremarkable, generic middle-class neighborhood that could be part of almost any city anywhere. The cabbie dropped us off where we told him to, accepted some stiff pesos from me, and zoomed away.

I took a moment to straighten my clothes. Such simple gestures served to compose my thoughts. Nonetheless, I could feel my stomach muscles tighten in anticipation as we set out to cover the two remaining blocks to the Brothers on foot. Images and sensations came in sharper, brighter. My mind was shifting into high gear.

"Remember," I told John, "I'll do the talking."

"Sounds good," he said. "Leaves the shooting to me if it comes to that."

I couldn't tell if he was joking.

CHAPTER ELEVEN

BUENOS AIRES, ARGENTINA

My first day officially on the job in South America brought me to a four-story brownstone building standing by itself on a small fenced lot plenty older than the others on the block. The black-lettered sign above the door read SCHULTZ ELECTRONICS. The windows on the ground floor had been bricked up.

As we entered the building, a metallic ring signaled our arrival, alerting whoever might've been listening. There was no need really, since a man was standing behind the counter. The store was loaded with the usual electronic store displays of television sets, radios, and stereo equipment. A Stevie Wonder song, "I Was Made to Love Her," was playing through the loudspeakers set up high on the walls. There were no customers in the store. We were as close as it came to that.

In a few seconds, I had taken it all in and now turned my attention to the man behind the counter. Tall and trim, about six two, in his mid-thirties with fair hair and big blue eyes. A good-looking guy dressed casually in dark slacks and a light blue shirt with the sleeves rolled up.

Argentine officials inspect the kilos of heroin found hidden amid the fish on the freighter ordered searched by Dan.

Looking up from replacing the batteries in a cassette recorder, the man smiled, displaying a gleam of even white teeth, and asked in Spanish, "Can I help you gentlemen?"

John hesitated for a moment and replied, "I'm looking for Avenida Rosa."

The prearranged code.

The words were barely out of his mouth when the man's clear blue eyes brightened. He chuckled warmly and came out from behind the counter, moving lithely on his feet like a gymnast.

"Ah, John!" he exclaimed in fluent English and embraced my compadre, his eyes warm with affection. "It has been much too long. What, three years? My brother and I were so happy to receive your call."

He patted John on the back.

141

"Hugo, you old son of a bitch! Still the same!" In a rare gesture, John smiled broadly and returned the embrace. "Hey, I want you to meet someone."

Hugo shook my hand. "You must be Mr. Addario. I am Hugo. Welcome, welcome! Nicholas, my brother, is out on a small delivery. He will be back any moment. Come, let us go in the back and wait for him."

He called on the intercom for a clerk to watch the front of the store.

I saw Hugo's blue eyes glance suspiciously at my attaché case. But he shrugged pleasantly and led us through the stockroom. Electronic merchandise lined the shelves and cabinets in the front, but as we went farther back into the spacious room, the nature of the equipment being stored changed dramatically.

There was all sorts of electronic gear, all in mint condition: telephone taps, radio transmitters, video cameras and recording devices, metal detectors, infrared equipment, microphones, timers, and considerable quantities of other paraphernalia. The gear was extremely sophisticated and very expensive, definitely not something you could purchase at Radio Shack.

At the end of the long room was a locked cage with rows of rifles, handguns, knives, and automatic weapons. An area had been cleared next to it for a workspace. The setup was most professional, the kind used for building wireless microphones and surveillance devices instead of merely repairing broken record players.

Seated on one of the workbenches was a young boy of about sixteen. He was soldering what looked like a telephone tap; it was the size of a silver dollar and could be slipped easily into a mouthpiece.

Hugo noted my interest. "You are admiring the facilities, Mr. Addario? It is adequate for our needs here." He motioned to the boy. "That is my nephew, Jose. He will be very good at this stuff someday."

I smiled and commented dryly, "Nothing like a family business."

Jose looked up at us and waved. Mickey Mouse grinned out from his T-shirt.

We followed Hugo down into the basement. He pushed open a door as thick as a bank vault and beckoned us to follow him inside.

There were no windows, and the walls were completely covered with electronic drapes so that no radio transmissions could come in or go out. All of the furniture was white plastic, given that even the tiniest piece of metal could act as an antenna. It was a fortress, a state-of-the-art electronic safe room with the type of interior decorating that would warm the heart of a Company man. Or an ex-Company man.

"You've done an excellent job here, Hugo," John admired, a shade of enthusiasm coloring his gaunt face.

He looked under the table and made a quick tour around the room before sitting down docilely beside me. I took a seat facing the door and kept my briefcase by my leg.

Hugo smiled, delighted. "I thought you would like it, John. We can chat here. No interruption. No interception." He poured coffee from a large plastic thermal container into waiting white plastic cups. "Have some real South American coffee, Mr. Addario. Not the brown water you North Americanos brew."

I tested what was the strongest, richest coffee I had ever had. I wondered if this particular Brother was pulling a little macho stunt on me, determining whether a gringo could drink it without turning green.

Hugo was gazing intently at me, lips curved in a brilliant smile. He really was good-looking and could have been a cover model for a fashion magazine. But I perceived a harsh coldness behind the sparkling blue eyes and was hardly reassured by his demeanor.

I took another swallow. "Great stuff. Where can I buy some of this? Anywhere near the American embassy?"

Hugo laughed, with a little pride and admiration. The younger of the Brothers, he was almost boyish in his mannerisms. "You can't buy it near the embassy or anywhere in Argentina. It comes from a certain mountain in Colombia where we have friends. We do favors for them, and they do favors for us. In South America, friends can get you almost anything you want. Without them, Mr. Addario, you settle for a life of Nescafé. You can't buy a cup of coffee such as this in North Beach, can you?"

"Not unless you have the right friends," I quipped in agreement.

Hugo glanced at John, who was sitting still for the moment with a grin frozen on his skeletal face. John shrugged to indicate that he hadn't told Hugo much about me.

"Have you been to San Francisco, Hugo?" I asked.

"Many years ago. I still know people there, though. It is a pretty city. The bay reminded me of Rio de la Plata," Hugo answered.

John lit a cigarette and nodded. Then the door opened, and Hugo's brother Nicholas strode in. John popped up from his seat, and the two men hugged each other.

Nicholas, the older of the Brothers, was in his early to mid-forties, built on a stockier, broader frame than his more handsome brother. He wore gold wire-rimmed glasses that, coupled with an ascetic cast to his Teutonic features, made him look like a history teacher about to deliver a lecture. "The Professor," a moniker bestowed upon him by John in a moment of abnormal humor and affection, grasped John by the shoulders and shook him lightly and playfully a couple of times.

"John, John. I have missed you! Let me look at you. You haven't changed at all. Right, Hugo? He still looks like a victim of the potato famine."

The Professor turned to me. He had the same blue eyes as his brother, but they were older, more intense, and more difficult to read. He extended a spatula-fingered hand.

"Mr. Addario, welcome to Argentina. You have come at the right time. I must thank you for bringing John back to us."

I shook his hand and said, smiling, "Thank you, Professor. As for John, you can have him."

The Professor managed a crooked smile at his first exposure to my brand of humor. "John is an old and good friend. He asked us to meet you, Mr. Addario, so we meet you. Please, let us all be seated."

When we were all settled, the Professor took out a pack of cigarettes and offered me one, but I explained I was trying to quit. He lit one and puffed away.

"I tried once. It was horrible. I was so jumpy and restless that Hugo begged me to begin again." He paused. "I was at Ezeiza Airport when you arrived this week. There are always so many people coming and going. This is a busy tourist season in Argentina. I hope there were no problems with your delayed luggage, Mr. Addario."

My mind raced through the memories of my arrival in the Argentine airport, aware that the Professor wanted me to know such a detail of my arrival had not escaped him. "There was no problem. Just a minor issue with one of the baggage loaders." I added purposefully, "However, I did notice something funny about one piece when I was unpacking. My Dopp kit had been turned around from the way I had packed it."

At the time, I had suspected nothing more than a customs inspector doing a spot check. Now I wasn't so sure.

The Professor smiled at me. Only this time, it was with the same warmth he'd shown to John.

"Good. Very good. You are very observant, Mr. Addario. I like that. Now we can be friends. My brother and I like to know the people we are dealing with. Someone who misses details can be dangerous for everyone. We know John. We trust John." He gave an apologetic shrug. "We didn't know you. Now we call you Dan, and you will please call us by our Christian names. Or, if you prefer, call me 'the Professor' as John nicknamed me so many years ago. *Si, mi amico? Noi siano italiano, anche.*"

"The same applies here, Professor," I said softly.

I wasn't surprised that the Brothers had given me a little test. They wouldn't have been the kind of people I needed if they hadn't checked me out first. Trained professionals in surveillance, interrogation, and removal, the Brothers were forever expecting infiltrators and assassins. They could wire plastic explosives as easily as a set of stereo loudspeakers.

I knew that although the Brothers were born in Argentina, they were of German-Italian descent. Not surprisingly, the records of their family were hazy. Both the populist presidency of Juan Perón and the current military regime had employed the Brothers as members of an elite squad annexed to the Argentine police. Their prime duty was to protect whichever government was in power by any means necessary; in other words, a kind of Secret Service force with Green Beret tactics. They had also worked for the Company throughout South America. The Brothers didn't limit their freelancing to Argentina or any one government.

I had a vague outline of their activities, and that was all I needed to establish their bona fides. I didn't want to know the Brothers' other interests or actions as long as it didn't interfere with the job I needed them to do. Besides, what I had in mind for them required a different job description. For now.

"Hugo and I welcome you to your first official day at work and wish you much success, Dan," the Professor continued.

A compulsive chain smoker, he paused to light yet another cigarette from the one he had just finished.

"How can we help you, Dan? Just tell us."

I placed my briefcase on the plastic table. Opening it, I took out some files and passed a photograph to the Brothers. It was my turn for a test.

"What do you know about Auguste Ricord?" I asked.

The Professor studied the picture. A look of distaste flickered across his face.

"We know who he is."

"Tell me about him."

The Professor's mental files were as good as my dossiers. A Frenchman who had joined the Gestapo in occupied France, Ricord was forced to flee to South America in the late 1940s. The Professor spoke succinctly of Ricord's exploits on his newfound continent, from his arrest in Buenos Aires in 1957 for running a prostitution ring, to his subsequent drug-smuggling operations throughout South America. There were powerful people in governments who'd been paid to look the other way. As a result, Ricord was always protected and continued to elude capture.

I nodded, pleased that the Professor's information matched my own, adding, "Ricord became involved in the drug trafficking through the Marseille routes. Now that the French Connection's dried up, he's moving cocaine and heroin out of South America."

"And quite successfully, from what we understand," the Professor stated knowledgeably.

"For sure. Ricord has the money and the connections to bankroll a South American network that would make the Marseille operation look puny. Our people are working through diplomatic channels to get him out of Paraguay. The longer he is allowed to live freely in South America, the easier it is for him to establish new routes. We know he's in Paraguay now," I finished.

I purposely left out the fact that Ricord had established himself as the owner of the Paris-Nice Restaurant located on the outskirts of Asunción, Paraguay. If the Brothers were as good as advertised, they'd have no trouble confirming Ricord's location and getting better information than my own agent had brought back. It would be a little test. If the Brothers couldn't find Ricord, or if they pretended they couldn't find him, they weren't good enough for me to work with or, alternatively, couldn't be trusted.

"We will find him and report to you," the Professor said, his expression tightening into a mask that made his skin look like polished porcelain. "Do you want us to take care of the bastard? We can deliver him to you in a box. No problem."

The chords in his neck were bulging; the steely control was gone, along with all pretense. I'd known enough stone killers in my time to be sure that the Professor was one of them.

147

That notion caused a prickling on the back of my neck. "No, no hit. I want you to locate and monitor Ricord. I want information, not a box. I want to know what he's doing, from the time he pees in the morning to who he screws at night. A US grand jury in New York just returned a secret indictment against Ricord, naming him as the head of a 2.5-billion-dollar heroin ring. The heat's on."

The Professor grounded out his cigarette angrily. His face flushed.

Eyes burning, he offered, "In that case, we most definitely will deliver him in a box. No charge. I may do it myself. No subcontractors, no middlemen. We hate these drug people. They are garbage," he said, almost spitting out those last words.

I was tempted. One nod from me and Ricord ceased to be a problem. I saw it as the most efficient way of eliminating a cancerous disease. Then I thought about the consequences. I didn't want, and couldn't risk, any complications.

"No," I repeated firmly. "No hit. The job is to locate and watch Ricord. There's too much White House focus on this guy. The president's personally watching over this. There's an election coming up, and Nixon wants some good press; he wants Ricord back in the States to stand trial, pronto."

Hugo spoke for the first time since his older brother arrived. "I would very much like to package this filth in a box," he said, pronouncing each word distinctly. "A niece of ours, Jose's older sister, had a very bad time a few years ago. Drugs are poison. The dealers are animals, bloodsuckers."

"I'm sorry," I said sincerely.

I remembered what it was like on a winter in the South Bronx with two addict informants in the back of my car, both crying and pleading for a quick hit. I remembered what it was like to look at the contorted, lifeless face of a teenage courier who had died a White Death when the cocaine packets inside his stomach had punctured, sending undiluted cocaine through the lining of his gut, hitting the nervous system like a Category Five hurricane.

The Professor stared at me. "You are a tough man, Dan," he said calmly, the madness vacating his eyes. "Yes. We will work together. We will go to Paraguay for you. This will be top priority. We have many friends there."

I put away my files. Some of the tension eased away from my stiff shoulders and, slowly, the sweat dried on my palms. I had been accepted, and I had accepted the Brothers in return.

Similar conversations would take place at regular intervals. Every time drugs or dealers were mentioned, the Brothers became furious. I never did find out exactly what happened to their niece.

Prior to that morning's meeting I had been concerned that the Brothers could easily strike a deal with Ricord, who had more money than the entire BNDD budget. I now dismissed the possibility. I'd known that John's relationship with them was strong and deep. Today, the Brothers had shown themselves to be unshakeable, moved by deeply rooted hatred of anything connected with drugs. I'd gone into that first meeting wondering how much they could really accomplish; instead, our challenge would be restraining them from doing too much.

There was another reason why I had wanted to connect with the Brothers. They had incredible contacts at all levels of society throughout South America. The Brothers spoke fluent English, Spanish, German, French, and Italian, and they possessed numerous false passports and identities that enabled them to travel to and from any country unquestioned and undetected. After working closely with them, I'd have said at the time that if someone had handed them the job of finding Josef Mengele, the Angel of Death would've been behind bars within a week.

I sat back in the chair and thought silently for a minute. Meanwhile, Hugo stepped out to bring back another thermos of fresh coffee.

I made a steeple, like a triangle, with my fingers and said, "I'm also interested in customs, police, and airport."

"Tastor," the Professor offered without hesitation, lighting a fresh cigarette. "Hannibal Tastor is the head of Argentine Customs. He is a man who keeps his feet on the ground and his ears at other people's doors. He enjoys the good life but is a loyal nationalist. You can talk to him, Dan. He's a very good friend of ours. Everything that comes in and out of the country passes under Tastor's eyes."

"He'll be at the reception tonight," I said. "I saw his name on the invite list."

"Perfect. Go to him. Tell Tastor that you are our friend," said the Professor. "Captain Jorge Rojas is also a close friend."

"The chief of police?"

"Yes. We knew him when he was only a police lieutenant."

I couldn't help but be impressed by the Brothers' apparent familiarity and friendship with the powerful police chief, who had a reputation of closed-mouthed aloofness.

"Rojas is the best man you can get to know in the police hierarchy," the Professor continued. "Solid, dependable, and moral, his business is clean. He comes from an old Argentine family and was raised in the old ways. You never have to worry about Rojas. Did you know that he and Tastor have an American education?"

I nodded. "Rojas even has a graduate degree. Means he must be a very intelligent man."

The Professor readily agreed. "He's an intelligent leader and he instills much pride and dignity in the police force. He is a soldier of honor, Dan, of the old school. Rojas is not unlike your Frank Rizzo."

I let the surprise show on my face. "You know Rizzo?"

The Professor smiled in satisfaction at my shocked reaction. "We have heard much about the controversial police commissioner of Philadelphia, my new friend."

"I'd already joined the feds by the time he became commissioner," I said. "But if I learn as much from Rojas as I did from Rizzo, we'll be in fine shape."

We all laughed. The two assassins, the ex-Company man, and the narcotics attaché. It was laughter of men who had been on both ends of a gun.

"I look forward to seeing Rojas tonight. And I'll be sure to mention our association," I told the Brothers.

I had already earmarked the American-educated Argentine police chief as a main connection and had met him briefly at a stiff formal meeting at police headquarters. Rojas had simply greeted me as the new attaché. He had extended his best wishes but had offered nothing in the way of cooperation.

"Yes, do that," said the older Brother. "I believe he will be more cooperative once he understands your mission here."

"I did tell him what my plans were."

"Perhaps you did, but perhaps also your plans were not explained in terms that are understood in Argentina. We will take care of that for you."

The Professor took off his glasses to clean them and then continued with the patience of a well-paid tour guide explaining the customs of a strange land. "You can't work in Argentina or in any part of South America like you did in the States. A police captain in New York can call a captain in Los Angeles for help. Or he can contact one of the Washington agencies for support. This is not the case between South American countries, or even between cities in the same country."

"Not even between different forces of the same government," volunteered Hugo.

"That is why," his brother picked up, "you must develop a personal network to get things done. A nice chat over Johnny Walker Red—that is your brand, Dan, yes?—does not guarantee your back will be protected when you most require it." The Professor replaced his eyeglasses and continued. "Now, the man you need at the airport is Rodrigo Mattera. He is a close friend of Rojas, a team player who follows the chief's lead. There is no problem with Mattera."

"These are important people, Professor. They can help me put away the dealers and suppliers. It's the big boys I want, the network bosses. If we can get at the source, we can eliminate most of the problem. And with your help, we can put them away, block their routes, and dry up their source."

The Professor's eyes were burning like lamps. "We are with you, Dan. Whatever you need, just tell us."

"I can't tell you how much I appreciate that," I said. "For starters, you are to locate and monitor Ricord. Find out where he is. You are to keep a low visibility and take no risk. The pay is one thousand American dollars a month for each of you, plus expenses. John can set up a vouchering system for you. Remember, no hit! Just find Ricord. If anything happens, if it even smells funny, tell me immediately."

The Professor smiled in assent. "We will do it for you, Dan. We will send you a message of our progress. The information will be sent to your residence. Don't worry, we have the address. We don't trust some of the locals who work in the American embassy, in particular the pretty young lady who's a translator in the communications office. Watch her carefully, Dan. Instead we will relay our messages through various vendors: the milkman, the paperboy, or the grocery delivery boy. Each message will be sealed. Later on, we can work out a more secure drop if there is a need. Okay?"

"Fine for now," I agreed. "Just what the doctor ordered."

We all rose to our feet. Through it all, John had merely sat silent and stiff as a statue.

"May I ask you something, Dan?" the Professor asked cautiously.

"Go right ahead," I said, picking up my attaché case.

"Don't your people wonder what happened to you?" he queried. "It is your first official day on the job and you have been out all morning."

I laughed. "I told my people that I was just following embassy hours. Come in at twelve and leave at three. I'm going there straight from here."

152

Actually, I'd told my staff that in fact I had an important meeting this morning and would not be expected in until later that day. All appointments were to be put on hold until then.

I shook hands with the Brothers, who both proceeded to hug John again. Hugo escorted us out of the store. He clapped me on the back and flashed his gleaming white teeth in a broad smile.

"Nicholas liked you, Dan. That is good. I like you too. We will speak again. Soon. Do not worry about that pig Ricord. We will bring you news of him. Take care, Dan. And John, please do eat something!"

Laughing, he watched us walk down the street.

CHAPTER TWELVE

BUENOS AIRES, ARGENTINA, 1970

Outside, the glare of the midday sun made me realize that the meeting had lasted just over three hours. John and I walked a couple of blocks. When I was sure we were out of sight of Schultz Electronics, I signaled him to stop. With a wry grimace, I took several deep breaths and slowly, exhaustedly, flexed my tense shoulders. The knot in my stomach was uncoiling and the pressure washed out of me, leaving me drained yet jubilant. I felt as if I had just been caged with a pair of deadly panthers and, not only had I survived, but I had them eating out of my hands and purring as well. I was also excited because I'd accomplished exactly what I'd set out to do that morning. The first step in netting Ricord had been taken.

John waited quietly, looking up and down the street.

"Your boys are cool," I said to him. "Come on, I'm starving," I continued. "Let's grab something to eat and go over a few things. Shit, all that coffee. My damn bladder's about to burst! And you guys with your cigarettes. Don't you know that they'll kill you?"

At this point, Operation Springboard didn't exist in the formal sense. That didn't come into play until a few weeks later into my South American posting, when I and the directors serving under me for the region were summoned to Caracas, Venezuela, for a conference with White House officials dispatched by President Nixon himself. A bevy of them were included, but G. Gordon Liddy and John Ehrlichman were running the show. They went around the room asking each of us to identify where the problems in our respective countries lay, where our primary efforts were focused. The meeting was about identifying the top traffickers in the region who were funneling drugs into the United States.

When my turn came, I went into some detail about Auguste Ricord, who, of course, everyone in the room was familiar with. I proceeded to lay out the challenges we faced in not only catching him but expelling him to the United States where he could stand trial. Something like that had never been done, or even tried, before. We needed a process, a plan.

And so Operation Springboard was born within the Bureau of Narcotics and Dangerous Drugs as a coordinated effort to bring the kingpins putting dope on American streets to justice. Ricord would likely be the first, but most certainly not the last, and that increased the pressure on me to deliver the goods in the plan I'd already set into motion with the Brothers.

Speaking of the Brothers, it's a good thing Gordon Liddy hadn't been at the meeting where they offered to kill Ricord instead of just find him for us. Liddy came down to Caracas loaded for bear. Left to him, he would've ordered Ricord assassinated. But I had a federal warrant issued by the US Attorney's Office for the Southern District of New York I intended to serve him instead. And that meant the first true major offensive in the war on drugs was about to begin.

But not all the soldiers saw the battlefield the same way. The regional director for Mexico at the time, who attended the meeting in Caracas, was still Joe Arpaio. Arpaio's stint as the BNDD's main man in Mexico had done nothing to stem the flow of drugs over the border because he was too busy cozying up to the politicians, handing over cash and guns that were supposed to better position the Mexican authorities to help us fight the war on drugs, without any accountability at all. That money ended up in the pockets of those politicians and the guns, in all probability, ended up in the hands of the very people they were supposed to help take off the streets.

Arpaio's case may be an extreme example, but it's far from an isolated one. Far too often, agents get too comfortable in a foreign country. I call that the "suck ass" effect, and I always tell my people to remember why they're there and who's paying them. They owe their allegiance to the United States government and nobody else, though you wouldn't know that from the number of American agents, diplomats, and attachés too busy ingratiating themselves into circles of power than fulfilling the jobs they had been dispatched to do. Foreign state governments are inherently part of the problem; they're often the ones protecting the very targets we're after, as was the case with Auguste Ricord in Paraguay. Working with those governments on a coequal basis toward achieving a common goal is diametrically opposed to feeling obligated, beholden, or subservient to them. That's what I saw all too often, and it's another reason why we started out behind in the war on drugs and have only fallen further back in subsequent years.

But I need to make one thing clear: Joe Arpaio didn't create our problems with Mexico, he inherited them. Congressional delegations, representatives from the Justice Department and BNDD, and other officials would go down there and end up being fed a dog and pony show, even as they were being wined and dined. They were taken on tours that showcased burnt-out cocaine labs, ravaged opium crops, and photographic evidence of huge heroin seizures. So everyone thought the Mexican government was doing a good job, that the US government's money was being well spent down there. And those delegations came home to a man or woman believing we were on the right track and that Mexico was cooperating to the fullest extent.

In fact, hundreds of kilos of heroin continued to pour across the border, the depth of the problem increasing all the time in spite of the staged events created to indicate otherwise. Mexico was doing just enough to keep us from suspecting they weren't really doing very much at all, a climate and mindset that people like Joe Arpaio found in their in-box when they arrived. He'd picked up where his predecessor left off, just as Arpaio's successor would pick up where he'd leave off.

Nixon got wind of this reality and asked the commissioner of US Customs, Myles Ambrose, what could be done. Ambrose convinced the president to basically shut the border down, ordering every single truck coming from Mexico into the United States to be stopped and searched. This went on for two weeks, halted only after fruits and vegetables spoiled by the ton and retailers couldn't get their shelves restocked with appliances and other goods. In the meantime, though, our intelligence indicated a precipitous drop in the amount of heroin on the streets. There was a genuine shortage. Junkies were going crazy, flooding methadone clinics for that drug or another suitable replacement to tide them over.

No, we couldn't keep the border shut down forever, but that one example showcased the effects of taking such drastic measures. Still, we needed to find a more enduring strategy toward the same ends, just as we needed to ensure that our officials assigned to foreign postings never forgot where their true loyalties lay.

Avoiding just that kind of predicament weighed on my mind a bit as I dutifully donned my rental formal attire for that evening's festivities. Tuxedos meant high school proms and weddings. I wasn't used to dressing up for a scotch and soda. Promptly, at eight, an embassy car and driver picked me up at the apartment. The ever-present former spook John was at my side, ready to help me through my South American social debut.

The American embassy was a large, renovated building complex built on a grand and elegant scale to blend in with its exclusive older neighborhood in downtown Buenos Aires. It was the working home of over fifty senior attachés, excluding the regiment of Marines that was attached to the embassy and the locals who worked there. At the gate, Marine guards in full dress uniforms checked all cars for IDs, and additional Marines at the main entrance escorted John and me to the grand ballroom. It was a long way from the streets of Philly chasing junkies and pushers, I'll tell you that much.

The reception was just beginning to get into full swing when we arrived. I took a deep breath and plunged into the throng. Waiters moved unobtrusively among the seventy or so guests, carrying trays of drinks and delicacies. I've never had a problem with alcohol, but I definitely needed to be at my best tonight. A drink or two to relax, in other words, but no more. The various embassy personnel and agents tried to be just as unobtrusive as they worked the party with dedicated fervor.

People sifted in and out from the central chamber. Long banquet tables and a full bar had been set out in the large reception area. Uniformed guards, both US Marines and Argentine police, stood protectively armed in the corridors and at the entrances to all rooms. A band featuring a terrific guitarist and pianist provided the music at one end of the long room.

Couples were dancing to the music in a cleared-off section. The distinguished US ambassador John Lodge was partnered to the ravishing French wife of the Argentine undersecretary. They were dancing so closely that a knife would've had trouble slipping between them.

The icy stare of a small mousy woman dressed in what looked to me like a mauve-colored satin sack slung over her shapeless body caught my attention. Her pursed lips could have been attached to a lemon instead of the martini she was sipping.

"Who's the tight-assed broad over there?" I quizzed John.

"She's the wife of your senior agent," he replied with a grin.

"What's her problem?"

"You," came John's curt answer. "She sees her diplomatic status going downhill with you on board. She was the Queen Bee around the embassy. With your wife and family arriving soon, she sees herself slipping down a notch on the invitation list."

I nodded, fully aware that the infighting among embassy wives could have caused even the most hardened politician to blush.

"Wait 'til she meets my wife," I laughed. "Her feathers will really be ruffled."

Joy was a dead ringer for Grace Kelly. The kind of woman born at the top of the invitation list from which the mousy woman was worried about slipping.

Without my wife present in Buenos Aires to guide me, I had worried at first that the formal clothes my secretary had rented would be out of place. Any qualms disappeared when I saw the formal reception area and the even more formal clothing the guests were wearing. This was wealth and elegance on a scale comparable to the big soirees hosted by Washington's social register. The Argentines especially were the epitome of grace and fine fashion. Some of them were better dressed and better mannered than their American hosts, although I was secretly proud that our top echelon was holding its own.

The CIA station chief was talking to the Argentine minister of interior about the upcoming football (that is, soccer) season. The minister's wife, a voluptuous raven-haired beauty, had unobtrusive diamonds in her ears and on her fingers. Indeed, one thing I found interesting and appealing was that the Argentinians rarely flaunted their wealth. One just didn't see garlands of diamond necklaces.

An arc of obsequious minor deputies and assistants surrounded the CIA chief and the minister. I was glad to see the face of one of my BNDD agents in the gathering. The CIA head worked the room like a veteran politician up for reelection. If there had been babies present, he would have kissed them.

Each of the CIA people was assigned a foreign guest to contact and engage in talk. I called them "social attachés." Each was fully briefed on the likes and dislikes of his "mark," and the next day complete reports would be filed about their cocktail chats. The CIA network in Argentina was one of the largest in South America because of heavy American investments in both government and private sectors. Argentina also supported US naval bases, and there were substantial American military forces stationed in the country. Where the military went, the spooks were sure to follow.

One of the first things I did when I arrived at the embassy that afternoon was to assign some of my own staff to do some fancy footwork at the reception. I was pleased to see that one of my four full-time operatives was currently working on Miguel Porlado, a young police lieutenant and one of Chief Rojas' top protégés. Frank Chiccilo was also engaged in discussions with his "target," Terencio Lescano, a banker who was the son-in-law of the powerful General Alejandro Lanusse.

The reception was high-level politics. Every Argentine guest was a potential contact to help me in my operations, an unsuspecting link in BNDD's South American network. John shadowed me throughout the evening. Content to remain in the background, he could have been mistaken for a waiter if anyone paid attention to him at all. I informed him that I didn't need his escort service at the moment and walked casually over to one of the savvier links in my network chain.

The tall, aristocratic man standing in the corner was in his late fifties, with more than a touch of gray in his dark hair and moustache. He was graciously attired in a formal black evening suit. A thin cigar was held in one shapely hand, a gold signet ring sparkling on his left pinky. The somewhat aloof, handsome profile turned slowly and piercing brown eyes slashed across my face.

"Chief Rojas? We were introduced before. I'm Dan Addario," I said, offering my hand to one of the most powerful men in all of

Argentina, with whom a mutual relationship based on trust and common mission could only serve my cause.

A smile warmed Rojas' severe features, though the brown eyes remained keen, suggesting the arrogance I'd first glimpsed in him from across the room. But Jorge Rojas, police chief of Argentina, took my hand in a firm grip, speaking impeccable English, his voice soft and quiet.

"Ah, our guest of honor. Again, it is a pleasure, Mr. Addario. Welcome to my country. Ambassador Lodge has spoken very highly and enthusiastically about your work. We have heard much of you from mutual acquaintances here and in the States, and everything we hear is good. I personally wish you the greatest success."

The praise was quietly and sincerely given, and I was flattered.

"How was your first day in the office, Mr. Addario?" Rojas asked, sounding genuinely interested.

I smiled, "The morning was very productive, but my afternoon was spent being introduced to everyone in the embassy."

A parade of people had filed past my office in the afternoon, and I had spoken at a small press conference arranged by the embassy's public relations staff. It was, in my opinion, a lost afternoon, though a necessary ritual to complete.

"Thank you very much for your good wishes, Chief Rojas. I'm sure we're going to work very well together."

I wondered if the Brothers had contacted Rojas yet. I decided to test the kinship they'd claimed with him.

"I've also heard a lot about you, Chief. In fact, your name came up in my meeting this morning when two friends of mine mentioned that they had worked with you before."

Rojas didn't bat an eyelash. "Yes, those two are useful individuals to know. It's a pleasure to work with professionals, men uncomplicated in their purpose. We often become too encumbered with our office and duties."

Dan pictured at the embassy with Ambassador Lodge, Argentine Chief of Police Rojas, and Argentina's head of Customs.

"Yes, I understand." I gestured toward the crowded room. "Overtime for us, eh Chief Rojas?"

"Part of the job description, Mr. Addario. But it does enable us to witness some interesting occurrences. For instance, I have noted that narcotics assistant Sumner is quite friendly to Lieutenant Porlado."

As I grew to know Rojas better, my admiration for the man's perception and dry wit increased. There was little that missed his eyes. He knew not just where all the bodies were buried, so to speak, but also how they'd gotten there.

"I like a man of action and strategy. But I respect even more a man who can adapt to his surroundings. You are unmoved by all this, Mr. Addario? It is a far cry from your hippies and protesters in San Francisco," Rojas added, his long, aquiline nose wrinkling slightly in disdain.

"I have to admit, this isn't too hard to take," I smiled confidently. "Besides, I had help from all those instant charm school classes the government made me take."

162

Rojas' eyes crinkled in shared amusement. He halted a passing waiter to take a glass of champagne. The waiter, a CIA plant, continued on his way.

"I am sure you know that I have spent some time studying at Langley. A very interesting place," the chief noted reflectively. "I was asked to take a course in statesmanship. Comes in handy at events like this."

I had no trouble believing that the CIA would ask a man who was born in South American high society to take diplomatic lessons. Rojas wore his tuxedo like a second skin. He exuded more authority than some American ambassadors.

"I can see you must've passed with flying colors, Chief."

Rojas chuckled. "Here in South America," he said after a pause, "we keep much of the old ways, but that too is changing. There is such change now, constant change. We have had a military regime for the last seven years, and now our president-general thinks to give democratic elections to the people. Do you know the Perónistas, Mr. Addario? They worship Juan Perón as if he were God."

It was a discussion that was to occur frequently over the next couple of years, and I always paid full attention to what Rojas said about Argentine politics. Politics play a crucial role in any drug offensive. The figures at the top of the food chain tend to be men of power not afraid to use it to further their own ends while keeping themselves protected. And Rojas was always able to foresee the winds of revolution, as well. That's how he survived in his position for so long. Some years later, the military regime of Argentina would be replaced by Dr. Héctor Cámpora, a fervent Perónist. Argentina, under the second Perón rule, endured another scourge that the chief would manage to outlast.

Rojas drew me slightly aside and lowered his voice. "There have always been drugs in South America, Mr. Addario. In the Colombian hills, farmers harvest coffee and cocaine side by side. Now there are certain powerful people who are able to organize and build the drug traffic that makes the problem a big one on an international scale."

"That's why I'm here," I said, my voice measured with conviction. "It's just the beginning. We aren't alarmists, Chief Rojas, but we do not underestimate the dealers. The situation can only get worse. You can't guard every border and harbor. Soon you will see refining labs and processing factories in those Colombian hills."

I watched his patrician face darken in grim thought.

"We will speak further of this," Rojas said, softer.

"Yes," I agreed. "This is hardly the place for business discussions. I feel we can work on this together, Chief. Shall we meet on Thursday? At your convenience, of course."

Rojas nodded. "I shall have my secretary make the appointment with your office, Mr. Addario. I am most interested in hearing your views." He looked around the room, then dipped his head politely. "Come. Let me introduce you to someone I am certain you would like to meet also."

We walked over to a quartet of men who were laughing at a joke. Rojas interrupted them with the ease of long friendship and returned to me with one of the men. Having been introduced earlier, I recognized Hannibal Tastor. He was of less imposing stature than Argentina's sophisticated chief of police. Of average height, Tastor was slightly squat with a paunch starting to push over his belt. Thinning, pomaded dark hair served to emphasize the protuberant round eyes set in a Peter Lorre face. When he spoke, however, the customs chief was articulate and clever, in direct contrast to his rather morose, hangdog appearance. As I shortly discovered, Tastor also enjoyed an inclination for colorful words and an expansive repertoire of dirty jokes.

From the records, I knew that Tastor had celebrated his sixty-fourth birthday a few months ago. A rabid anti-Perónist, he'd spent some time in the Argentine prisons during Juan Perón's reign. And anyone who survived Perón's political prison camps was one tough son of a bitch, which made him my kind of guy.

We spoke of trivial matters at first, then the conversation gradually eased into the same vein as my talk with Rojas. Rather than the diffident approach I took with Rojas, I adopted a more aggressive, less philosophical tone. Soon Tastor was slapping me boisterously on the back and nudging me slyly with his elbow.

Drugs were barely mentioned during the course of the talk. Not because Tastor was being ambiguous or crafty so much as his disinterest was plain to me. The customs chief was just not particularly concerned with drug trafficking. He would do what he could to help, but it was not of any major importance to him personally. I offered no counterargument, preferring Tastor's honesty. We agreed on a meeting later in the week. When I hinted that I wanted to talk to the airport chief too, Tastor helpfully drew me over to Rodrigo Mattera.

Mattera was a tall, heavyset man whose dark, solemn face seemed cast in a perpetual frown. There was an air of reservation and quiet about him that was as impenetrable as Rojas' old-world dignity. During the entire conversation, Mattera looked unwaveringly at me, his slate black eyes intelligent and enigmatic. He didn't smile or joke. He didn't drink or smoke. He listened, questioned, and voiced his thoughts flatly, unemotionally.

"I do not like drugs, Mr. Addario. I despise the dealers. They are trash and profit from dope," he said gravely, in his slightly accented English. "I am a friend of Rojas, Tastor, and Los Hermaños. I will go over my calendar and schedule a meeting with you." As an afterthought, he added, "Would there be any problem with that?"

I was quick to reassure him that I would be delighted to meet with him. I found Mattera's directness and no-nonsense demeanor refreshing. His terseness and almost fatalistic view cut through the usual polite, but meandering, small talk. Another man I could work with and, especially, rely on.

I found myself talking to Mattera about his own strong conviction that the current US administration's approach to drug enforcement was a valid and viable policy, that he had worked enough years in the field to know nothing kills an operation more than indecisiveness and indiscriminate change. It was my final important (or business) conversation of the evening, and I came away with a deep sense of achievement. The entire day had been enormously successful for me, and I was pleased with the pace of my assignment. More quickly than I had anticipated, key players were being slotted into crucial roles. The necessary groundwork had been laid. I'd reached out to the people I needed for support, and the initial responses were positive.

Rojas dominated the law enforcement scene, and my initial meeting with him couldn't have gone better. Tastor was no problem, and if Mattera was not exactly pouring out good will, he was a man of the same mind I could definitely work with. I wanted to enlist his aid; I wasn't interested in marrying his sister. I didn't think Mattera liked me much and was surprised, in later years, when a close associate of the airport chief told me that he'd always spoken highly of me.

Auguste Ricord still weighed heavily on my mind, but I felt easier now. I had begun to activate the force that would eventually help me snare my prey. Not bad for a first day on the job, but it wasn't over yet.

CHAPTER THIRTEEN

BUENOS AIRES, ARGENTINA, 1970

I was looking for John when John Lodge, the American ambassador to Argentina, ambled up to me. A train of aides and foreign officials trailed in his wake. He held two lovely young ladies on his arm, neither of whom was his wife.

John Davis Lodge was one of the famous New England Lodges, known for their old money and exemplary services to the United States. His brother, Henry Cabot Lodge Jr., for example, was ambassador to Vietnam. The Lodges were a remarkably good-looking family, and John Lodge had his fair share of the family wealth and good looks. Tall, silver-gray haired, and trim, he spoke with a resounding Bostonian accent. At sixty-five, he was still an incredibly vigorous and magnetic man who believed in the glory and might of the USA. A devout adherent of democratic truth and justice, he deemed it his patriotic duty to spread the word to the less fortunate. He also believed in having fun, and John Lodge certainly knew how to enjoy himself.

He grabbed my shoulder and said with a hearty laugh, "What? All by yourself, Dan? We can't have that! Why, you're the man of the hour. Rita, come here. Dan, I want you to meet Rita. She's with the German embassy."

Lodge literally thrust the statuesque beauty who had been clinging to his side into my arms. The young woman instantly transferred her affection from him to me. I forced a smile, distinctly uncomfortable and trying not to show it.

Grinning broadly, Lodge tapped me on the arm. "Now that looks better! How are we doing, son? Have you been around the room? Just hang on, Dan. The evening is still young. Have you eaten? The food is great. Most of the stuff is from the Claridge Grill. You won't find *cazuela de mariscos* like that back home. Have another drink. Someone get Dan a drink! Scotch, Dan. Have a scotch."

Judging by the ambassador's breath and his ramblings, he'd had quite a few himself. Lodge halted a passing waiter, confiscated drinks, and shoved them into everyone's hands within his reach.

I realized that all the talking had made me thirsty, and I drank the scotch gratefully. Rita, meanwhile, was staring soulfully up at me, her eyes carrying a message I pretended not to get. She really did have a fantastic figure! But I made it politely clear I wasn't interested and sauntered off.

My family joined me two months later—Joy and all three kids. And not long after they arrived, we moved from my spacious apartment into a far more spacious walled, gated villa kept under twenty-four guard. Their flight was uneventful, which turned out not to be the case the following summer when we were returning to my South American posting after a brief visit back to the States.

While we waited to board our flight from San Francisco to Buenos Aires in the summer of 1972, our black Labrador Smokey got out of his kennel and was running free on the tarmac and around the airport. Nobody could catch him, and before I could try, our flight boarded after an hour delay. When we took off, we had no idea whether our dog had been found and returned to his kennel, no idea whether he was on the plane with us. As we were landing, though, the pilot made

*Dan pictured with
President Manuel
Noriega of Panama.*

an announcement over the PA that allowed us to breathe a reassuring sigh of relief.

"Smoke on the plane."

The problem was the message had the opposite effect on Buenos Aires airport authorities, who thought the plane was on fire. We landed to see a bevy of fire engines at the end of the runway to put out a fire that was, in fact, a black Lab.

The embassy complex included a tennis court where Ambassador Lodge regularly thrashed the competition, in large part because the CIA guys he was fond of playing let him win. I never asked John if he ever faced Lodge from across the net but, if he had, I'm sure he would have put on just good enough a show to leave the ambassador feeling he had won fair and square.

Not so with my son Bobby, who arrived in Buenos Aires as a solid player, ranked locally back home, for a twelve-year-old. That came up in conversation between Lodge and me, so, of course, a match was arranged. And, being a kid, Bobby knew nothing of official protocol when it came to letting the boss win. Bobby beat Lodge soundly, and I never heard so many excuses, from a problem with his sneakers to loose racquet strings to a court that hadn't been cleared of dirt and was still damp from a recent storm.

I watched that match quietly rooting for Bobby to win with all my heart, wondering if I was going to end up paying the price for the ignominy he'd served up to Ambassador Lodge.

On that night of my welcoming party, Lodge turned away to speak to someone else, and Lou Burdette, who'd been skulking in the crowd, sidled up next to me. He was a rotund, muscular little man with close-set eyes and fleshy lips. His shape was not unlike the fat cigar jutting out of his mouth. He spoke without removing his cigar so that every word came out the side of his mouth.

Burdette was one of the two US Customs representatives in Argentina. Unpleasant and crude, he would have been better cast for undercover work on the New York waterfront. I'd already heard plenty about Burdette. Both he and the Washington Customs people hated the BNDD and, every chance he had, Burdette regaled in spying on the bureau for his home office. It was part and parcel of the infighting between the drug enforcement agencies—the BNDD and Customs. I mentioned earlier how internecine battles among rival agencies was one of the primary reasons for the United States falling so far behind in the war on drugs, and this situation more or less typified it.

Burdette had been described to me as a loose cannon. I never understood why the Customs Department assigned a person like him to an important diplomatic post. He enjoyed all the grace of a rhinoceros and maintained about the same level of diplomacy. When he caught me looking his way, he stormed over and seized my hand in a viselike grip, all the while pumping it like a man working a jack on a flat tire.

"How are you liking this, Addario? Pretty nice, huh? We outdo all the other embassies when we give parties. Saw you talking to Hannibal

Tastor. Beware, he's one wily son of a bitch." A calculating look came into his beady eyes. "So what gives? Setting up something? I can tell you are by the look in your eyes. Hey, I can help you. I've got the contacts here who know Buenos Aires inside and out."

And probably have just as big a mouth as you, I thought in disgust, modulating my tone when I responded.

"Nothing, Burdette. Just a little social chatter. You know, chitchat about the weather, kids, and the pretty *señoritas*."

I smiled warmly at the woman still leaning against me like an extra appendage I couldn't shake.

Rita smiled back. I wondered how much English she understood.

"Look, I know it's tough for you, being new out here," Burdette pressed on. "You just need a little guidance and support. We Americans have to stick together against all the spics."

"Spics?"

He nodded. "You need any help getting the lay of the land, just ask."

I frowned. "I think I'm good. But thanks for the offer to help, Burdette. I'll think on it. Maybe we can do some interdepartmental jobs."

"You do that, Addario. We will have to sit down one of these days, real soon, and go over stuff. I could really help you."

"Okay, sure."

"Hey, I'm not kidding here," he said, sounding perturbed that I wasn't responding with the enthusiasm he'd expected. "Talk to people. I can pull strings. Just tell me what you're working on and I'll get you help pronto."

I pasted a smile on my face. I would've loved to tell the little cretin to take a leap off the embassy roof, but protocol dictated a different tactic.

"That's real generous of you, Burdette."

"What's generous?" asked Lodge, cutting into the conversation and then jerking his head toward the musicians with disdain. "Dan, what's that music those guys are playing?"

Another full glass of scotch had magically appeared in his hand to replace the one he had finished.

"'Amarilla,' Mr. Ambassador," replied one of the Argentine officials. "It is a very popular tune."

"No offense, but that's not how a piano is supposed to sound," said Lodge. "Come on, Dan! Come on, everyone! Let's let them hear how good old American music sounds."

He ushered us toward the musicians, and I found myself swept along by the crowd. John appeared suddenly beside me, his sallow face looking wan.

"What's going on?" I whispered to him, under the cover of all the noise.

Burdette, who had been shuffling alongside me, said out of the side of his mouth, "It's showtime!" as if he'd seen this all before.

I glanced at John, who shrugged slightly.

By now we were standing around the musicians. Lodge spoke rapidly in Spanish to the pianist. The man listened attentively and then relinquished his seat to the ambassador.

Lodge sat down with a flourish and shouted happily, acting like one of my kids.

"Chuck, take the guitars. Give Mickey one. Where's Dan? Dan, come over here. Bring Rita with you. That's right. Come sit down right beside me. Hell, you're the guest of honor tonight."

I was half drawn, half pushed down beside the ambassador. The guitarists handed over their instruments to the Americans. They all wore expressions of placid acceptance of the situation, as if they too had seen this before.

Rita perched herself gingerly next to me on what little room was left on the bench. She was almost sitting on my lap and had to put her arms around my shoulders to keep from falling off. Pulling away would've been rude, so I let her hang on.

Lodge tried a couple of notes on the grand piano. Smiling from ear to ear, he waved everyone over.

"Come on, everyone. Is everyone here? Now, everyone, sing along! Especially you people out on the sides!"

He tested a few bars, then launched into a rousing rendition of "Home on the Range" in a booming baritone voice. I nearly slid off the piano bench in shock.

Everyone joined the ambassador. *"Home, home on the range. Where the deer and the antelope play…"*

I felt a poke in my ribs from next to me on the piano bench where I was sandwiched between Lodge and Rita.

"Dan! Dan! You're not singing!" goaded the ambassador. "Come on now, you're the guest of honor. Have some fun!"

I glanced around. We were indeed the center of attention. Burdette was smirking from the sidelines. Most of the Argentinians were singing gustily along. Tastor was literally belting out the words, clearly familiar with this show, while John watched me from across the room with detached amusement.

Ha-ha! I wanted to say to him. *Very funny.*

Here I was, in a country that formed one of the front lines in the war on drugs, sitting on a piano bench while a plan was underway in earnest to deliver Auguste Ricord to me.

"Where seldom is heard a discouraging word…."

But it was about to, and then some.

CHAPTER FOURTEEN

BUENOS AIRES, ARGENTINA

A couple of days later, the Brothers sent word that their sources had located Ricord just outside of Asunción, the capital of Paraguay. "Are you sure?" I asked them on a secure phone line. "How do you know?"

"We have very good people there," replied the Professor. "We are going to fly down and personally check the information."

The Brothers had passed their first test effortlessly. They had found Ricord much faster than my own staff could. Before they could take any further action, though, the Paraguayan government mysteriously arrested Ricord without forewarning. Initially, this was cause for celebration. Hearty congrats were exchanged like cigars, plenty of pats on the back came my way, including a cable from the White House congratulating me on doing what no one else had ever managed to do. Everyone was elated. The ambassador called me into his office and offered a toast. BNDD headquarters in Washington called to congratulate me. But a considerable challenge remained ahead of us:

How do we get the notoriously uncooperative Paraguayan government to cooperate further?

Then the legal maneuvering began. The BNDD's chief legal counsel cabled from Washington advising me that, because no formal extradition treaty existed between Paraguay and the United States, Ricord might go free unless and until the Paraguayan government pressed charges against him. The Paraguayans backed off. No formal treaty, no release of prisoner to US custody. Then the French government tried. Again, no treaty, no release.

I sent word that the US ambassador to Paraguay, Raymond Ylitalo, should try to negotiate an informal extradition. If the Paraguayans would simply turn Ricord over to me, I could do my job. Let the diplomats worry about a formal treaty. No cable came back. I repeated my request.

"Your request is under consideration," came the curt reply.

I was not reassured. I'd already heard from the White House.

"Is the car stalled?" queried the one-sentence cable, all that celebrating suddenly a distant memory.

Our challenge was that we were operating in brand-new territory here. No foreign national had ever been extradited to the United States from a third-party country on drug charges, much less from a country with which the US maintained tenuous diplomatic relations at best. I was worried that Ricord would slip out the back door. He had plenty of money to buy his way out of prison and out of Paraguay. He had already purchased some mid-level customs bureaucrats very capable of abetting his escape. I even considered spreading some of BNDD's money across the same palms myself to arrange for Ricord's departure instead.

On a hunch, I dispatched Chiccilo, one of my senior BNDD agents who was especially well versed in field operations and really knew the territorial politics, to Asunción to check on the case with the Paraguayan minister of defense and police chief, along with Ambassador Ylitalo.

175

Chiccilo's first cable back reported, "Ricord under arrest at Tacumbú prison. No special treatment. US ambassador doing everything possible to assist. Recommends my coordinating all matters with his chief counsel. Minister of Defense and police chief very cooperative. Since US and Paraguay have no narcotic extradition treaty, still the same legal problems. Please advise."

I replied that the State Department and BNDD were working on the legal issue. Chiccilo should stay and watch the mark, make sure he stayed right where he was.

That evening, the paperboy brought a report from the Brothers.

"Ricord's living the life of an exiled king. He is staying in a mansion on the outskirts of town. The house is surrounded by a ten-foot stone wall. There are a dozen armed guards on the compound. He is moved to a cell at Tacumbú prison only when US diplomats request a visit with him. We have started electronic surveillance. Last evening, Ricord dined with the police chief of Paraguay, Graciella [the former Miss Colombia] and Lus Marina, mistress to the police chief. They dined on veal, salad, fine French wine, and cocaine. Enclosed are pictures."

"Shit," I murmured.

It was obvious the Paraguayan government was not going to do anything to help beyond the show they'd already put on. I was at a loss. Without that help there was no way to get Ricord out of the country, and it was only a matter of time before he'd manage to disappear. I ordered the Brothers to keep following his every move. Now that I had Ricord in my sights, there was no way I was going to let him slip away. No way.

I knew I was going to have to lean on my connections to push Paraguay to the absolute limits. I wasn't taking any chances. I went to the top rung of the ladder: President Richard Nixon. He wanted Ricord as bad as I did. Ambassador Ylitalo was doing everything he could to push for extradition, but was getting nowhere. That meant we needed to find some leverage.

"Sir, we have a problem," Ambassador Lodge informed President Nixon.

He proceeded to explain to him exactly what the Brothers had reported. There was silence on the other end of the phone before the president's voice returned.

"I will be back with you soon, Ambassador," Nixon said.

The phone clicked off.

But the president did indeed get back to Lodge with instructions that I needed to lay the groundwork to get a clear line on Ricord, even though Asunción was still showing no signs of playing ball with us. The United States maintained a military attaché in Asunción, but even the US military's influence was limited. Still, when the Paraguayan military requested to purchase millions of dollars of equipment, primarily communications gear and spare parts intended to be used for disaster relief, search and rescue, and the interdiction of narcotics traffic, Nixon saw his opportunity.

With the deal in place and the equipment loaded on a ship sailing down through the Panama Canal to Paraguay, we had our chance. I placed a call to Manuel Noriega, who was beginning his rise to power, propelled by his meteoric ascent through the ranks of the Panamanian army, thanks to an alliance with Omar Torrijos, the dictator of Panama. Noriega at the time was chief of Panama's powerful military intelligence service, having been appointed to that post in August 1970 and heavily rumored to be a CIA paid asset almost from the beginning and, thus, a close friend of the United States.

The rumors proved to be true.

Noriega was one of the CIA's most valuable assets in Panama. He had been a useful partner in fighting drug distribution, which was ironic in that he had acquired a great amount of his fortune through the same channels. Noriega had the reputation of being the strongman of his country, regardless of what the official pecking order suggested. As the head honcho, he could accomplish anything he wanted. Now, we just needed him to want Ricord put in jail.

"Thank you for taking my call, General," I said.

"What can I do for you?" he said, his voice matter-of-fact.

"I need you to help me convince the Paraguayan government that it is in everyone's best interest to extradite Auguste Ricord," I told him.

"I agree. I do not want that *estupido* in my country. How can I help?" he asked.

"There's an American ship coming down the canal, scheduled to arrive in Paraguay tomorrow morning. I'd like you to intercept it."

"I will phone you when it is done."

Wielding the power that would ultimately propel him to Panama's highest office, Noriega agreed to hold up the shipment bound for Paraguay at the Panama Canal until such time that the Paraguayan government agreed to expel Auguste Ricord. True to his word, the next day I received a call from Noriega that he had the ship under his control. It was now time for the negotiations.

I called Ambassador Ylitalo.

"It's time," I told him.

Ylitalo swaggered into the Paraguayan government offices, where he was greeted by the secretary of a top military official we'll call Ortega. The secretary's name behind the desk was Carolina. Ylitalo knew her well. He had been in front of her dozens of times trying to get General Ortega to help us get Ricord. So Carolina knew that her boss wanted nothing to do with Ylitalo and had had enough of the attempts.

"He is out for the day, I am sorry, Ambassador," she said, following orders.

"I think he's here," Ylitalo said with a grin.

"No, *señor*," she insisted again. "He isn't."

"You tell your boss I have his boat and if he wants it back to get his ass out here," Ylitalo said, smiling again.

It was obvious Carolina knew something because she picked up the phone and whispered into the receiver. Not but a second later, General Ortega threw open the door, his face twisted like a trapped rat.

"Hello, General. May I come in?" Ylitalo asked him.

"It seems I don't have a choice," Ortega replied with a shrug.

Ylitalo explained the current predicament that the Paraguayan government now found itself in. "Let me make this simple for you. The equipment for Ricord. No Ricord, no shipment. You give us Ricord, we release the goods."

Ortega fumed as though he was going to erupt. But he didn't.

He extended his hand to Ylitalo. "You have a deal."

"You've made the right choice, sir," Ylitalo said and he walked out of the room.

Paraguay had agreed to turn over Ricord, arguably the world's most notorious drug trafficker. On the surface, it was time to begin the celebrating anew.

But not so fast. Since no extradition treaty existed between Paraguay and the United States, no clear path existed for us to bring Ricord to justice. If there had been a treaty, that would've been the end of things there.

But there wasn't. So we needed to work around the problem.

We needed Ricord declared persona non grata and expelled by the Paraguayan government, so he could be sent to the United States through a foreign country that maintained strong diplomatic ties with us. Argentina was the most obvious option, but not a viable one because no American airline currently flew in and out of the country. So instead, exhaustive efforts secured Brazil's cooperation to have Ricord flown first to Buenos Aires, where he'd be placed, under heavy guard, on a flight to São Paulo.

Why São Paulo? Because Pan Am maintained regular nonstop flights to the United States from there. And the particular flight Ricord was going to board contained federal agents, a deputy assistant US attorney from the Southern District of New York who'd obtained the warrant, and a doctor. We were prepared for the likely eventuality that our prisoner would scream he was being kidnapped. But a federal judge had already ruled Ricord's seizure in São Paulo to be legal.

179

By today's standards that may all sound routine, but back then it was utterly unprecedented. And the naysayers were already second-guessing me. I knew that if this thing went south, my ass was out.

But it didn't.

Ricord protested and screamed through virtually the entire flight. We were met at Kennedy Airport by the chief prosecutor for the Southern District of New York, who arraigned Ricord right there at the airport, since according to the law he had to be rearrested and arraigned as soon as he touched down on United States soil. We weren't about to squander our case on any procedural oversight.

Ricord used his considerable stash of drug money to hire top attorneys who fought his arrest on every conceivable ground, insisting that he had been unlawfully kidnapped and should be released with all charges dropped. The judge, though, ruled that this fell under the category of a diplomatic kidnapping and that all proper laws and procedures had been followed in the process. In 1972, Auguste Ricord was sentenced to twenty-two years in prison and served ten years of that, at which time he was issued a medical pardon. That enabled him to return to Paraguay in 1983, where he died of illness two years later, his drug activities long dead and the infamous Marseille distribution network portrayed in *The French Connection* long disabled.

* * * * *

The Ricord bust was indeed cause for celebration, given the volume of drugs it kept from reaching the United States and off our streets. But there was plenty that happened in my tenure as South America's regional director for the BNDD that was anything but celebratory.

I had an agent—let's call him Sergio—I'd personally selected out of New York to head our Bogotá office in Colombia. He was from Spain originally and was a great guy with a wife and a couple kids who nonetheless jumped at the chance to take the reins as Special Agent in Charge of the most dangerous front in the burgeoning war on drugs.

Auguste Joseph Ricord appears in court on drug trafficking charges, 1972.

And he managed to thrive there, despite being dropped into the worst climate for drug interdiction imaginable. Corruption in Colombia stretched from the bottom to the top of the ladder, including the military who sold themselves out as soldiers for the drug traffickers to secure their crops, labs, and cash.

Against those odds, Sergio had developed a number of top-flight informants, one of whom provided intelligence on where the biggest cocaine production labs were located in the Colombian jungles. In addition to drugs, these jungle strongholds held huge caches of American dollars because our currency was the only negotiable tender in the drug world. That cash went to pay corrupt cops, military officials, soldiers, and politicians. Sergio's plan was to go after the cash as well as the drugs. He didn't need to retrieve it, only to destroy it, to break the drug trade's back.

But that was sure to roil the Colombian government at the highest levels. Corruption in foreign governments we deal with is another of the primary reasons why the war on drugs has been successful only in fits and starts, often feeling like three steps forward and four steps back. The government official you just dined and shook hands with is reliable and trustworthy only until the next envelope stuffed with cash is pressed into his palm. Many of these countries were and are controlled by money gleaned from the lucrative drug trade. That money can make even democratic elections suspect, the drug cartels being expert at installing puppet governments or seizing on the vulnerabilities of those officials they might not yet control once in office.

What could we do about this? I'll give one idea here: How about going after the money, all that cash drug traffickers need to buy their guns, soldiers, and politicians, and generally fund their entire operation? They stockpile massive stores of American dollars, especially in the hundred-dollar bill domination, tons and tons of it just waiting to be passed to this official or that. Here's what I propose:

Change the color of American currency, at least the hundred-dollar bill. Once the change takes effect, drug operations would grind to a halt. With their stockpiles of American cash rendered worthless, everything would stop.

This may sound like a radical change, but how many regular people ever use hundred- or even fifty-dollar bills? Not many. And the ones who do would have a specific period to turn in their old large-domination bills for new ones in the proper color, or perhaps ones imprinted with a strip or watermark to distinguish them from the old bills.

A version of this was actually proposed by former secretary of the treasury Donald Regan in a *New York Times* op-ed on September 18, 1989:

> *To get at the cash dealings of drug wholesalers, retailers, street pushers, etc., we should quietly print new $50 and $100 bills—either of*

a different color, or size, than the current ones. Then with only a 10-day warning, we should make all $50 and $100 bills obsolete—no longer acceptable as legal tender. Everyone would have to exchange their large bills for new ones. Banks and other financial institutions would have to keep a record of any cash transactions over $1,000. Reports would be furnished to the Comptroller and I.R.S. by name and taxpayer identification number.

This would panic those with huge cash holdings. If the cash is legitimate, no one should have any fear. Yes, it might cause confusion for a couple of months, but what honest citizen wouldn't be willing to put up with a little inconvenience so as to trap these criminals? This would hit the criminals where it hurts most—in the pocketbook.

Sometimes, after all, radical problems require radical solutions.

Back in Colombia, Sergio was meeting with a trusted informant in Bogota who turned out to be a double agent working for the loosely configured groups that would soon grow into the infamous cartels, based in Medellín and elsewhere. The informant shot and killed Sergio at that meeting before escaping. I flew into Colombia, only after making the hardest phone call of my life to Sergio's now widow. What could I say? How could I convince her that her husband hadn't died for naught? It comes with the job, but it's something you never get used to.

That doesn't mean I didn't get plenty of practice.

I had two brothers working for me, one in charge of the BNDD office in Panama and the other working undercover in Caracas, Venezuela, named Raoul. Raoul had an informant who was dealing kilos of heroin out of the nation of Curaçao, then a Dutch possession. That informant arranged for him to penetrate the network, but things went bad in a hurry. There was a gunfight in which the informant was killed and Raoul shot in the leg. They got him to the hospital in time to save his life, but he later died of an infection.

This time, I hopped on a plane and flew to Panama so I could tell his brother, my Special Agent in Charge there, in person. Although understandably traumatized, he was so grateful not only that I'd come in person, but also that I'd held off giving the tragic news to his mother.

"She has a bad heart, Señor Addario. The news would have killed her."

CHAPTER FIFTEEN

WASHINGTON, DC, 1973

On July 1, 1973, in the next phase of the war on drugs, the Drug Enforcement Administration was born in a merger of the Bureau of Narcotics and Dangerous Drugs together with Customs and Border Protection. The move was conducted under the auspices of President Nixon and the newly formed entity would fall under the jurisdiction of the US Department of Justice, its mission statement being of singular purpose: To carry out drug investigations on both foreign and domestic soil.

It was a major step forward, at least on the surface, since this was the first time a single federal agency or entity had been chartered for the express purpose of interdicting and combating illegal drugs. Nixon was backed by a Congress that took note of the increasing drug problem and how it was affecting the country. They thoroughly supported him when he decided to merge over six hundred agents into one powerhouse organization of such singular mission.

This was how shit was to get done. This was the first step to changing the tide in the war on drugs for good.

But like any best-laid plans, bureaucracy and politics always manage to mess things up. Right from the beginning, the merger was riddled with politics. The Customs commissioner, Myles Ambrose, for example, outranked the commissioner of the BNDD in political stature and power, thanks to his close association with President Nixon. Thus, Ambrose became the interim, and later permanent, head of the newly formed DEA, which probably wouldn't have been a problem if he didn't decide to pull rank on all of his agents. But he did, meaning the agency was riddled from its very conception by the same bureaucratic infighting and internecine struggles that had roiled previous incarnations. He came in and began moving personnel, even simply changing their positions or demoting BNDD employees to raise the ranks of his Customs agents.

Sound familiar? No one in those first days of the DEA stepped up to fight for the former BNDD guys, and Ambrose's friendship with Nixon kept all of us from doing anything about it, efforts that would have surely yielded nothing worthwhile, in any event. We had been thrown under the bus and had no choice but to stay there, lest we risk being run over by the wheels.

The true tragedy of this lay in the fact that the directors I had appointed in my tenure as regional director of South America had by this point really ingratiated themselves into their respective cultures, including me in Argentina. It wasn't just a job for us; we had made it our lives. I had no time or opportunity to groom a replacement when I was recalled, because to replace me Ambrose appointed none other than the incompetent Customs agent Lou Burdette, who lasted all of six months and did irreparable harm to the office in his brief tenure. It was just one example of the steps Ambrose took that created a blueprint for failure.

Meet the new boss, same as the old boss, right?

I just didn't get it. Auguste Ricord had been followed across the world, chased for years, and shortly after I finally caught him, I learned I was out. It was the DEA's new director of foreign operations, Jack

A photo sent to Dan from President Richard Nixon commemorating his service.

Cusack, who called me with the news of my recall slash firing. I knew that shit was going to change with the merger, but this?

"Dan, you know, we can never thank you enough for how you handled that case with Ricord. The president was thrilled," Cusack said.

"Thank you, sir."

"And you know we have a lot of respect for you here at the agency," Cusack continued.

I sat silently. I knew when Cusack started with so many compliments that he was about to rip the rug out.

"However, Burdette is now in charge and he has some changes he'd like made."

"The new administration always does," I said, waiting for the bomb.

"Well, Burdette has decided to place the Customs guys as the heads of all the offices," he said.

I could tell he was waiting for me to reply, but I stayed silent.

"Lou Burdette," Cusack continued, "is going to be the new deputy in charge of South America. However, the commissioner would like you to stay and take the assistant deputy position."

"Hell, no!" I said, unable to restrain myself.

There wasn't a chance I was going to work for Burdette, the man who sat around on his ass while I caught Ricord. He was useless, a prototype for everything that had gone wrong with efforts to fight the drug war up until that point. After all the years and time I'd put in to straighten out and reorganize the office I had overseen as regional director, there was no way I was going to step down and work for that pisser. He was nothing more than a political appointee who knew which wheels to grease and which asses to kiss.

I let Cusack know how I felt in a more diplomatic way, of course. Well, maybe not too much more.

"I understand how you feel, Dan. This is just how these things work," he said, trying to excuse the absurdity of the decision and absolve himself of any culpability in reaching it.

With the wrong person running the coordinated South American efforts I had initiated, what did he and the rest of the politicos think was going to happen? Didn't they realize that all the drug routes I had shut down would reopen and even expand throughout South America with Burdette in charge? That was as inevitable as the sun coming up the next day. I just didn't want to be there to watch it happen; I couldn't, not if it meant watching all the progress we'd made in my tenure go to shit. I wasn't about to let myself be complicit in a regression likely to set things back to where they'd been when I'd taken over.

I felt like I'd been stabbed in the back. I guess, to a large degree, I was naïve, believing I was past the politics of all this, had grown beyond it. But yet another purported solution had ended up creating far more problems than it solved. Apparently, no one involved in the formation of the Drug Enforcement Administration had bothered to anticipate the obvious. Because politics dominated their lives, they didn't realize they were appointing nothing more than a politician in Myles Ambrose to be the country's top drug cop. This was their world, and they were too myopic to see the bigger picture of what they were destroying in their attempt to create something better.

The way we were fighting the war on drugs was akin to sending soldiers out into real battle with empty magazines in their assault rifles. The difference in the military, though, was that the generals calling the shots viewed the battlefield through an objective lens, as opposed to a political one—for the most part, anyway. A shooting war is all about figuring out how to win, whereas in the war on drugs we seemed to be doing everything we could to lose, including squandering so much of the progress the BNDD had made.

"Well, we don't have any regional director positions open right now," Cusack told me, sounding respectful of my efforts while expressing no real regret. "However, we can transfer you back to Washington, DC, until something opens up."

"Okay, then," I said, still livid, trying to rationalize the situation I'd been forced into. "It'll be good to be home for a while."

* * * * *

"Ugh, Dad! We have to move again?" Dan asked.

Dan and his younger brother Bob had really been enjoying their time in South America. They were on a spectacular soccer team and were top players on their respective teams. They had made friends and settled in, and now it was time to uproot them again.

Mark had especially ingratiated himself into the Argentine landscape—literally. Our family's villa was located directly across the street from the one occupied by the president of the Goodyear Tire and Rubber Company, surrounded 24/7 by armed guards. Those guards weren't enough to prevent the man's kidnapping, big business in Buenos Aires carried out by criminal gangs who were after the biggest ransoms they could realize and who knew that companies like Goodyear always paid.

One day I got a frantic call at the embassy from Joy telling me that Mark had disappeared after school. I rushed home, fearing the worst, wondering if the US government would front the ransom money so I could get my youngest son back. What seemed like the entire Buenos Aires police department descended on the neighborhood and started going door-to-door to see if anybody had seen anything. They found Mark at one of these homes, enjoying a backyard barbecue of *chorizo* with the family, including a schoolmate. My wanderer of a son spoke fluent Spanish and fit right into the scenery. Another time, Mark wandered off into the mountains. We searched for him futilely and were just ready to go out again when Smokey, our trusty black Lab, brought him back.

I think Smokey would have made a better successor for me in Argentina than Lou Burdette.

"Boys, don't make your father feel bad. It will be great to go back to the States. To settle down on home turf for a change," Joy said, patting me on the back.

She knew how badly I felt about ripping the boys out of an environment in which they'd thrived.

"I don't like being without you, Dad," Bobby said, his bottom lip quivering.

I decided at that moment that for this move, I would bring them home at the same time instead of allowing them to finish the school year at their English-speaking school in Buenos Aires. A couple of weeks later we packed our bags and moved to Vienna, Virginia.

* * * * *

Because of my experience in Argentina, I was placed on the Latin and South American desk at the newly christened headquarters for the Drug Enforcement Administration in an old office building around 9th Street near the White House. I was responsible for getting people and supplies to all of the local DEA offices. I also worked as the liaison between Congress and the regional directors, which had the bonus effect of educating me on which of our elected representatives were really serious about winning the war on drugs.

Manning a desk allowed me to get more time with my family. I was working the typical nine-to-five for pretty much the first time in my entire law enforcement career. While that was a difficult transition to say the least, I have to say that it was wonderful to spend more time with my kids and be there for them, more than I had in the past several years.

My boys were really into sports. Dan was still excelling at swimming and I took the opportunity to be his swim coach again. He also played football and basketball. During our time in Argentina, Bobby had learned to play soccer and was a stupendous player. He could kick left- and right-footed and was fast as lightning. He helped take one of the teams he played on back in the States to national championships. Barely nine years old, Mark was following in the footsteps of his brothers, starting to excel in both football and basketball.

Athletics was my boys' tool for adjusting in new schools and meeting peers. They always melded so well and made friends quickly because of their athletic ability, a true blessing for our entire family.

* * * * *

While life was more normal than it had been, Jamaica was becoming a hotbed for marijuana runners. Although not my wheelhouse, it was a problem that needed to be stopped. The Drug Enforcement Administration didn't have an office in Jamaica and with the escalation of marijuana exporting, it was time to open one, opening the door for my return to the foreign service.

Jack Cusack sent me down to Jamaica to meet with the prime minister to achieve two goals: get him, and the American ambassador, to allow the DEA to set up an office down there and to let us train the local drug cops in the principles of narcotics interdiction. Turned out the prime minister had been briefed extensively on my background and experience. Cusack wanted him to know I wasn't just some flunky, since he'd no doubt heard of the DEA's regressive efforts to fight drugs in South America. So I had his respect before I even walked in the door, and I was gratified to learn that he was very serious about fighting the marijuana problems infecting his nation and pouring especially potent weed into the United States.

I was back to doing what I did best: troubleshooting. Being dropped into a problem area and leaving it better off when I left than when I found it. As for Jamaica, I was able to get both the prime minister and American ambassador to support a DEA presence down there and laid out the parameters of how we could solve, or at least mitigate, the marijuana problem that was overcoming the entire nation.

I never saw Jamaica as a long-term posting; it was more a drop-in assignment that ended as soon as I'd accomplished the mandate given me by Jack Cusack. But my success down there had positioned me for another high-profile international posting where the drug business threatened to consume entire societies. If South America was a hotbed, then this next foreign assignment was hell itself:

The Golden Triangle.

PART FOUR

THE GOLDEN TRIANGLE

CHAPTER SIXTEEN

BANGKOK, THAILAND, 1974

I arrived in Bangkok, Thailand, in the autumn of 1974. My assignment was to somehow, somewhere, put my finger into the dike of the Golden Triangle, formed by the remote border area of Thailand, Burma, and Laos, and stop the flow of heroin into the United States.

First, though, I had to go through the whole training process again to regain my top-secret security clearance, which had been taken back upon my return from Argentina. Once again, I underwent sessions with the State Department and CIA, pretty much identical to what I'd experienced before, with the exception of briefings specific to the area in question. That was hardly boilerplate, given the Southeast Asia region I was taking over was smack dab in the middle of a war zone, even with the Vietnam conflict waning.

What all those briefings didn't cover was the fact that I was going to have to plug a much bigger hole than anticipated, thanks in large part to the fact that the regional director I was replacing had let things slide badly, to put it nicely. To put it more bluntly, he was a real asshole who was brazenly disobeying Jack Cusack's instructions and ignoring the mandate he'd been given. There's a phrase the FBI uses to describe agents who get too close to their subjects, often because they actually hail from the same area; the bureau calls that "going native." Well, my predecessor had married a Thai woman and lost himself in the culture, forgetting what his real job was in the process. He was also suspected of smuggling jewels out of the country in diplomatic pouches, even as huge quantities of heroin were being smuggled into the United States on his watch.

The problem was we had no idea what the outgoing regional director knew; he wasn't saying. You know how they say a fish rots from the head down? That's the condition I found the entire Golden Triangle in when it came to fighting the war on drugs. I was going to need to bring in a new deputy and new agents. The current agents had taken their lead from the top, and I found their replacements in the form of operatives I'd worked with at various previous postings. Men I could trust, in stark contrast to the mess the Bangkok office had become.

My official title was Regional Director of Southeast Asian Operations, working out of the US Embassy in Bangkok, dropped into yet another hostile environment that also brought Manila, Tokyo, Hong Kong, Kuala Lumpur, Jakarta, and Vientiane under my domain, each of which I'd be visiting no less than once a month to make sure my directives were being followed and progress was being made. I'd come to relish the opportunity that provided for me to get the job done from the ground up and to facilitate my transition process.

Jack Cusack himself accompanied me when I made the move. Cusack had inherited the previous regional director prior to the merger that created the DEA, so he wanted the people who mattered in the respective countries I was responsible for to know that there was a new sheriff in town. His presence and direct involvement also indicated the top priority he intended to give our so far failed efforts to stop the flow of narcotics out of the region.

It was no secret on this particular ground that my predecessor had done nothing to interdict drugs coming from Vietnam, the same predecessor who was literally flying out as I was flying in, affording no opportunity for a smooth transition. It was left for me to learn about that major distribution channel in those closing days of the Vietnam War. Our agents in New Jersey and Manhattan had alerted us to a new trickle of heroin entering the country through the East Coast. When I first stepped off the plane in Bangkok, though, all I knew was that the trickle had become a torrent. Large quantities of first-class heroin were appearing along the Eastern Seaboard, and it was obvious it was coming from the Golden Triangle. Who were the ringleaders stashing the heroin? How was it being transported? How had the pipeline been organized?

In that festering steam bath that was Bangkok in autumn of 1974, it was up to me to find out.

Bangkok was a mixture of beauty and bestiality, the acrid odor of embalming fluid and the intoxicating scent of jasmine. The Vietnam War, of course, created the dichotomy, an aberration fueled by an unfortunate combination of bad timing, a bad place, and bad politics. But I also remember a beautiful little girl who sold garlands of jasmine at the corner of Sukhumvit and Wireless Road, halfway between my residence and my office at the US Embassy. I'd stop for flowers every day, pay her more than the pittance she was charging, exchange smiles, and be overwhelmed by the smell of the jasmine.

Jasmine and formaldehyde, a strange juxtaposition to say the least.

Each morning I stepped out into the sauna of downtown Bangkok, watched the carefully ironed pleats in my safari garb disappear, and uttered a silent prayer that at least one good lead would be on my desk when I arrived at the embassy. More often than not, though, I'd arrive at my desk with nothing substantial to go on. I had hope, but my patience was waning. I had my people spread around in bars, brothels, and military posts, and had a high degree of confidence that they'd turn up good leads. Throughout my career, I had operated on the premise that good agents would always come through; a good source would always deliver, if given the time.

And we needed every source we could come by, thanks to a Shan warlord named Khun Sa.

"Over the two decades of his unrivalled hegemony in the Shan state, from 1974 to 1994," the *Economist* wrote on November 8, 2007, shortly after his death, "the share of New York street heroin coming from the Golden Triangle—the northern parts of Myanmar, Thailand and Laos—rose from 5% to 80%. It was 90% pure, 'the best in the business,' according to the Drug Enforcement Administration. And Khun Sa, the DEA thought, had 45% of that trade."

"The Kuomintang, the Chinese Nationalist forces," the same article continued, "had lured him into opium in the 1950s when he trained with them along the Chinese border. Soldiering and drug-dabbling seemed ideal for him: a chain-smoking country lad of little education, but with a way of making friends and a streak of uncompromising violence. His *nom de guerre*, Khun Sa, meant 'Prince Prosperous.' Through the 1960s, mostly in the Shan state, he gathered men and changed armies as it suited him in the wars for drug-routes and territory."

The *New York Times* elaborates further in Sa's obituary, which ran on November 5, 2007:

> He entered the opium business in 1963, when the Burmese government authorized him and others to form militias allied with the central government as a way of outsourcing the job of fighting rebel groups. Within a year he broke his ties with the Burmese Army and established an independent fief in the northernmost reaches of Burma, near the border with China.
>
> His early career was characterized by failure. He challenged the dominance of the Nationalists in the Golden Triangle drug trade, but lost in battle. He was captured by the Burmese central government and imprisoned from 1969 to 1974.
>
> Soon after his release he rejoined his supporters in the northeast and set up a base in Baan Hin Taek, along the mountainous border near the Thai city of Chiang Rai. His drug network soon came to dominate the Burmese heroin trade.

Part of the warlord Khun Sa's camp as seen from the air.

Drugs meant money and money meant power, the kind of power that would make it difficult for any Thai government entity to openly oppose Khun Sa. Individual politicians who dared do so risked death.

My job was to change that, or at the very least devise a strategy to reduce the staggering flow of drugs, particularly heroin, coming into the United States out of the Golden Triangle. It was the world's largest opium-growing region, covering an area the size of Nevada, from the green mountains of western Myanmar to the valley of northeastern Laos. Nearly 70 percent of the heroin on the streets in the United States at the time originated from there.

How exactly, though, did the region become such a hotbed for drug manufacturing and distribution worldwide? According to the encyclopedic website Facts and Details:

Opium was introduced to China by Arab traders during the reign of Kublai Khan (1279–94). The drug was highly valued for its medicinal qualities and was grown by some ethnic minorities in south China to raise money to pay tributes to the Chinese Emperors.

Opium as a major cash crop was introduced to the Golden Triangle by the British in the colonial period. It was grown as a cash crop for the French as well as the British. But it was Chinese who once fought for the Kuomintang troops with Chiang Kai-shek against Chairman Mao's Red Army that introduced big time production and smuggling....

In 1949, the remnants of Chiang Kai-shek's defeated Kuomintang (Chinese nationalists) army retreated to the mountain of Burma along the Chinese border and tried to organize attacks against the Red Army. To raise money the Kuomintang encouraged peasant farmers to raise opium, which the Chinese nationalists sold for huge profits. Later the Beijing-backed Communist Party of Burma financed their operation with money from the opium and heroin trade.

Another problem unique to the Golden Triangle was America's complicity in the problem thanks to the CIA, which had long held entirely different priorities than drug enforcement agencies and was willing to turn a blind eye to drug trafficking so long as it served their more military-oriented goals. From 1963 to 1973, the CIA trained Hmong tribesmen to fight against Communists in Laos, and the Hmong, in turn, ended up financing some of their efforts by selling opium. So, at best, the CIA condoned and thus supported the problem I'd been sent to Thailand to solve; at worst, they were directly complicit in it.

In essence, we had created the monster, and now I was here to destroy it. The only problem was, I couldn't figure out how the Asians were exporting the heroin. Over the years, I had seen dope smuggled in furniture, cars, clothes, and kids' playthings, yet everything we searched in our region came up empty. It wasn't until I heard a rumor picked up on the mean streets of New York by a DEA tipster that I had something to go on:

"The heroin is being smuggled into the United States in the bodies of GIs killed in Vietnam."

This was the most horrific smuggling rumor I had ever heard, but in my business I'd learned that the meaner the rumor, the more likely it was to be true. I didn't share the tip with the American ambassador or the CIA station chief. I'd learned from my time in Argentina that the best way to keep drug-busting secrets was to keep them from the State Department and the CIA, since their interests far too often diverged from mine and now the DEA's. When it came to stopping narcotics, they often had other priorities, higher in their minds.

Their biggest priority was stopping Communism from prevailing in the now disproved "Domino Theory." During the Vietnam War, though, it wasn't so much a theory as it was the basis of an edict. Just as the FBI of the same era turned a blind eye to the criminal actions of their informants enlisted to bring down the Italian mob, the CIA looked the other way when it came to the allies they perceived as helping them save the world from Communism. The Agency enjoyed far more clout and had convinced, effectively brainwashed, Washington into believing that their efforts were far more important than stopping the flow of drugs into the United States. That their war, in other words, was more important than the one I was fighting.

As a direct result of this, drugs ended up being shuffled to the back burner to the point where some of the biggest smugglers turned out to be CIA informants who flew kilos and kilos of heroin out of the Golden Triangle with total impunity. Here's how the website Collective Evolution aptly framed the historical perspective of what I was being dropped into:

In Southeast Asia (SEA), during the Vietnam War, the CIA worked alongside Laotian general Vang Pao in an effort to help make Laos the world's largest exporter of heroin. The CIA then flew drugs all over SEA, allowing the Golden Triangle (parts of Burma, Thailand, and Laos) to become the world hub for heroin.

Agents from the Bureau of Narcotics and Dangerous Drugs managed to seize an Air America aircraft [a false-front airline used for covert CIA operations] that contained large amounts of heroin, but the CIA ordered the agents to release the plane and halt any further investigations.

The CIA wasn't just involved with the transportation of the drugs, however. The heroin was refined in a laboratory built at the CIA headquarters in Northern Laos. After about a decade of U.S. military intervention, SEA represented 70% of the world's opium supply. Unfortunately, many of the operatives became addicted to the heroin themselves. At the same time, SEA also became the main supplier of raw materials for the U.S. heroin industry.

The CIA's involvement, even complicity, in criminal activities, though, didn't start there.

"It goes all the way back to the predecessor organization OSS and its involvement with the Italian Mafia, the Cosa Nostra in Sicily and Southern Italy," the CIA's Victor Marchetti told *Frontline* on May 17, 1988. "Later on when they were fighting Communists in France… they got in tight with the Corsican brotherhood. The Corsican brotherhood of course were big dope dealers. As things changed in the world the CIA got involved with the Kuomintang types in Burma who were drug runners because they were resisting the drift towards Communism there. The same thing happened in Southeast Asia, later in Latin America. Some of the very people who are the best sources of information, who are capable of accomplishing things and the like, happen to be the criminal element."

"Early on," recalls Ron Rickenbach, former official for the US Agency for International Development on the same *Frontline* segment, "I think that we all believed that what we were doing was in the best interests of America, that we were in fact perhaps involved in some not so desirable aspects of the drug traffic; however we believed strongly in the beginning that we were there for a just cause." He continued:

> *These people were willing to take up arms. We needed to stop the Red threat and people believed that in that vein we made, you know, certain compromises or certain trade-offs for a larger good. Growing opium was a natural agricultural enterprise for these people and they had been doing it for many years before the Americans ever got there. When we got there, they continued to do so. It was then the presence of these air support services in and out of the areas in question where the product, where the opium was grown that greatly facilitated an increase in production and an ease of transshipment from the point of agriculture to the point of processing. So, when I say the Americans greased the wheels, essentially what I'm saying is we did not create opium production. We did not create a situation where drug trafficking was happening. But because of the nature of our presence, this very intense American means that was made available to the situation, it accelerated in proportion dramatically. I was on the airstrip, that was my job, to move in and about and to go from place to place and my people were in charge of dispatching aircraft. I was in the areas where opium was transshipped, I personally was a witness to opium being placed on aircraft, American aircraft. I witnessed it being taken off smaller aircraft that were coming in from outlying sites.*

It was Fred Platt, a former pilot operating out of Laos, who provided the best explanation to *Frontline* for the financial incentive behind the practice undertaken by this loosely amalgamated group of allied smugglers: "When a farmer raised a crop of opium, what he got for his year's worth of work was the equivalent of thirty-five to forty US dollars. That amount of opium, were it refined into morphine base, then into morphine, then into heroin and appeared on the streets of New York, that thirty-five-dollar crop of opium would be worth fifty, sixty, a hundred thousand dollars in 1969 dollars—maybe a million dollars today."

Which aptly sums up the Golden Triangle maelstrom into which I'd been dropped.

* * * * *

I moved into the home previously occupied by the previous regional director but didn't like the place from the first time I laid eyes on it. Although it had a wall enclosing the grounds, that was hardly an impediment to the burglars known as *kamvoys* from climbing over and plundering the house's contents. This particular area was rife with them too, busy and congested. And as a foreigner living there, I might as well have put up a sign saying "Open for Business." It was that bad.

Joy and the kids hadn't made the move to join me yet and, fortunately, a CIA agent rotating out had an Akita, a great watchdog he wasn't able to take home. So he gave me the dog and we bonded immediately.

One night, a noise woke both of us, and I realized someone was in the house.

"Who's there?" I called out.

When no response came, I knew it had to be a burglar. I got my gun and the Akita, whose name was Thor, and padded out of the bedroom, where we confronted one of those *kamvoys* armed with a knife.

Before he could use it, Thor chased him out of the house and took a bite out of his ass. You've never seen anybody run so fast—I think he might have leaped over the wall to get away instead of just climbing it.

No way was I going to subject my wife and sons to such a threat, so I moved into a guarded compound well off the beaten path with lavish grounds dotted with banana and palm trees, bird-of-paradise flowers, and a sprawling outdoor pool. I felt a lot better about settling them there than that initial residence and set about continuing to get the lay of the land.

My so-called "tour guide" in that respect was General Pao Sarasin, one of the highest-ranking officers in the entire Thai army and one of the most powerful people in the country period. It turned out he was the son of the country's former prime minister and that his family owned the Coca-Cola franchise for all of Southeast Asia. He was a man of means no less committed to his duty and, thanks to those means, never needed to be in debt to anyone—incorruptible, in other words. My predecessor had pretty much avoided dealing with the general and, for his part, the general wanted nothing to do with the man he'd heard the same rumors about that we had. In meeting me, though, he knew he'd found someone he could work with, someone who maintained the same priorities he did.

One of the first things I realized had to be done was setting up an office in Burma. My predecessor had basically ignored one of the key spokes of the Golden Triangle, and I had no intention of repeating the same mistake. So I flew into Rangoon to convince the Burmese government, and our own American embassy, to let us open an office there, where we'd station an agent who'd report directly to me on whatever intelligence he was able to collect. We got approval, on the condition we'd agree to call our agent a "cultural attaché" instead, primarily there to arrange for "crop substitutions" where we'd swap coffee beans for opium seeds and subsidize the difference in profits out of our budget, something you can do only if you have the cooperation of the host governments.

I went back to the States to pick up Joy and the boys and, once we landed in Bangkok, wouldn't you know it, good ole Smokey got loose again, running around the airport tarmac with the Thai police in hot pursuit. He didn't get along with Thor at all, so I found another home for the Akita that may well have saved my life.

Mark especially took to his new surroundings right away, to a point where, a few weeks into my family's arrival, he disappeared yet again, this time at a beach on Penang Island off the coast of Malaysia. We immediately suspected he'd been kidnapped and called out the cavalry. Not surprisingly, Mark was found slightly later a half mile down the beach in a fishing village hanging out with a group of fishermen, eating cooked fish and already speaking decent Thai.

But lighter moments like that were short-lived. I had a maid we called "Can Do," because that's what she said whenever we asked her if she could do something. It was Can Do who realized something was wrong with Smokey when he came in from playing in the garden. I was home at the time and she'd barely called out to me when he keeled over and died.

Our gardener later found and killed the cobra that had strangled him, and I relocated to another house, my third in Bangkok, because there was no way I was going to let my boys play around in a yard populated by deadly snakes. We were finally settled in, but Smokey's death had left its mark on all of us, especially the kids. He was a great dog and I missed him every day.

But I didn't have much time to grieve. From what I'd been able to uncover initially, pouches of heroin were being found not only in Thai dolls belonging to the children of military and diplomatic personnel coming home from the war zone, but also in furniture, vehicles, household items, even the linings of clothing. It wasn't our people who were doing the smuggling. They were only the innocent unwitting carriers of the contraband.

But I had also learned something else, something that turns my stomach to this day—specifically, the fact that the heroin was being smuggled into the United States inside coffins and even inside the bodies of military casualties (as portrayed in the movie *American Gangster* starring Denzel Washington as Harlem-based drug trafficker Frank Lucas). I had to acknowledge the ingenuity of whoever these bastards were, while similarly being struck by their utter depravity. As reprehensible as the practice was, whoever was behind it knew no one would tamper with the revered, flag-draped coffins destined for hallowed ground. No one would dare defile the corpses of these returning heroes, some of them still teenagers.

Dealing with that problem was the mandate Jack Cusack had given me. And succeeding with that mandate meant I was going to need more than the agents currently stationed in Thailand. I was going to need a guy willing and able to get his hands dirty—real dirty—to find who was behind smuggling heroin inside the bodies of our KIA.

That guy was Fred Moore.

Fred had been a narc for over twenty years, and he knew the dark streets better than any undercover agent I knew. I got him papers as a US Army medical corpsman and had him assigned to the military hospital so he'd be imbedded in the army. He more than looked the part of an army medic: raw-boned, sinewy, with these eyes that looked at you like he had X-ray vision.

I brought him to Bangkok when I heard the rumors about the coffins. His job was to tell me how heroin was being smuggled into the United States in the bodies of our fallen heroes, something I absolutely couldn't wait to put an end to.

CHAPTER SEVENTEEN

BANGKOK, THAILAND, 1975

Moore based himself about thirty minutes from downtown Bangkok. We used the neighborhood of Patpong for our meetings. Patpong was a seedy mix of sex shops and topless joints intermixed with restaurants. I used the same location for the meetings with all my undercover guys. A place called the Bookstore that fronted a series of massage parlor booths.

Moore and I met at the Bookstore after he'd managed to gather his initial intelligence dump. He was seated in the back behind a row of mystery books. He had a baseball hat pulled down low and a pair of aviator sunglasses on, even though it was pouring rain outside and had been for days.

"I got some intelligence on the coffin matter," Fred said, before even saying hello. "This could burn my cover, but I think we ought to move on it," he said.

I could hear moaning coming from the adjacent massage parlor, a common sound that pulsed through the walls of the Bookstore.

"I was having dinner at Mitch and Nam's rib joint," Moore continued, "when this black guy I'd met there before comes over to my table for some small talk. He wanted to know if I was still working at the hospital. He seemed a little nervous so I bought him a drink to keep him talking. He said he had me checked out by some of his brothers in the military and that I checked out okay."

"What's this guy's name?" I asked.

"They call him Cowboy Jim."

And just like, with no further introduction, he laid out this story.

"There's a network of military brothers here in 'Nam, in large part hailing from Oakland and North Carolina. Seems that one of the brothers in the network worked in my hospital morgue, but he's being rotated home. I'm being recruited as his replacement: embalming, suturing, icing. That sort of thing."

Moore went on to explain how the Cowboy took him to the hospital to meet the embalmer, Charles Walker. In the room were more than a dozen bodies zipped up in black body bags. The bodies were fresh kill from 'Nam. Cowboy was the size of a football linebacker, with a shaved head and Southern drawl. Walker couldn't have been any more opposite: a skinny white guy, with glasses and a lab coat. Cowboy gave Walker a simple nod and Walker jumped to attention and unzipped one of the bags and rolled the cadaver onto the table. The body was that of a white male, about 150 pounds or so. The body was already embalmed and had been stitched down the middle from sternum to groin. Walker sliced up the stitches and cut open the chest cavity. He then reached inside the corpse and pulled out two clear plastic envelopes—about two pounds of heroin, covered in body slime.

This particular body was on its way to New York for a family service, first passing through Oakland customs, without any problem. The plan was for one of the brothers to meet the body in Oakland, show a phony ID as a relative, and then accompany the coffin to the East Coast. Somewhere during the trip, the brother would remove the heroin and disappear.

I could hear the anger resonating in Moore's voice as he told the story. These men, these kids, who died for our country deserved better. He believed that, and so did I.

"Walker said they've been working this gig out of here for five years. Five years! Customs never thought about checking a coffin. Walker and the Cowboy thought that was kind of funny, how easy it had been," Moore went on.

I am glad they found it funny. Because they wouldn't be laughing soon. Bastards!

"The Cowboy offered me Walker's job. He told me that I would be a millionaire by the time I got home."

"I'm sure they pay better than I do," I told him.

"Dan, you can't believe how I felt in that room. There was very little ventilation. The damn smell was getting to me. I thought I was going to pass out. I told him that I had to go outside to talk. I didn't want to seem too eager. Hell, I was almost too sick to seem eager. But, then we got in the fresh air and it all worked out."

Moore walked out and I browsed through the books, then grabbed the first of a series of cabs back to the embassy. Whenever I met one of my agents, I would go to the meetings in several different taxis, hopping in and out at random points. It was melodramatic but prudent. At this point, I didn't realize the extent or source of the problem in this far-flung place on the map; I'm not sure anybody did. But I'd come to believe I had what I needed to put a sizeable dent in the export of drugs coming out of there.

* * * * *

The heavy rain had subsided, but the streets remained flooded. I watched the reflection of the three-wheeled *tuk tuk*, the last taxi on my thirty-minute ride to the hospital, bouncing off the ruts in the road. It had been over a week since our last meeting. A week of rain and planning.

Moore was waiting for me near the MP's post. I showed my diplomatic passport and embassy ID. I told the MP I'd come to pick up medical records of a dependent of a State Department official who had overdosed on heroin. I explained that Moore was assigned to help me find the records. The MP stood aside as Moore and I faked personal introductions.

The morgue was on the second floor of the cinderblock building, rows of embalming tables and uncovered slabs under a twenty-foot ceiling. On some slabs, several bodies were stacked atop one another. The windowless room was air-conditioned, but the scent of formaldehyde and rotting flesh was making me sick. I stepped away from the slabs and into the corner to pull myself together. Moore understood, having been in my place only weeks ago. He said nothing while he waited for me to gain my composure.

After a few minutes, I said, "Show me."

He pulled out one of the slabs. The two of us picked up the body bag on the slab and carried it to the embalming table. Moore unzipped the bag. The kid could not have been more than twenty years old. He had a crew cut and a clean-shaven face. He reminded me of my oldest son Daniel, and all I could hope in that moment was that I'd never see one of my kids like this.

Later, when I first had to put my hand into the chest cavity of a dead Marine myself and pull out a slimy packet of premium-grade heroin, I ran to the corner of the lab and threw up. It wasn't only due to the strong whiff of formaldehyde. Sometimes called embalming fluid, it smells like death itself. But when combined with the stench of rotting flesh, it can make one instantly vomit.

But looking back today, I realize that the disgusting part wasn't the odor so much as the realization that the heroin was secreted there by a team of fellow Americans, a nefarious group of former noncommissioned officers who had organized one of the most malevolent drug smuggling rings I had seen in all my years fighting the war on drugs on the front lines.

Moore sliced open the stitches that ran from under the kid's chin to his belly button. He pulled out a plastic packet about a half-inch thick and six inches long. Inside was a double-sealed plastic envelope. Inside the envelope was a soft white powder.

I punched a hole in the envelope with a small knife and put a dot of the powder on the blade. In the breast pocket of my bush jacket was a tiny glass vial of solution called Marquis reagent. I flicked the powder into the vial. The clear solution turned a bright purple. This was textbook field-testing for heroin, and this was indeed heroin.

Fred put the packet back into the cadaver and rewound the stitching. We placed the body bag back on the slab.

"Well," Fred said, "at least you've got the proof you need now."

* * * * *

I went back to the embassy to figure out my next step. I'd started picking up information locally that confirmed the rumors, stories, hearsay, speculation. Heroin was leaving the country in everything from corsets to coffins, all right. And I spent virtually all of my time those ensuing months uncovering and verifying all the information I could in an effort to track down its source.

I knew I'd have to tell the ambassador something to position myself to take the next step, but I wasn't sure what. I wasn't one of the ambassador's favorite attachés, but he wasn't my favorite ambassador either.

Ambassador Charles S. Whitehouse was tall, stately, and gray-haired, with a patrician air about him, elegantly attired at all times. A lot like Ambassador Lodge back in Buenos Aires, only without the gravitas. He called us together on the morning of February 13, 1975, before I had the chance to issue my report, but not in his office. Instead, we met in an electronic safe house smack in the middle of the embassy compound. The only entrance was a foot-thick concrete door, guarded by two Marines twenty-four hours a day. The safe house, actually a large room, had no windows and was completely curtained. It was a lot like a bank vault. Once you entered, you couldn't leave until the ambassador said so, and even then only after a special code, which changed daily, was entered into the door locks behind the guards.

Just before anyone entered this room, it was swept electronically for bugs. The process was repeated after everyone left as well. It was a surprisingly sanitized meeting place, made all the more sanitary by its stark white furniture, including an oval table and twelve chairs. Even the surrounding curtains were white. In that room, one felt clean, protected, important. And once we were in the room, a red light flashed on over the doorway, indicating that we had been sealed inside.

Around the table this morning were the ambassador himself, a US Air Force general, the CIA station chief, the consul-general, and me. The ambassador reported that earlier in the day, Washington had informed him that the United States would be pulling out of Vietnam within the next three months. Just like that, the war would be over. Whitehouse explained that the orders were for the pullout to be as orderly as possible. We didn't want to panic either the civilians or our troops. Also, within the Golden Triangle itself we had about 55,000 US support troops. Whitehouse told us we'd be moving out a minimum of 10,000 people a month, dependents first and then the uniforms. That was the grand design, and the ambassador now looked at us for opinions.

Air Force Lieutenant General Heinie Aderholt said he would issue orders immediately. The consul-general said he'd take care of the red tape that would be required to arrange travel for military wives who were Thai or Vietnamese. The CIA man said nothing.

Until that morning, I hadn't mentioned the fragmentary information I'd been getting about heroin shipments back home. Because I couldn't yet point a finger, I'd been considering it prudent not to bring it up. But now, stripped of the luxury of investigative time, I had to tell this group everything: about the coffins, about the gutted Marines, about what had to be done before anybody was transferred out of there. I looked up at the red light over the door. As far as I was concerned, it was green.

I blurted out a rough sketch of what was transpiring, enough to paint a picture without coloring it in entirely. When I was finished, everyone just looked at me skeptically, not quite believing what I was saying. They bought into the notion of drugs being smuggled in dolls, furniture, personal possessions, and even inside coffins. But the concept of smuggling drugs inside the remains of our war dead was more than grotesque. To these people, who weren't familiar with the kind of people who played this grisly game, it was simply too incredible to believe. As I tried to convince them of the truth, I shared my sense of disgust, but I also told them how bad people can be counted on to do bad things, and despicable people can be counted on to do despicable things.

I wasn't trying to shock them. The CIA man, for certain, was unflappable; he could recount ugly deeds that would repel even me. What I was trying to do was set up a request I needed to make to everyone seated around the oval table: before any dependents or military people left for the States, their effects had to be thoroughly searched. Also, I wanted body pat-downs at the airport and at dockside, as well as drug-sniffing dogs at all departure points.

I remember the consul-general's expression. "Are you including State Department personnel and their dependents when you talk about body searches?" he asked.

"Everyone who leaves," I said. "Everyone, even my own family. Even me. No exceptions."

I went on to explain that I wasn't exaggerating when I said that stuff could be planted in the personal effects of anyone without their knowledge.

The consul-general didn't like my answer. Neither did the CIA station chief. They both sat there scowling, as if I had questioned their integrity or, worse yet, their loyalty. I briefly thought about the possibility that being locked in a vault might arouse a fit of paranoia.

"Look," I explained. "If we ourselves can show we're willing to be searched, then nobody else can put up a beef."

I looked to the ambassador and General Aderholt, as the senior ranking civilian and military men in the room, for affirmation. The general nodded curtly in agreement.

The ambassador, meanwhile, looked at me for a long while, and then said, "All right, Addario. All personnel."

"There's always a chance a good lead will develop and we'll break this ring before we start sending people back in large numbers," I said. "But we can't guarantee we'll come up with anything that quickly."

The consul-general said, "If you do, you'll save a hell of a lot of people a hell of a lot of trouble."

"I'll do what I can," I obliged.

And in twenty-four hours, obliging him suddenly became possible. Life is all about timing.

* * * * *

The ambassador was prone to discount my notion that drug enforcement should be a major priority in the Bangkok embassy. If I had briefed him on everything I had seen at the hospital and what my investigation had compiled so far, he'd go by the book and brief the CIA and military intelligence people. And they'd recommend arresting the Cowboy and Charles Walker and seizing that single half kilo of heroin in the cadaver. Case closed. But what good would that do? Shut down two peons? I wanted to grab the connections in Oakland, North Carolina, and the eastern US that our intelligence indicated were the operation's strongholds. I wanted to knock off the entire stateside network. I wanted to kill the dragon, not just wound it.

The next afternoon I sat in the ambassador's office telling him all that I thought he needed to know about drugs being smuggled stateside in the bodies of deceased GIs at this juncture. He seemed uninterested in everything I was saying, preoccupied with rubbing his chaffing bald head.

"I have an informant in San Francisco who says he's got evidence that heroin is being smuggled into the US inside the bodies of our casualties. The informant is retired military. He's willing to come here to further the investigation. I recommend that you let me bring him over here."

That informant, Lionel Smith, was an ex-GI from Philadelphia. I had recruited him into the DEA years earlier. Like Moore, Smith was African American. He was also a damn good investigator.

The ambassador pushed his wire-rim glasses up his bird-beak nose. "Okay," he said, merely humoring me.

Whatever the reason, I was willing to accept it if it completed my mission. I headed back to my office and drafted a cable to DEA head-quarters in DC requesting that agent Lionel Smith be sent to Bangkok on temporary duty to "penetrate possible smuggling of heroin in cadavers…. Details to follow."

And Smith's arrival came just days after I forwarded those details.

* * * * *

The Threme massage parlor was a Super Bowl of sex: a hundred rooms, a hundred girls, plus carpeting, ornate fixtures, the works. I asked for a private room in the back where Fred Moore knew to meet me. Moore had managed to flesh out more of the details of the operation from Charles Walker, the base embalmer. Apparently, it was being run through the auspices of something called the "12-20 Organization," based in Durham, North Carolina, with two men named Carl Jackson and Milt Atkinson as the kingpins. All of the members of the 12-20 Organization (I never learned the basis of that name) were either active military or Korean War veterans who knew army trans-portation methods and supply units to a T. And they had contacts that allowed them to hop aboard a flight on a Military Air Transport Service plane anytime.

Moore said the key Bangkok connection, the deliveryman who provided the heroin, was a Thai-Chinese man named Ramrudee who owned the Lucky Star nightclub on Soi Nana near the Nana Hotel. Walker told Moore that he would be hearing from Ramrudee at the hospital soon. Now we had to wait.

Two weeks passed without contact being made. By then Lionel Smith had arrived and was registered at the President Hotel. His cover was a dishonorably discharged army NCO, and he quickly ingratiated himself into the Lucky Star scene.

A third week passed in tense silence. Moore heard nothing at the hospital. Smith picked up nothing at the Lucky Star. I began to wonder if the 12-20s were wise to our deployment. Perhaps someone saw Moore and me together?

Finally, a break. A call came in to me at the embassy.

"I need to see you straight away," Smith said tersely. "Usual place, fourteen-hundred hours sharp."

I met Smith at the massage parlor. He had made himself comfortable, even kicking back and having a beer. Some things don't change. The best informants are the ones capable of completely losing themselves to the local culture. Normally you develop, or turn, local sources who are already ingrained in that culture. In other instances, you opt for an outsider, normally a professional like Smith, adept and even expert at imbedding himself into a world he makes his own.

"What do you have for me?" I asked.

"I've been playing a lot of cards at the Lucky Star. Mostly GI games. Big pots. The players go real heavy," he said, taking a swig of his beer. "One of the players, a GI named Chino, told me that he was into our man Ramrudee for eight grand. Can you believe that?"

"That's a lot of cash for a GI."

"Hell yeah, it is. But he said that he was told not to worry about it because Ramrudee was going to ask him to do him a favor. But Chino doesn't want to do anybody any favors. See, he just got his orders back home. He figures he'll be out of Thailand before Ramrudee knows where he's gone. But I'm telling you, Dan, this guy is scared shitless… and I don't blame him."

Chino and his family were due to be shipped home to Durham, North Carolina, in three days. We set up a twenty-four-hour surveillance on Chino's residence with the help of General Pao Sarasin, commander of the Thai National Police. General Pao's surveillance teams consisted of taxi drivers, motorcyclists, noodle vendors, monks, and street beggars. The Thais could run two-dozen people in a stake-out and no two would look alike.

After thirty-six hours, General Pao phoned me to say a load of hand-carved Thai furniture had been delivered to Chino Dexter's house. The packers showed up on the morning of March 18, 1975. After they left, a delegation of Thai police, DEA agents, and drug-sniffing dogs stepped in. Mrs. Dexter looked at the dogs and fainted on the spot.

A pair of two-foot-high, hand-carved Thai end tables had particularly appealed to the dogs. Thai Police Colonel Pasat Panarachun upturned one of the tables, pried off the bottom, and found ten kilos of heroin, pure as the driven snow; under the bottom of the other table was fifty kilos of the finest quality. The total US street value was more than thirty million dollars.

The fall of Vietnam, you see, had created a desperate fervor within the entire Golden Triangle because a major distribution channel that pushed heroin into the United States was closing up. No more corpses to stuff with drugs or vulnerable GIs to use as couriers. Instead, there was a frenzied rush to make one last score by finding potential carriers among the tens of thousands who would be returning stateside. In some cases, money was dangled. In others it was blackmail, over a gambling or other debt that would be summarily erased if the GI or support staff personnel agreed to carry drugs home in furniture or hidden somewhere else. Our problem, fundamentally, was that the

Dan pictured with General Pao Sarasin and the head of the Thai narcotics squad.

military status enjoyed by a lot of the kingpins behind the operation could enable them to move around Southeast Asia like ghosts. Hop on military flights and pretty much head anywhere in the region without their names ever appearing on a manifest and no trail left behind them. Jump on one flight and come back on another before anyone even noticed they were gone.

General Pao arrested Ramrudee at the Lucky Star and brought him in for interrogation at the Bangkok police barracks where the general had based himself. I hadn't been present for the arrest but was there for the interrogation, and I let Pao run with the initial questions, chomping at the bit to get my hands on this bastard. When I was given my cue, I walked into the small room. Ramrudee was handcuffed to the table but wasn't fighting. He had accepted his situation and knew that he had a card to play. We wanted more than just

Ramrudee, and these guys typically knew that their sentence could get pretty light if they sang. And Ramrudee sang the song we wanted to hear: he told us all about the ringleaders of the 12-20 Organization, Jackson and Atkinson back in Durham.

I had all I needed to take down this syndicate. Before anyone knew what was coming, we started with a wave of arrests in Bangkok and stateside, not unlike the takedown raids during my first assignment ever on the streets of Philadelphia as part of Operation Intake. It was the same, only different, because when operating as a foreign agent overseas, you're only permitted to do what the host government lets you do. That government, in the person of General Pao in Thailand, determines your role. Plenty of host countries see you as no more than a conduit, an intermediary confined to the embassy. They don't allow you to go on raids, carry a gun, or participate in interrogations. General Pao set a different standard, one aimed at identifying the players and dismantling the operations of criminal organizations like 12-20, which is exactly what we did in Bangkok. It wasn't just about arrests and seizures; it was about disrupting the flow of drugs from their source to the streets.

I now had to report to the CIA about the takedown that I'd been keeping secret right up until the wave of arrests on two continents. It wasn't mere paranoia that kept me from letting the Agency in on our plans for the international coffin bust; I just couldn't be sure whether I'd inadvertently targeted any of their informants. The CIA's mission sometimes ran parallel, but often conflicted with, our own. As I alluded to earlier, the Agency often turned a blind eye to the actions of their informants, sometimes even tacitly abetting those actions since their informants were under the impression that their status gave them impunity, even immunity. I couldn't bring the CIA into the circle I'd formed with General Pao because I was afraid they might tip off one of our targets and blow our whole bust. Indeed, it's common knowledge that the Agency will make a deal with the devil for its own gain. But this time I was the one holding the pitchfork.

BANGKOK, THAILAND, 1975

* * * * *

I knew that although one of the biggest heroin pipelines out of Thailand had been shut down, new ones would pop right back up. And with the Vietnam War ending in the fall of 1975, a perfect opportunity was about to open up that was ripe for smuggling. Over 55,000 troops and their dependents were returning to the United States, and we needed to cut off the pipelines that opportunity afforded.

I went to the ambassador to get the go-ahead to begin the process he'd already approved to search everyone and everything going back to the States. He said he'd get back to me, but I could tell neither his head nor his heart was really committed, that he was about to renege on his promise. First and foremost, the ambassador was a politician loath to making the kind of scene certain to roil the higher-ups back home. As a result, thousands of pounds of heroin reached the United States and those drugs spread through the country like wildfire.

We had pretty much lost the Vietnam War. Now, thanks to delays and inaction, we were also clearly losing the war on drugs.

CHAPTER EIGHTEEN

BANGKOK, THAILAND, 1977

More needed to be done. If we couldn't stop the smugglers, perhaps we could cut off the supply. We had to do something about those heroin labs. Our Burmese office, led by that "cultural attaché," was up and running now, coordinating their efforts with ours.

The heroin that had been smuggled into the United States in the bodies of our dead GIs was being manufactured at labs located deep in the jungles on the Thai-Burmese border. So deep that the farmers actually brought their harvested opium flowers to those labs via pack mule. No vehicles could traverse that territory and no helicopter could land. We knew that the drug shipments were extracted from the jungle aboard trawlers traversing the narrow rivers that sliced through the whole of the Golden Triangle. Beyond that, we had no idea where exactly these labs were located.

With General Pao's help, we found a willing informant in the person of a Thai-Chinese chemist who'd worked in those labs and knew where they were located under the highest security precautions imaginable. Every day when they arrived at the labs, the workers had to take all their clothes off and shed any personal possessions. They were issued clothes they took off prior to leaving, at which point they were allowed to put their own clothes back on and collect their personals.

There was no way we could possibly plant anyone in the labs with a bug or recording device, which meant we had to get creative. The only personal items workers in the lab were allowed to take in with them were these Thai walking sticks used to help negotiate those treacherous jungle paths, feeling about the ground for snakes or equally poisonous lizards. If we could somehow plant a device in one of those sticks belonging to an informant and then, somehow, get that stick into a lab, we'd be in business.

Our first challenge lay in the fact that the stick we used had to be made out of wood native to Thailand. While this kind of thing may seem simple and old hat now, it was anything but that back in the 1970s. Far from it. We had to send walking sticks composed of native wood back to Washington, where the electronic detector devices could be built in. Once they were tested and returned, I worked with General Pao to coordinate the informants who would be charged with leaving them behind when they departed their stations at the end of the day. Then Thai army overflights would hone in on the signals, enabling them to positively identify the precise locations of the labs.

Showtime, as they say!

Not so fast, was the message from the ambassador, after I'd issued a report I had to make.

"What do you plan to do about these labs?" he asked me.

"Well, the Thais have all the intelligence. General Pao wants to go in and strafe the labs in coordinated air strikes. The Burmese army would be waiting at the nearest points of flight to put a double block on whoever gets out."

The ambassador was so livid, his hands were trembling and his face had reddened. "You can't do it."

"Why?" I asked him, doing my best to hide my own disgust and anger.

223

"Washington's concerned with human rights."

"I'm not going to do it. General Pao and the Thais are going to do it."

He was so pissed off, he started tying the cord for the venetian blinds into knots. "I'm gonna throw you out of the goddamn country. Pack your bags."

I took that as my cue to leave his office, but not the country. Hardly. Instead, I got ahold of three of the congressmen on the Select Committee on Narcotics, including Charlie Rangel, and told them what was going on.

"If he throws you out of the country, Dan," another of them told me, "he'll be on the next plane out."

Knowing I had (political) backup, I called the general and told him to go ahead with the strikes, coordinated with four Huey helicopters the US government had given the Thai police to help them fight drugs. They bombed the hell out of those labs, eradicating (for a time, anyway) the flow of heroin that was running rampant.

That's the ideal strategy to pursue, having powerful elements of the host country handle the raids and strikes with the required equipment and ordnance being supplied by the United States. The problem, as I'd learned in South America, was that in some countries, like Chile and Colombia, the governments weren't about to sacrifice economic concerns to fight the flow of narcotics. Since it's not practical to expect the US military to conduct strikes in foreign countries, even if requested, that leaves us with the old Chinese saying that "you fight your battles with other people's swords." We needed to encourage high-ranking players in the host countries who knew the game to take the necessary action themselves. We could supply reconnaissance, intelligence, sourcing—pretty much anything—but it had to be up to those countries to handle the coordination and attack themselves. We could spoon-feed them everything they needed and the hope is that those willing to take action are powerful enough, like General Pao, to overcome those in the host governments who don't want to risk being aligned with, and perhaps perceived as being manipulated by, the United States.

Take the *Mayaguez* incident as an example in May 1975, shortly after the Khmer Rouge ousted the Khmer Republic in Cambodia and took control of Phnom Penh. The incident began when the crew of the US merchant ship *Mayaguez* was taken hostage and then President Gerald Ford ordered US Marines to effect a rescue. The mission required the rescue force to refuel in Thailand, which on its own was enough to spark full-scale riots, once the American complicity and involvement became widely known. The Thais who hit the streets and attacked the US Embassy added fuel to the fire of the anti-American fervor stoked by the closing days of the Vietnam War. If that's all it took to turn an entire city like Bangkok on its ear, imagine what American troops bombing drug labs might do.

I was trapped in the embassy in Bangkok for several days with a skeleton crew, genuinely fearing for our lives in the event the building was breached—a very realistic possibility given the size of the crowds massing beyond our gates. As we sorted through files for burning and shredding, we could hear small-arms fire and explosions beyond. Meanwhile, I got a call from some bureaucrat back in Washington inquiring about some issues pertaining to an embassy car. Not exactly the moment to worry about fiscal restraint, I told him, and hung up.

My next call came from Peter Law, an MI6 agent who was then Britain's narcotics attaché in country, offering us refuge if things got really hot.

"We've got Gurkhas guarding our gates," he told me, referring to the famed Nepalese soldiers who'd struck fear into the hearts of the Japanese and Nazis during World War II.

"I think we're okay," I said. "And we wouldn't be able to get out now anyway."

"How about we send the Gurkhas down there?"

It was tempting, but I begged off. That call did end up fostering the formation of the Foreign Authorities Narcotics Group (FANG) comprised of us, the Brits, the French, the Canadians, and the Australians. We'd meet twice a month at a big restaurant in Bangkok called the Galaxy to discuss areas of common interest and how we could coordinate our efforts in fighting the drug war. The Galaxy was known as the "No-Hands" restaurant because once the fantastic food was served, as honored guests it was fed to us on chopsticks by beautiful Thai women in evening gowns, one for each of us. Of course, that wasn't the only thing they could do for us, if we so chose. It might seem crass, even immoral, to accept such favors, or even to flirt or be fed in such a way. One thing diplomacy teaches, though, is that it was our obligation to accept such hospitality, that it would be a serious affront to have refused it. When you're working in an overseas post, you have to live not only by the host country's rules, but also its traditions, norms, and mores. In Bangkok, this was how they did things, which meant we did them that way too, lest we risk losing the trust and cooperation of officials like General Pao over pretty much nothing.

But we had another problem. The general's efforts had led to the accumulation of, almost literally, a warehouse full of confiscated drugs. Leaving it in place was a recipe for theft and temptation on the part of Thai officials, so we put into place a plan I'd first utilized in Bolivia during my posting in South America. We made a show of carting all that dope into a field, alerted the media and local officials, and set it ablaze as the cameras rolled. At times the bonfire seemed to reach the night sky, a noxious smoke cloud filling the air, pictures of which ran across the country and world in the days that followed.

Point, and example, made, as they say.

As for the ambassador, in the wake of the lab bombings coordinated by General Pao with those US-supplied helicopters, he was even more livid than before, but there wasn't much he could do about it because Congress liked what we had done and were doing. So much so that an American delegation spearheaded by Congressmen Charlie Rangel, Lester Wolff, and Morgan Murphy returned to the Golden Triangle, requesting a meeting with General Pao and Khun Sa himself.

We took two helicopters to Khun Sa's camp located in a kind of nebulous no-man's-land between the three countries that formed the Golden Triangle. The scope of the camp was jaw-dropping, populated with what looked like a couple hundred thousand troops outfitted in military fatigues. This was Khun Sa's private army, and Khun himself appeared dressed in uniform as well. I looked at this thinking how easy it would be for him to just take us all hostage then and there. Maybe feed us to the snakes.

But Khun Sa understood politics as well as drugs, that sometimes drugs *were* politics. In this case we had come packing a plan that was kind of an offshoot of the policy we employed of subsidizing farmers to get them to stop growing opium: we made an offer on the spot to buy Khun's entire opium crop. His eyes gaped at the suggestion, no doubt seeing all those dollar signs the tens of millions would make. This was a huge deal, unprecedented at the time and one that could drastically curtail the supply of drugs coming out of the Golden Triangle. And we thought we had Congress on our side, ready to embark on this new strategy to fight the war on drugs.

But they refused to come up with the funding we needed, and Khun Sa's opium fields remained open for business.

* * * * *

A bumpy flight back to Bangkok proved a harbinger for a later flight during another trip I made to Burma. We were flying into Rangoon on a jumbo jet that had originated in India, packed with passengers lugging vegetables and even livestock, including goats and chickens. As we came in for a landing, I could tell we were coming in too fast. Sure enough, we overshot the runway and ended up mired in a mud paddy. I thought I smelled smoke and figured the plane was going to blow up. But when the emergency escape chutes were deployed, the passengers insisted on taking their livestock with them, slowing the process to a crawl, leaving me certain the plane was going to explode with me still on it.

We finally made it out without further incident, but I resolved to take a military flight back home. As we reached the skies over Bangkok, the CIA officer who'd accompanied us left his jump seat to strap on a parachute, tilting a gaze back at us as he opened the rear door.

"See you on the ground," he said, and off he went, leaving the rest of us to reach the ground the more traditional way, without incident this time.

When we returned to the embassy grounds, the CIA officer was waiting for us with a grin stretched from ear to ear, having beaten us back.

"What took you guys so long?" he asked us.

* * * * *

We had a little party at my house that night where the alcohol was flowing freely, but none of my guests were feeling the effects. It turned out that my gung-ho maid Can Do had watered down the booze in order to sell what she'd siphoned off. Apparently, the black market for liquor was going like gangbusters at the time, something I should have figured given how many bottles purchased from the PX we gave away as gifts to further curry favor with the locals.

I guess Can Do wanted to curry a little favor of her own.

Meanwhile, one morning not long after we had to fire Can Do, I got a call from the Marine guard at the embassy that there had been an accident. I rushed there to find one of my agents, Jim Lightfoot, had been killed when his service weapon accidentally discharged. Apparently, he had rested it atop a filing cabinet and it had fallen off while he was reviewing some documents, going off and mortally wounding him when it hit the floor. The seemingly accidental nature of the incident notwithstanding, Jim's death hit me as hard as that of the agents I'd lost in Colombia and Panama when I'd been regional director for

South America. He had a Thai girlfriend listed as his next of kin, and we had no information about what family members to call stateside. Those calls are something you never get used to, and Jim's death has haunted me to this day, as I've never gotten past the possibility that his pistol might not have accidentally discharged at all and that foul play was somehow involved.

But who? And why?

Before I could do a deeper dive into those questions, I got a call from General Pao.

* * * * *

The general informed me that he had a Thai-Chinese prisoner in custody who was heavily involved with organizing drug shipments on those trawlers that traversed the waterways of the Golden Triangle. The general had called to invite me to the man's execution, to be carried out both as a warning to others and to demonstrate to Washington that the Thai government was serious about stemming the flow of narcotics. I had no choice but to report this to the ambassador.

He was livid. Again.

"How could you do this?" he barked, throwing a fit and blaming me.

"I didn't. The orders came from the Thais."

"I don't care. I want it stopped. The human rights advocates will crucify us."

"We aren't responsible. The Thais want to show they mean business."

"Well," he said, exasperated that there was nothing he could do to intervene, "no way you're going to attend this. Send your regrets."

I begged off with General Pao, apologizing profusely for fear of offending him. But he was a worldly man and understood entirely. The execution went forward, a picture of the executed man handcuffed to a post plastered on the front page of the Bangkok newspaper the next day to serve as warning for anyone else considering conspiring with the country's drug lords.

The ambassador, of course, didn't see the bigger picture, that enabling allies like General Pao was a key component of winning the war on drugs. Disabling and hampering the flow of heroin from the Golden Triangle would have cut 30 percent of the heroin coming into the United States. But that policy ebbed with my departure once my four-year rotation was up. And, beyond that, bombing drug labs was a policy and strategy our government just wouldn't support or embrace. I had originally proposed a joint operation to wipe out those jungle labs on the Thai-Burmese border. I was working out details and getting things into place when I got the no-go from the White House. President Jimmy Carter's drug advisor, Peter Bourne, said that the raid would violate the administration's "human rights policy," echoing the words of the ambassador when I'd informed him.

I had to fight the CIA over them letting their informants fly drug shipments with impunity. And now I had to fight with my own government to stop the very flow of drugs I'd been sent to Southeast Asia to stem. It wasn't so much I wasn't getting the job done as they weren't letting me do it. Everyone seemed to see everything as a classic zero-sum game: somebody wins and somebody loses. We couldn't win both the war against drugs and the war against Communist expansion at the same time. And that meant the war on drugs had to play second fiddle to what was becoming a hotter and hotter funeral pyre, while I was really starting to wonder whether the best and brightest in Washington really cared about winning it.

They threw a lavish party for me at the embassy on the eve of my departure. Everyone I knew in Bangkok was there, including the Thai generals I'd worked with alongside General Pao, and numerous politicians as well. The generals presented me with a medal on behalf of the king of Thailand that was the highest honor a noncitizen can receive for whatever reason that's specified. In my case, that was, simply, "for services rendered." No reason to advertise the upshot of my close

The King's Award, the highest honor a non-Thai citizen can receive.

association with General Pao, given the riots that had resulted over the *Mayaguez* incident.

As the rainy season approached, so did the end of my four-year tour in Thailand. I have to say, I was not going to miss the weather. The air was so thick I had to push aside the steam that rose off the cobblestone streets. And I swear, if I stood downwind I could smell the war and a metallic odor from all the bloodshed.

It was time to go home.

After four years in country, all three of my boys now spoke fluent Thai. Smokey didn't make the trip home with us, that cobra having ended his days lapping around airport tarmacs. There would sadly be no more "smoke on the plane."

As for me, back in the States these foreign challenges were about to be matched by domestic ones in the form of a gang as violent and vicious as anything I'd encountered overseas:

The Hells Angels.

PART FIVE

THE HOME FRONT

CHAPTER NINETEEN

SAN FRANCISCO, 1978

Although some of the Hells Angels' history remains a disputed mystery to this day, the gang's origins appear to date back to 1948 in Fontana, California. Formed from the remnants of another gang called the Pissed-Off Bastards, they took their name from a fighter squadron known for its daring exploits in World War I as well as the just-concluded World War II. It was a group of the veterans from that war, coming home displaced and disenfranchised, who found the action and freedom they craved by forming biker gangs. Motorcycles were cheap and the open road beckoned: the route these men returning home chose to ride into their futures.

It wasn't until nine years later, though, in 1957 that Ralph "Sonny" Barger founded the gang's Oakland chapter and set the Angels on the road to infamy that persists to this day. Violence became their calling card, defining the colors they wore and reputation they built for retribution, revenge, and all-out domination of any scene or road they inhabited. The first turning point was their disruption of the annual American Motorcycle Association race in California in 1957, followed in 1963 by their violent takeover of the town of Porterville that many say was the basis of the classic Marlon Brando film *The Wild One*.

But the biggest turning point came when three hundred Angels roared into the coastal town of Monterey in late summer of 1965. It was there, after a wild weekend of partying and violence, that four Angels were arrested on rape charges. The gang couldn't afford lawyers to defend them, so they took to selling speed to raise the money they needed. The case never went to trial; the arrested bikers weren't even charged. But they'd finally landed on law enforcement's radar, including that of California's attorney general, Thomas C. Lynch.

Meanwhile, drug dealing was so easy, and so lucrative, the Angels just kept doing it. These outlaw bikers, who somehow saw themselves as latter-day incarnations of Western frontier heroes in the tradition of Billy the Kid and Jesse James riding choppers instead of horses, had found the ideal way to finance the sustenance of their lifestyles. They went from being a loose amalgamation of disparate groups to a highly organized, centralized gang that began to spread from coast to coast. They looked at the road and embraced a twisted romantic notion of the new America, carving out their own version of the American Dream.

"When you're asked to stay out of a bar you don't just punch the owner," Hunter S. Thompson observed in his seminal *Hell's Angels: The Strange and Terrible Saga of the Outlaw Motorcycle Gangs* (Ballantine Books, 1966), "you come back with your army and tear the place down, destroy the whole edifice and everything it stands for. No compromise. If a man gets wise, mash his face. If a woman snubs you, rape her. This is the thinking, if not the reality, behind the whole Hell's Angels act."

Until then, the Angels had stuck to their roots in California. But their growing popularity among a disaffected, rebel element of the postwar generation, together with Barger's vision for expansion, spurred them to grow to ninety-two chapters in twenty-seven states. Barger foresaw a modern-day outlaw gang that would trade the badlands of the Old West for the fledgling interstate highway system, allowing members to move unencumbered and undeterred through the nation.

"When we award charters in new states," Barger wrote in his quasi-biography, *Hell's Angel: The Life and Times of Sonny Barger and the Hell's Angels Motorcycle Club* (Fourth Estate Ltd., 2001 edition), "it's always done by national vote. When a prospective club lets us know they want to become Hell's Angels, we'll check them out to see if they're stand-up people. We'll send officers out to meet with them, and in return they'll send guys out to meet with us. We might invite them to a run or two, and likewise we'll send some of our guys to party with them. At some point—time varies—we'll vote on their membership status. The same process that lets in individuals applies to entire new chapters as well.... Once we sanctioned each official Hell's Angels charter, it became their responsibility to keep anybody from starting up an illegal charter in their part of the country."

But Thompson's definitive study presents a wholly different take on the Angels, based on his time spent living in their midst to research the book that launched his career:

California, Labor Day weekend...early, with ocean fog still in the streets, outlaw motorcyclists wearing chains, shades and greasy Levis roll out from damp garages, all-night diners and cast-off one-night pads in Frisco, Hollywood, Berdoo and East Oakland, heading for the Monterey peninsula, north of Big Sur. The Menace is loose again, the Hell's Angels, the hundred-carat headline, running fast and loud on the early morning freeway, low in the saddle, nobody smiles, jamming crazy through traffic and ninety miles an hour down the center stripe, missing by inches...like Genghis Khan on an iron horse, a monster steed with a fiery anus, flat out through the eye of a beer can and up your daughter's leg with no quarter asked and none given; show the squares some class, give 'em a whiff of those kicks they'll never know...Ah, these righteous dudes, they love to screw it on...Little Jesus, the Gimp, Chocolate George, Buzzard, Zorro, Hambone, Clean Cut, Tiny, Terry the Tramp, Frenchie, Mouldy Marvin, Mother Miles, Dirty Ed, Chuck the Duck, Fat Freddy, Filthy Phil, Charger Charley the Child Molester, Crazy Cross, Puff, Magoo, Animal and at least a hundred more...tense for the action, long hair in the wind, beards and bandanas flapping, earrings, armpits, chain whips, swastikas and stripped-down Harleys flashing chrome as traffic on 101 moves over, nervous, to let the formation pass like a burst of dirty thunder.

Melodramatic, perhaps, but accurate in depicting this criminal scourge that had appeared on the scene to battle local authorities ill-equipped to match their firepower and national authorities ill-prepared at that time to deal with an organized menace that stretched across the entire country. Almost right from the beginning of Barger's reign, the Angels' business model was defined by drug dealing. Initially, they played the role of mob hit men and enforcers, providing muscle for drug dealers they would later usurp and replace. After all, why take a small cut of the action when you can own it all? Barger knew full well that the field was there for the taking, no rival gang anywhere near capable of matching the Angels in terms of firepower or muscle.

"'I've said it before and I'll say it again,'" Sonny Barger once said, as reported by *Rolling Stone* magazine in 1972. "'I'm gonna live in the world I want to live in. You people who run things ain't got nothin' to be proud of, you've left things in one hell of a mess.'"

"Sonny Barger," the same article continues, "got quoted more than any other Angel, which still wasn't much. The Angels never went around telling people what they were like inside or what their motives were; anything that wasn't obvious was none of your fucking business. But once in a while, there were at least clues to where they were coming from. Back in 1966, for example, Sonny led a herd of Angels into the middle of an antiwar march in Oakland. Several of the marchers were hurt. The country has enough 'peace creeps,' Sonny said, and a couple months later he sent a letter to Washington offering to volunteer his men as 'gorillas' in Vietnam. He was turned down; the country was too busy drafting 'peace creeps' to take on outlaw bikers best known for their police records."

Because these Angels of the '60s, '70s, and even into the '80s had another advantage: they weren't at all reluctant to use all their fire-power and muscle when it came to claiming and solidifying territory from coast to coast.

* * * * *

I was just a few years short of fifty-five, the mandatory age of retirement, and was determined to end my stint in a location where I was sure my family would be happy. Jack Cusack helped secure me my old post as the DEA's regional director of San Francisco. My family was understandably thrilled; after all, it was the first time since my three boys had been born that I'd be going back to where I'd most recently been.

Almost like going home again, even though it wasn't Philadelphia.

We were going to be able to live a normal life, free of gated compounds, armed guards, and corpses stuffed with heroin. My sons were going to be able to stay in the same school, keep the same friends, play in the same leagues from year to year. I won't say it was a dream come true, because moving around comes with the job I still loved, but it was pretty close.

Dan was sixteen and looking forward to driving, something I wouldn't let him do in Thailand. Bobby wanted to get back to a place where he could play tennis, and Mark was looking forward to having new lands to explore. My mom was also excited when I shared the news that we were coming back to the States. My father had passed away several years earlier, and she was now living in Florida with my brother and sister.

We didn't have long from the time I found out about the new location and the move. We pretty much packed up all our stuff and boarded a plane back to San Francisco, arriving without a home to start our new lives.

The DEA put us up in a motel. We had two rooms, not really ideal for a family of five. Joy began house hunting while I started to get a handle on the status of my new office.

It didn't take Joy long to find us a fantastic house, a two-story contemporary home back in the hills of Orinda, a stone's throw away from our original house in the same town. This home overlooked the Orinda Country Club. The back was all windows and allowed us to watch the golfers on the fifth hole of the most elite country club in the area. The membership had risen to ten thousand dollars a year, which was too rich for my blood. However, Bob had gotten a job in the pro shop and golf course. The club granted our family a pool membership that Joy and the boys took full advantage of while I was happy staring out at the Orinda trees, hills, and unobstructed views.

Then one day, working in my office on the twelfth floor of the Federal Building at 450 Golden Gate Avenue, I was reviewing all of the ongoing cases under my jurisdiction. I had a small black-and-white television on in the background. Most agency guys always had the news on; we needed to be aware of what was going on in the world.

I wasn't paying much attention at the time, until the newscaster said, "Fire in Orinda Hills." My head snapped up. I needed to make sure my family was safe. Even from the small black and white, I could tell how bad it was. The city had been so dry that the dried grass made perfect kindling. My eyes were glued to the television.

"The fire was started when the engine of a car caught fire. The car, owned by XYZ auto shop, was being test driven by three young boys," the newscaster explained.

My heart stopped. There, on the tube, was Dan. I could tell he was terrified. I hopped in my car and raced to the scene.

Dan had tears in his eyes. He threw his arms around me.

"I'm so sorry, Dad!"

"It's not your fault, but what a way to be welcomed home!" I replied.

Dan flashed me an insecure smile. "Can I still get a car?"

* * * * *

An associate who was leaving the country couldn't take his dog, a Rhodesian ridgeback named Streaker, with him, so he gave the dog to us. Nothing could replace Smokey, but Streaker gave it his best shot. And it didn't take me long to fan the flames of my old relationships in the city, picking up right where I'd left off with the reporters like Paul Avery, Herb Caen, and Warren Hinckle. Not a lot of the politicos and power brokers knew much about what I'd done in the Golden Triangle, but they knew enough to help me fit right back in, laying down the welcome mat. Beyond that, plenty of the guys in law enforcement I'd worked with before I left for Southeast Asia had now risen to captains, deputy chiefs, and other positions from which we'd be able to accomplish even more together.

Starting with one of the most unique cases of my career.

Unique because it started when Dan, then a high school senior, was jogging with Streaker up in the Orinda Hills where homes like ours were nestled with plenty of space between them. Enough so that you really didn't see your neighbors much, including one named John who lived above us in those hills.

John was jogging with his dog, a beautiful Doberman, when he ran into Dan and Streaker. Dan recognized John as the neighbor of ours known for restoring classic cars because he was into the very same thing. Then Dan and John struck up a conversation and by the end of it, Dan had a job restoring cars for him.

"Got any buddies at school with the same interest?" John asked him. "Because I've got some extra work right now."

241

He couldn't wait to get home to tell Joy and me.

"Dad, please, please can I work for John?" Dan pleaded.

"Of course you can get a job. But who is this John?" I asked.

"John, our neighbor," Joy jumped in.

"Oh. Okay," I replied, still having no idea who he was.

"The job is in the city, Dan," Joy continued, the concern clear in her voice.

"Joy, Dan's almost a man. He could use some more responsibility," I replied.

Dan's head was teeter-tottering from me to his mom, stopping only when Joy nodded in approval.

* * * * *

While Dan and his friends started working for John, my office was heavily working cocaine cases. The San Francisco office was a big one; I was supervising, just for starters, four teams of twelve agents each spread out through the city and Marin County to the north, and the busts were coming hot and heavy. We started hearing about some exotic car place in San Francisco that had become a major conduit for cocaine distribution, but I didn't make the connection to John right away. Not until one of my office's undercovers bought some kilos from a guy identified as my neighbor, the neighbor my oldest son met while jogging and had offered him a job on the spot. We hadn't been living in Orinda for very long, and the solitary nature of our hillside retreats must've kept John from learning what I did for a living. But I ended up finding out what he really did. It was a great bust and a really nice case.

The San Francisco office was a model of efficiency, in large part because of a US attorney named Billy Hunter, an African American former wide receiver with the Washington Redskins who looked like he could still mix it up between the football hash marks. Billy, who in later years would go on to become the executive director of the NBA's

Players Association, ran a tight ship, and all the law enforcement offices in these parts were battle hardened by the war we'd fought and mostly won against LSD before I'd left for the Golden Triangle. The FBI, DEA, and ATF (the Bureau of Alcohol, Tobacco and Firearms) often riddled by internecine rivalries in what were supposed to be joint operations, got along just fine here. No squabbling over credit, jurisdiction, or seizure allocation. As far as federal investigations went, no way Billy Hunter would've tolerated anything less, no way.

Of course, Billy didn't hold much sway over the San Francisco PD, a portion of which thought we'd cut them out of the classic car cocaine bust. Their response was to selectively leak rumors that my own son was involved and that I'd covered it up. I fumed but kept my cool, in part because nobody who mattered was buying that shit and, in part, because I knew I was going to have to work with these guys again.

* * * * *

We had taken down the car shop, but the town was still flooded with supply. I got a call from my informant that he had traced the dope to the northwest section of the city, where all the strip clubs were located. One of the most exclusive clubs in the area, and arguably the very first club to go topless in the entire country, was called the Condor and was frequented by politicians, dignitaries, and celebrities. Taking down all those who were participating was going to make some headlines, especially since the Condor and many other clubs like it were owned by a mobbed-up guy named Gino Del Prete.

I had long suspected that something wasn't kosher at the clubs, because most of these types of joints had plenty illegal going on inside. But suspecting and proving are two vastly different things. The Condor was taking in so much cash, you'd need a Brinks truck to haul it all away. I decided to send in informants to ingratiate themselves with Del Prete.

Del Prete was a Joe Pesci-type character around fifty or so. He didn't try his supply, and that made him a tough mark. However, eventually my agents worked their way into his inner circle. Not an easy task with a professional criminal, but they managed the task because they were able to cozy up to Del Prete through golf outings we'd arranged at the best courses in the Bay Area. An avid golfer, he just couldn't resist taking the bait.

But we never nailed Del Prete at the Condor. Patience paid off yet again when six months later, we got him on cocaine charges at another bar he owned called Sneaky Pete's after we got a warrant to install a wiretap. We needed to make sure our warrants were solid on this case. With such an elite group of perpetrators, I had to get this right. We ended up writing warrants on all kinds of dignitaries, celebrities, and politicos, in addition to Del Prete, and knew the shit was going to fly.

It ended up flying faster and harder than we'd thought. We were thrilled to finally take down Del Prete, to get him and his shit off the streets. But the judge and all of Del Prete's political connections must've had other plans. He was sentenced to less than a year in jail because he had more than his share of political balls in a vise, and the last thing they wanted was for him to turn on them and cooperate with us. Saving Del Prete meant saving themselves, for all intents and purposes.

Years later, I ran into Del Prete at a social function. I hadn't seen him since the trial, but he came up, threw his arms around me, and gave me a big hug.

"You saved my life," he said. "I'm only alive today because of you."

And, thanks to my setting Del Prete on a straight and narrow path away from a life of crime, he lived all the way until March 2018 when he died at the age of eighty-seven. Sometimes busts lead to pleasant surprises. Sometimes, you end up helping someone you hadn't meant to help at all.

* * * * *

Plenty of the hotshots and politicos who frequented Del Prete's joints were also loyal customers at the swanky Robert's Restaurant. It was the top French restaurant in town, and their food was delicious. I always looked forward to a night at Robert's.

That was soon to change when my informant called to tell me that Robert's was serving more dope than fine food.

Ugh! There goes my favorite hot spot!

I sent in agents to get a better grasp of the situation. The most obvious strange activity was coming from the bathroom. It seemed to be a very popular place. Now, in my experience the best place to hide something is in the bathroom. Even criminals know a thing or two about privacy.

My agents decided to stake out the bathroom and found white residue on the sink that turned out to be cocaine. But we had no idea where the restaurant's supply was coming from—the servers, chef, owner? Whoever was dealing was keeping it quiet. The cocaine residue gave us enough probable cause for a wiretap, and I went to the US attorney's office to help execute the perfect warrants.

While I was waiting for all the i's to be dotted and t's crossed, an informant was able to buy a bag of blow off of a waiter. *Score!* We were finally able to pinpoint one of the dealers. I had the informant introduce one of my undercover agents to the waiter, and it didn't take long for my agent to become one of his top "customers." Eventually, after dozens of buys, my agent received information that a big load of cocaine would be coming into the restaurant.

The waiter was dumb enough to give my agent the date and time. That was when we planned to strike. We always wanted to get them when they had the most amount of illegal substances on them.

All my men were in place over an hour before the actual drop. We waited until we saw a suspicious truck pull in and out. Once the courier was gone, we served our warrant and tore the whole place apart. We searched the wine, produce, and meat. Nothing.

There was one place we didn't search…

"Check the linens," one of my informants shouted.

My team followed the advice and, lo and behold, there was the coke! We arrested the owner, the waiter, and other staff, putting yet another supply chain out of business. Unfortunately, we were never able to find the source of that cocaine, which meant the dope going out through Robert's would just find another route into the city.

Sometimes, when you chase the dragon, you're left holding on to the tail. And I was about to take on one of the biggest dragons I'd ever gone after.

* * * * *

The cooperative nature of the rival agencies in San Francisco allowed the DEA, FBI, and ATF to all have undercovers who'd infiltrated the Hells Angels at the same time. We learned from the undercovers that the Angels weren't just into drugs; they were also dealing weapons, running extortion rings, and steadily increasing their foothold in all things racketeering. We weren't just looking at a major drug operation here; we were looking at a continuing criminal enterprise, or CCE, turning this into a major RICO (Racketeer Influenced and Corrupt Organizations Act) case for Billy Hunter to make. Before he could, though, we assembled a task force that comprised equally the FBI, ATF, and us at the DEA. The system was finally working as it was intended to. I'd come off working in that very manner with General Pao in Thailand, and now it had followed me home, so to speak.

Of course, the difference, and sometimes the frustration, about being involved in foreign operations was that your level of participation depended entirely on the host country's policies and attitude toward the United States. Thailand's General Pao was a prime example of how things looked when we all worked cooperatively, which was hardly the case in all countries. Indeed, many less trusting governments pretty much confined guys like me to the embassy grounds, twiddling our thumbs while they conducted raids aimed at confiscating drugs and arresting the perps. So you never really knew what was going on outside those embassy walls, how much those to whom you were beholden to nab the bad guys might've been similarly beholden to those they were supposed to be arresting. You trusted them, you had faith, because you had no other choice.

But me and my counterparts at the FBI and ATF, by contrast, had the freedom to get our hands as dirty as we wanted. Our multijurisdictional task force worked hand-in-hand and Billy Hunter had assigned a terrific deputy United States attorney by the name of Robert Dondero, who was assisted by Robert Mueller, who, of course, would go on to run the FBI and plenty more after that. I liked Bob Mueller a lot. Both of us had been tested on the battlefield as young men, me in Korea while Mueller had done a hard stint in Vietnam. He was a no-nonsense, no bullshit guy, as honest as they come.

Our task force worked for over a year assembling the evidence we needed for probable cause to get the search and arrest warrants we'd been after. The grand jury finally came back with forty indictments

Dan pictured with Bob Mueller circa 1978 around the time they worked the Hells Angels case.

for a massive simultaneous raid, not unlike the one I'd been involved in all those years ago in my first case in Philly, which in this case was designed to take all forty Hells Angels down at the same. The logistical challenges of pulling that off were already immense before we considered the worst-case scenarios of trying to put forty bikers in county lockup before arraigning the lot of them in court.

We decided to hold the Hells Angels at the Alameda County Naval Base, located on an island in the bay off Oakland and accessible only by a single road or the water. Since even the mighty Angels couldn't ride their bikes over the ocean, all we had to do was heavily secure that lone road in order to deter what all of us feared might be a bloodbath once the hundreds and hundreds of gang members based in the area caught wind of their brethren being nabbed.

The raids were carried out by multiple squads without a hitch, and we managed to gather all the suspects as planned at the naval base. But word of our operation must've leaked, because an armada of rented boats packed with reporters and cameras surrounded the island like they were ready to attack it. Fortunately, none of those boats were carrying any heavily armed Hells Angels and we were able to transport all forty gang members to a single courtroom to meet their high-priced lawyers who'd flown in from all over the country. It was the rowdiest courtroom I've ever seen. The Angels, both the perps and those in the peanut gallery, wouldn't sit down. They were swearing, hooting, laughing—anything they could do to be disruptive. The courthouse just wasn't set up for such crowds and chaos.

Well, a terrific jurist named Sam Conti put his foot down. After slamming his gavel down hard enough to almost break it, he warned the Angels that one more outburst and he'd order all suspects back to their cells, where they'd be arraigned via closed-circuit television. Since the Angels crave publicity for their cause to further expand the mythology that surrounds them, that got the job done. The arraignments went off without further hitch, though to be on the safe side, I assigned a twenty-four-hour security detail to guard Judge Conti for weeks afterward.

Here's how the *New York Times* described what had gone down in an article that ran in 1981.

> *The indictments were voted on June 13, 1979, on evidence gathered by agents of the Drug Enforcement Administration, the Federal Bureau of Investigation, and the Alcohol, Tobacco and Firearms Bureau of the Treasury Department. The charge in each case was violation of a Federal law, the Racketeer Influenced and Corrupt Organization Law, enacted in 1969. The RICO section of the criminal code, as it became known, was an effort by the Nixon Administration to meet law enforcement problems. In the Hell's Angels cases, the charge was that the organization operated an illegal manufacturing plant and distribution system for methamphetamine. However, the indictments listed a range of vicious crimes that were described as a part of the major plan to sell drugs.*

While the multiple trials and retrials yielded mixed to disappointing results, our task force had established the template quickly followed by other jurisdictions, as federal authorities continued to wage war on the Angels in increasingly effective fashion. Most notably, this included Operation Rough Rider that led to the arrest of nearly 150 gang members across fourteen cities, including thirty-eight in San Francisco, in 1985.

"'The Hell's Angels have been around for a number of years; now they are getting much deserved attention,'" Lee Laster, the FBI's assistant director in New York, said at the time in a *Chicago Tribune* article that went on to say, "Undercover agents bought $2 million in methamphetamines, cocaine, marijuana, hashish, PCP and LSD from the Hell's Angels during the undercover operation."

I've used the word "patience" before in describing the way you have to go about your business trying to win the war on drugs. Even for me, though, five years was a long time to wait.

* * * * *

Busting big dogs like the Hells Angels made the work I did for thirty years so worthwhile. You know that with every bust you make, every dealer and kingpin you turn or take off the street, you're saving lives and I mean that literally. How much damage can a gunman do in a crowded restaurant with an assault rifle? Well, a few kilos of heroin can kill just as many people. That conviction had spearheaded my entire career, which, as the Hells Angels case came to a close, was nearing its finish. I was fifty-four, and the DEA's mandatory retirement age at the time was fifty-five.

Little did I know that that career was about to come to a premature end.

CHAPTER TWENTY

SAN FRANCISCO, 1982

I wanted to finish out my career in San Francisco, another year I wish I could have stretched out longer. But a new administrator was put in charge of the DEA and it was like déjà vu all over again. Another new regime and yet another reorganization with political cronyism behind the hire.

The Reagan administration brought in a guy from the internal affairs office of another city, a guy who wouldn't know cocaine if it blew up his nose in the kind of blueprint for disaster I was all too used to. The first thing this blowhard did was to begin transferring people across the country. People he had never met and didn't have the courtesy to meet, all of them informed of their new assignments via wire. I mean, this guy couldn't have picked me out of a lineup!

Nice way to inspire loyalty and confidence, by reassigning a lot of your top agents to the boondocks so you could replace them with your own cronies, right?

As for me, well, I was offered an okay administrative position, assistant regional director of New York, but hardly an inviting prospect at the time. I was less than a year from mandatory retirement. By the time I moved my family to New York and got settled in my new job, that would be down to maybe seven or eight months, so what was the point? I wasn't going to move my family again over those nine months in what was essentially a demotion. Joy and the boys loved San Francisco, and so did I.

I never had a single conversation with the new administrator, who lacked the decency, and the balls, to talk to me directly. Had we spoken, the only input I would have had would have been to recommend that he quit before he did any more damage than he'd done already by reassigning agents and supervisors with hundreds of years of experience among them. How did he expect to replace that? How did he expect to win the war on drugs after replacing some of the best soldiers and generals the DEA had fighting on the front lines?

Maybe he didn't really care, any more than he cared about replacing the kind of veteran leadership and experience he'd flushed down the toilet. You want to hear a prime stratagem for winning the war on drugs? Make the administrator's position apolitical. A ten-year fixed term, like the director of the FBI. Our mandate at the DEA was on the same level as that of the FBI or CIA, maybe even higher in some cases given the incredible damage drugs were doing to society even back then. But the DEA has never been treated as an equal, more like a bastard stepbrother ripe for dispensing jobs as paybacks for political patronage.

Imagine General George Patton being replaced on the eve of the Battle of the Bulge. That's an apt metaphor for the attitude various presidential administrations had taken toward the DEA. They gave us a job to do and then seemed to do everything in their power to stop us from being successful. The perpetual lack of continuity at the top led to an ever-changing dynamic in which the DEA kept reinventing the wheel instead of just changing the tire, its policies subject to the whims, foibles, and priorities of every new administration.

Strange.

The FBI's mandate was to fight crime; the CIA was about spying. And they both prospered from the continuity that helped define them. The only continuity displayed at the DEA, on the other hand, was the utter lack of it.

* * * * *

My going-away party was held at La Pinterra in North Beach, a restaurant frequented by all manner of cops, politicos, and even wiseguys. The San Francisco PD blocked off the street to make things as convenient as possible for the arriving guests—that was the kind of juice enjoyed by the place's owner, Adolph "Pee Wee" Ferrari. He loved holding court with us when we came in for lunch at the end of the long family-style tables that dominated the restaurant.

On this day, I was greeted by all manner of officials and politicians, chiefs and deputy chiefs, and agents I'd worked with in the past

Hillary Clinton and Tipper Gore pictured on either side of Dan and Donna.

as well as the present. But it was Pee Wee himself who gave me the best retirement gift of anyone.

"You wanna go see Frank?" he asked me, knowing from those lunches I'd had with him that I was a huge fan of Sinatra.

"Isn't it sold out?"

"Let me make a call," Pee Wee offered and off he went to make a phone call.

Sinatra was playing at a hotel casino called the Cal Neva he owned a piece of on the California-Nevada border.

"Okay, you're fully comped," Pee Wee said when he got back to the table. "Food, booze, the room, and tickets for the show."

Those tickets turned out to be at a table right next to the stage and the one occupied by Frank's wife and her guests. Talk about a great way to end my career with the DEA!

* * * * *

I started giving some thought to entering politics, but I got my private investigator's license first and then did a stint with the media, as a reporter with both the NBC and CBS San Francisco affiliates at different times.

"You know Manuel Noriega. You worked with him, right?" the manager of the CBS station asked me one day, a guy named Russ Coughlin.

"Sure, back in the day. Why?"

"Because things are starting to heat up down there. Rumors that President Bush is planning an invasion if Noriega doesn't turn himself in on drug charges."

I'd heard the rumors that the general had been linked to any number of drug gangs, offering them protection and the support of his military. No longer just a general, he was now president of Panama.

"What do you want?" I asked Russ.

"Do you think you can get an interview with him? Can you arrange for us to get down there so we can get his side of the story?"

I left a message for Noriega and one of his top aides got back to me, saying he'd agree to the interview only because he knew I wouldn't do the usual hatchet job on him that everybody else was doing. He agreed to the meeting with me, Russ, and a cameraman in attendance. The interview was supposed to take place inside a military airport. We were whisked there as part of a Panama police convoy and waited for hours.

Nothing happened. Noriega never showed.

It was afternoon when the aide approached me and said we'd passed the test, the Panamanian authorities having confirmed that the three of us had come alone and weren't setting a trap where the general might be extracted out of his own country. Our police convoy departed the military base for the old abandoned CIA headquarters that Noriega had claimed for his own. There were armed guards everywhere, and the general had added barbwire fences to the perimeter of the complex.

Once inside, we were escorted to this big office where we were thoroughly searched. Only when we were again deemed to be "friendlies," a panel of a wall opened up and Noriega stepped out.

"Why is the US picking on me?" he asked me as soon as the camera was rolling and the interview was underway. "I've always been helpful to you."

"That's why we're here, to get your side of the story."

"Tell your president, tell Bush that I'm willing to step aside. I'll go away. I'll step down. I don't need all this aggravation. He wants me to go, I'll go. Why is Bush so pissed off?"

Apparently, from what I'd been able to learn, this had all actually been caused by Noriega's refusal to use his troops against Nicaragua. Noriega told me that the US had requested that he do so through former undersecretary of state Elliot Richardson, and that he had refused. Noriega insisted these claims about him turning a blind eye to drugs and that he'd turned to Communism were just an excuse to remove him from power. He was sure an invasion was coming and had agreed to do this interview in large part for us to bring word that he was willing to leave power peacefully.

We finished the interview, flew home, and completed all the editing in time to get it on the air that very night locally. We figured the story was a lock to be picked up nationally but CBS refused, allegedly caving to pressure applied by the White House. And not very long after that, the US invasion of Panama did indeed take place.

While working at the station, I frequented a restaurant called Reno's owned by Reno Barsocchini. He'd enjoyed a decent minor league baseball career that culminated with him playing for the San Francisco Seals and helped win him the friendship and business of Pete Rose, Johnny Bench, and numerous other baseball legends, including one of the biggest of them all, Joe DiMaggio, the Yankee Clipper himself, who was living in San Francisco at the time. He was in there all the time signing baseballs, and Reno had been best man when Joe married Marilyn Monroe.

"But never talk to him about her," he warned me. "Not the Kennedys or Frank Sinatra either."

I got to know Joe pretty well. He learned about my background and nicknamed me "Cuffs." We watched Joe Montana's San Francisco 49ers win the Super Bowl at Reno's that year, and I found Joe DiMaggio to be a really good guy, maybe a bit uncomfortable with all his celebrity who nonetheless liked it when fans came over and asked him to sign a baseball.

You may be wondering where my wife Joy was through this stage of my life, and the truth is we had separated. I was living in a condo on the Wharf in San Francisco, while she had remained in the hills of Orinda with the boys. There wasn't a single incident I can point to; it was more an accumulation of things, a buildup of stress over having to move around so much over the years. I think she blamed me for constantly uprooting our family, putting myself and my career first. I think Joy was bitter over that, maybe rightfully so, and saw an opportunity to make a clean break with my retirement from the DEA. She'd been living my life for so long, she just wanted to live her own. I can't really blame her, because she knew I wasn't going to change, although it was ironic we split up after I finally stopped moving around and settled down. My divorce with Joy didn't come all that long after my divorce from the Drug Enforcement Administration.

You hear about this kind of thing happening a lot in the world of law enforcement, even more so in the military. Wives were left holding the family together while wondering every day if their husbands would be coming home. No, the war I was fighting didn't require me to serve on foreign battlegrounds humping through the jungle, desert, or mountains with an M16 and body armor while my family stewed and worried at home. That was a whole lot different, but it was also very much the same for the pressures it created. Wives like Joy toughed it out because they were very much soldiers too. Then when the endless series of deployments finally ends, they find themselves exhausted, drained, with nothing left to give and unable to adjust to a world where the pressures that had held them together finally went away. The problem was that that often left a void, a vacuum, a hole they suddenly realized was suffocating them.

I don't blame Joy for anything; in fact, I'm grateful she stuck it out and held the family together for as long as she did. We had three great sons, and the experiences we shared were enough for anyone's lifetime, which might've been another part of the problem. Indeed, life in the field, in foreign countries, was so intensified that a day might seem like a week, a week like a month, and a month like a year. So, I guess all those years in the field amounted to a lifetime in itself, and she'd just had enough.

I kept my hand in my old world through a network of retired agents, identifying trends of where the drugs were coming from and passing that information on to SFPD narcotics officers mostly. There was nothing I was especially privy to, just stuff I was able to glean from bulletins I saw and rumors I heard. I was asked to speak to groups about narcotics a bunch of times and accepted most of them. Even though drugs were no longer part of my life, I'd spent too long fighting this war not to keep an eye on the developments surrounding it.

I gave up my career as a television reporter to take a job as district manager for the private security firm William J. Burns International Detective Agency with 250 security agents working under me. Among our many tasks, we were responsible for safeguarding the Golden Gate Bridge, the Bechtel Building, and the headquarters for Pacific Gas and Electric, and we were also assigned to collect all the change from the city's traffic meters on a regular basis. I was running things for the entire Bay Area, which gave me the opportunity to revisit some old haunts and reconnect with some old friends, which got me started thinking again about pursuing a career in politics, like my father had back in Philadelphia. I'd watched so many politicians screw things up from fighting the drug war, I figured maybe I could do better.

* * * * *

When it came to women, I didn't think I'd ever be able to do better than Joy. But then came this night at a bar in the Marina District called Mulhearn's that was owned by a former professional basketball player. I met up with this old friend of mine who'd also become a private investigator on the same night I spotted this tall, elegant, gorgeous woman stride into the place like she owned it.

"That's Donna," my friend told me. "She's a good friend of my wife's."

He introduced me to her and, Christ, I felt like I was in junior high again. She seemed impressed by my friend including "DEA" in his introduction.

"Oh," Donna beamed, "my family was involved with the CIA."

"Can I buy you a drink?" I stammered.

I forgot what she ordered and I stayed tongue-tied through most of the night, but managed to ask if I could see her again when she said she had to go. She smiled at me, got up, and headed off to use the telephone—at least, that's what I thought until she came back with a page of the phone book torn out with her number circled in red.

"Here, call me. And don't lose this."

* * * * *

I was practically shaking when I carefully stuck that page of the phone book in my pocket. All told I'd come out of the biggest transitional period of my life, both personally and professionally, pretty well. I started to see the road ahead and didn't spend as much time looking back.

Donna became the perfect partner with whom to walk down that road. We dated for six months maybe, and I could tell she was starting to get antsy. Her best friend was Reno Barsocchini's daughter, and Joe DiMaggio's goddaughter, Rena. They got to talking about things and, *boom!*, Donna hit me with an ultimatum.

"If you don't marry me, I'm leaving."

I just looked at her.

"And I'm taking the dog."

That was the deal killer. I had the wedding set up for the next week in the San Francisco city hall rotunda, the same place where Joe DiMaggio married Marilyn Monroe. Presiding over the wedding was City Supervisor Terence Hallinan, who was just about to become San Francisco's district attorney. He had to get special authorization to perform the service, and I'm pretty sure our nuptials were legit.

Pretty sure?

Anyway, this felt like a door opening to the next stage of my life, and I figured I was done fighting the war on drugs, at least on anything approaching the front lines.

But then I got that phone call.
About my son.
How Daniel had died.
And everything changed again.

CHAPTER TWENTY-ONE

SAN FRANCISCO, 1993

"I'm calling for Dan Addario," greeted a female voice.

"Speaking."

"Are you the father of Daniel Addario?"

"Yes. Who is this?"

"The Coroner's Office, sir. I'm afraid I have some bad news."

The rest of her words remain a blur to this day, but not the message they carried: my thirty-four-year-old son had died of a drug overdose, specifically opiates. I remember my heart skipping a beat, then hammering against my rib cage. I remember losing my breath and feeling my stomach sink. I was lucky I was sitting down or I'm pretty sure I would've collapsed.

I'm repeating that section here because of how many times I played it again in the days, weeks, months, and years that followed. It felt like a dream, a nightmare. My thoughts went fuzzy as the room wobbled. I figured I must've heard wrong, because this couldn't be my son.

Not Daniel.

None of us had any idea he'd become addicted to opiates. Not me, not his brothers, not Joy, and we were all devastated as a result. Dan was doing absolutely great, having a carved out a niche for himself working for a guy named Nick Leonoudakis, who owned a string of parking lots throughout the city, including the whole Candlestick Park concession where the Giants still played at the time. Nick was grooming Dan, along with his own son, to take over the business and had already put my son in charge of some of his prime garages. My younger sons Mark and Bob had been working with Dan when there were events at Candlestick, seeing him up close and personal on a regular basis. But they didn't have a clue, not even an inkling, that he was an addict.

But he was. And now he'd become a victim of the very scourge I'd spent my life fighting. No matter how close I'd grown to the drug issue in Philly, New York, Detroit, South America, the Golden Triangle, and two stints in San Francisco, nothing had prepared me for this. I'd been fighting that war on the front lines and, from that vantage point, never saw the human costs of drugs. I saw statistics, I saw dealers, I saw junkies, I saw distributors, I saw corrupt politicians, cops, and soldiers. But the victims, where the real pain of this scourge lay, remained distant for me. Like everybody else, I figured this was the kind of thing that only happened to other families. I'd come back to our home in Buenos Aires, or Bangkok, or San Francisco never thinking for a moment that my own oldest son would get hooked on the very drugs I was committed to keeping off the streets. I started out numb and progressed through all the stages of grief before I settled on the one that would move me into a new phase of my life that kind of resembled the old.

The funeral and memorial service were jam-packed with Dan's friends, the number even more impressive when you consider he'd spent so much of his youth overseas. Those friends, the ones he'd made when we finally settled down in San Francisco, wanted to do something special for him. They raised around five thousand dollars to help fund construction of a baseball field in Orinda. A plaque in Daniel's honor still hangs on the backstop fence behind home plate today, passed by everyone who comes to either play or watch a game. This while I felt like I had struck out as a parent.

How could I not have seen it? How could I not have known?

I can't tell you how many times I've asked myself those questions, particularly because of the often sordid world in which I'd spent my life. That's the thing that really got me. Being around this stuff for so long, so many years. I'd started my career developing the ability to spot a junkie a mile away. But I never saw the signs with Dan. I look back and think maybe if I'd been around more, maybe if we hadn't moved around so much, maybe if I'd been more like a regular working stiff, this never would've happened.

But Dan was in his early thirties when it happened, building a great career, surrounded by wonderful friends with a nice place to live. He was the textbook example of what you're supposed to be doing in your thirties. And when I did see him, I didn't have a clue there was anything wrong. I truly never saw a single sign.

Maybe because there weren't any, which is one of the defining factors of the opiate crisis we're facing today. The paradigm shift has left us with a whole new profile for the most at-risk drug addict. My son Dan displayed no outward or physical symptoms typical of the addicts I'd busted or worked with over the years. As for more behaviorally oriented symptoms, here's a list compiled by DrugAbuse.com:

- Increased aggression or irritability
- Changes in attitude/personality
- Lethargy
- Depression
- Sudden changes in a social network
- Dramatic changes in habits and/or priorities
- Financial problems
- Involvement in criminal activity

Dan displayed none of these either. That became a recurring topic of conversation between his friends, since they too had seen none of these on display. And Dan's not alone in that respect. As *Psychology Today* reported on February 17, 2014, in an article entitled "The Opiate Addict in Your Office":

> *The depiction of the opiate addict as unemployed, homeless, or hustling to buy dope by doing street crimes, certainly has its place in society and our history, since opium and heroin became pervasive in the US in the 1900s. But there are far more opiate abusers who have jobs, families, and even an outwardly-displayed sense of stability. Their hidden secret is what ultimately kills them if they don't reach out for treatment before they overdose for the last time.*
>
> *The Substance Abuse Mental Health Services Administration (SAMHSA), which oversees the federal government's response to drug abuse, estimates that 10 to 12 percent of employees use alcohol or illegal drugs while at work. This number does not incorporate a shadow figure—people who abuse opiate drugs, under a physician's prescription, at work too.*
>
> *The problem with opiate use is a bit like what recovering alcoholics say about beer: "One is too many; a thousand is not enough." What starts as a perfectly reasonable use of the drug for pain relief, soon starts to slide into taking too many, too often. Once the patient slips from, "one pill every four to six hours," to "six pills a day," and then on to double figures, what started as a legitimate medical use has given way to addiction.*

CNN, in a February 27, 2018, post by Jessica Ravitz, adds this about heroin use today:

> *They're not slumped over in alleyways with used needles by their sides. Their dignity, at least from outside appearances, remains intact. They haven't lost everything while chasing an insatiable high.*
>
> *They are functioning heroin addicts—people who hold down jobs, pay the bills and fool their families.*

For some, addiction is genetic; they're wired this way. For others, chronic pain and lack of legal opioids landed them here. Or experimentation got them hooked and changed everything.

What addicts have in common, according to experts, is a disease that has more to do with their brains than the substances they use. About 85% of people can take a pain pill, for example, and never crave it again.

This is a story about the others, those traveling the dangerous road of functional addiction. What works for them now, experts explain, can easily and lethally be derailed.

Hanging in the balance are people you may never imagine: peers, co-workers and neighbors. Loved ones, bosses and teachers. Respected members of your community who, for the benefit of everyone's understanding, want to be heard.

That same CNN article went on to profile a young man named "Todd" who, according to the article, enjoyed "loving and successful parents, good schools, a great upbringing in the Midwest: Todd can't point to anything that drove him to drugs. He was a typical suburban high school student who dabbled in weed. Then, at 15, he popped a Percocet his mother left lying around while she was recovering from surgery."

Maybe that's the way it was for Dan too, or something close. I'll never know for sure. What I did know back in 1994, though, was that I couldn't stay on the sidelines anymore.

* * * * *

San Francisco, 1994

And that meant a return to the world of law enforcement, this time as chief of detectives for the San Francisco District Attorney's Office, under the just elected Terence Hallinan, who'd married Donna and I in what indeed turned out to be a legitimate service.

It wasn't just about drugs, I'd realized; it was about making a difference. And I thought making a difference any way I could made for the best therapy in the wake of Dan's death. His sudden passing had me feeling so helpless, I just needed to get back into the world where I could achieve something positive.

Thanks to my father's status as a ward boss, I'd grown up in the world of politics and figured that might provide a better venue for me to hit the front lines of the war on drugs again. I ran for city supervisor, a position comparable to the one my dad had held for a number of years and counted among its past ranks the likes of Gavin Newsom and Dianne Feinstein. There were twenty-seven candidates running and I finished around twelfth. But the experience was eye-opening in any number of ways. Meeting the people, getting into the neighborhoods, gave me a fresh appreciation of the problems people were facing beyond drugs, which had been my singular focus for so long. Being out on the campaign trail meant listening to any number of different points of view on a whole variety of subjects, and I came away with a much deeper understanding of our city's diversity, all the varying community dynamics and the competing agendas across a myriad of fields that extended way beyond illicit narcotics. That said, far too often I also saw the true cost of drug addictions in families not that much different from mine. This scourge doesn't discriminate; it's an equal opportunity killer.

Before I married Donna, though, I'd hooked up with Terence as one of his top fund-raisers. The position of chief of detectives for the DA's office invariably went to a cop, normally a high-ranking one like a captain or deputy chief. It was a plum job with a tradition all its own. The morning Terence was sworn in he was also scheduled to announce the appointment, and the same city hall rotunda where he'd married Donna and I was packed with uniforms in eager anticipation of the announcement.

You could have heard a pin drop. But what really dropped were the mouths of all those police officials when Terence called my name.

*Dan pictured with
San Francisco
District Attorney
Terence Hallinan.*

I'd barely stepped up to shake his hand when a mass exodus followed to the doors.

As chief of detectives for the entire office, my primary responsibility was to investigate any case the various assistant district attorneys were working on. My job was to interview witnesses and victims, collect hospital and police records, and make arrests whenever necessary. I had about fifty investigators working under me and a couple dozen additional support staff. The investigators were mostly culled from the ranks of former police officers and other law enforcement venues. The investigator jobs were highly sought after, the ranks swelling with experienced detectives moving on to the next stage of their lives, just like me. We had our pick so we boasted the cream of the crop, all happy to be working in an apolitical office absent the kind of pressures that come with being a police detective. The only people we had to answer to were the people of San Francisco. Besides Terence, of course.

Bob Mueller, who I'd worked with as head of the DEA's San Francisco office in the late seventies when he was an assistant US attorney, had been elevated to the position of director of the FBI. Unbeknownst to me, Mueller came to San Francisco in 1994 to meet with a panel of judges at the Hall of Justice where my office was located as well. Shortly after that meeting wrapped up, he paid me an unannounced visit.

"How you doing, Dan?"

"Great and great to see you," I told him. "Congratulations on the new job."

We reminisced about our days together waging war on LSD and the Hells Angels, after which he asked me to update him on the current state of the drug problem in San Francisco, what was moving and popular at the time. It was just a friendly visit, but I could tell that Bob Mueller was interested in anything I could tell him about current trends in the drug world.

Drugs were only a part of my investigative caseload, instead of a whole in themselves, as they always had been in my career in law enforcement up until that point. I think that was probably a good thing, because it was refreshing and even reinvigorating to roam outside my comfort zone. And, let me tell you, the bad guys were just as bad. I might not have been chasing the same dragon I'd been after for almost thirty years, but many of those I investigated packed just as much of a bite.

Literally, in one case.

I was involved in a famous dog mauling case in which a lawyer couple's Spanish guard dogs attacked and killed a coed who lived in the same condo building. She was just walking past them on the grounds when they pounced. The case got splashed all over the national news for the myriad of issues and causes it attracted, not the least of which was the fact that the dogs' owners made for a powerful, politically-connected couple. A pair of terrific assistant US attorneys, two of thirty working out of our office, convicted them of manslaughter before a media circus. I attended the wedding of one of those AUSAs, Kimberly Guilfoyle, when she married the current lieutenant governor of California, Gavin Newsom, prior to going on to become a major personality at Fox News.

I also spent several months following up complaints lodged by parents with the DA's office that their sons were being molested by pedophile priests. These were difficult cases to investigate because you needed to make probable cause, and the archdiocese, under Archbishop William Levada, had already done everything it could to stop that from happening. Levada's plan was to cover things up in large part by sending the accused priests to a parish in Mexico. That was his approach to dealing with the problem: by not dealing with it at all. Terence was pissed the diocese was trying to sweep everything under the rug, and my instructions were to go at this full bore.

The interviews with the kids were tough, but the more of them I did, the more committed I became to putting away their abusers, which included the police chaplain, of all people. A man who was beloved by the law enforcement community and used to go out drinking with the cops all the time, he was also a personal friend of mine and Donna's who we saw at civic lunches and other events. I was able to accumulate evidence of his sexual advances toward merchant seamen who came and went from the Port of San Francisco. Similarly, I was able to collect detailed background information on all of the accused pedophile priests and ultimately traced them to the Catholic diocese in Mexico where they'd been stashed. We ended up convicting about a half dozen of them. As for Levada, he made cardinal and Pope Benedict XVI ended up transferring him to the Vatican, where he became the new pope's successor in the post of Prefect of the Congregation for the Doctrine of the Faith, the very position that had spring-boarded Benedict to the papal chair.

The roadblocks put in our path, and all the corruption we encountered along the way, reminded me so much of a drug case. Dealing with the San Francisco archdiocese and the Catholic Church wasn't much different from dealing with South American or Southeast Asian governments you weren't sure you could trust. It was also a matter of facing a system that demeaned our efforts to bring the guilty to justice. More pedophile priests remained free than we were able to prosecute. We didn't have the support of the politicos until after we'd made our cases, and even then people were afraid to speak out, whispering to power instead of shouting down the ugliness that had been allowed to permeate the church.

Not much different than the war on drugs.

I watched as casual users and junkies got stiffer sentences than the kingpins who'd been the source of their drugs. The bishops and cardinals, like William Levada, who protected the priests reminded me of the politicians who curtailed the DEA's efforts into looking at the pharmaceutical industry—Big Pharma—for purposeful overproduction of opiate drugs. The current administrator, I'd heard, had put the kibosh on letting agents charged with getting drugs off the streets go after the pharmaceutical companies putting drugs on the streets, and therein lies another reason why we've been losing this war.

The Drug Enforcement Administration's top guy, the administrator himself, doesn't have to be confirmed by Congress. Unlike the directors of the CIA and FBI, it's more of a political position, and most of those who've held it reflected that. So every time a new presidential administration came in, or the job opened up after the first term or midterms, a new administrator was appointed and the DEA was left to start from scratch again. No continuity, no consistent strategy. The priorities of the administration become personality and politically driven, which is no way to run an agency, never mind win the war on drugs.

Same thing with the post of drug czar. In theory it's a very worthwhile, even necessary position. Not, though, when it's a transient position filled by hacks who are there because of patronage instead of performance. Both the drug czar and administrator for the DEA should serve ten-year terms, like the FBI director does, to assure the kind of consistency of message and continuity of strategy that have been woefully lacking almost since the DEA's formation. Imagine what the right people in those positions could accomplish if left in place for ten years, the progress they could make without starting from scratch maybe five or ten times running. Winning any war starts with picking the right generals. And for the war on drugs we've either not picked the right generals or pulled them out before they could get the job done.

The opiate crisis snuck up on us because we never saw it coming. Even in the district attorney's office, when it came to drugs we were looking at cocaine and heroin. Prescription drugs like opiates just weren't on our radar. Remember, they weren't then and aren't now listed as Schedule One drugs like heroin, cocaine, and meth. We weren't looking at over-the-counter prescription opiates because we had been focused since the time of Auguste Ricord on how to inter-dict foreign drug pipelines and put a stop to the manufacture of illegal drugs at their source. Big Pharma just didn't enter the picture along-side the Golden Triangle, Colombian drug cartels, Afghan poppy fields, or kingpins like Ricord himself, even though it was putting as many drugs out there as any of them, if not far more.

And it isn't even an old problem. Way back in my days working the streets in Philly, we'd busted those pharmacies that had essentially become distribution centers, veritable pill mills, for amphetamines and barbiturates. Remember, that was an ongoing operation we ran that went on for months, years even. It's doubtful the typical DEA administrator or national drug czar would have remained in place long enough to see that through.

That's what I liked so much about working for the DA's office: I felt like I was making a difference, enjoying the freedom to work cases the way I wanted to without fear of being yanked off for political rea-sons. I was seeing firsthand how we should've been fighting the war on drugs on a regular basis instead of a sporadic one. I kept flashing back to my experience building our interdiction programs in South America, only to have the political hack who replaced me go back to square one and blow up everything I'd achieved. How many more kilos of drugs hit the streets in American cities, suburbs, and even rural areas because he'd opened up the very spigots that I'd fought to close?

I didn't have to worry about looking over my shoulder with the DA's office, because I knew I had Terence Hallinan watching my back. This was true even when he handed me a case that the parents of two college students had filed against the San Francisco PD for an incident that occurred on Union Street, where some drunk cops got into a beef with these kids and ended up assaulting them. Not surprisingly, the top cops in the department tried to cover it all up, and a grand jury Hallinan had impaneled ended up returning indictments against the top cops in the department, including the chief of police himself.

"You're a chief too," Terence said to me of the incident that had already become famously referred to as "Fajitagate," since that's what the whole altercation had started over—a bag of takeout fajitas. "So call the chief of police and tell him you're coming down to arrest all three of them."

And that's exactly what we did through the media frenzy that followed. We got them on obstruction of justice charges and all three resigned, even though the charges were ultimately dismissed. I considered that mission accomplished because they'd been held accountable and were ultimately disgraced by their actions.

"I saw the names of the chief of police and the two deputy chiefs," Hallinan recalled at the time upon learning the indictments had come down, as reported in the July 14, 2003, issue of the *New Yorker*. "I felt like the guy who had dropped the bomb on Hiroshima."

The article went on to say that "for the first time in American history, the entire command structure of a major police department had been indicted in a single stroke."

On the lighter side of things, I was also in charge of investigating actor Woody Harrelson after he and other protestors climbed the

Golden Gate Bridge and shut down traffic going to and from Marin County for hours.

"It was not our intention to stop traffic," Woody told the *San Francisco Examiner* in January 1997. "We were up there engaged in a political protest. But we did not stop the traffic. The CHP [California Highway Patrol] did. We can't be blamed for their decision."

No charges were filed and we actually ended up becoming friends and even went out for dinner after the office declined to prosecute the group. I gave him a DEA baseball cap at the restaurant.

"Listen, Woody," I said, "I don't want to see you climbing the Empire State Building or the Brooklyn Bridge wearing this."

"Hey," he said, with his trademark smile, "you never know."

I remained as chief of detectives for the district attorney's office for both of Terence Hallinan's terms, eight years in total, which ended in 2003. That brought my official career in law enforcement to an end, but it didn't end my fight to find a way to win the war on drugs.

Far from it.

CHAPTER TWENTY-TWO

SAN FRANCISCO, 2003

Terence actually ran for another term, and I had every intention of remaining his chief of detectives had he won. But he was trounced by one of his own people, Kamala Harris, whom he'd mentored as an assistant US attorney.

He thought he could win again, thanks to his overwhelming support from the gay and African American communities, in large part because of his stellar history in civil rights that included marching in Selma with Martin Luther King Jr. But Kamala proved too strong, and Terence resisted the advice I and others had given him to spend more time courting the Italian and Chinese communities.

I packed up my office in more ways than one. I was closing in on seventy-five at that point. Even though I didn't feel old, far from it in fact, it wasn't exactly an ideal situation to get the engines running from scratch again. Donna and I remained in the Bay Area for a time, during which I took my old private investigator badge out of storage. I worked some missing persons cases, did a bunch of favors for people, handled some work for celebrities that included investigating the death of David Carradine overseas, and also took on a few assignments from the NFL. That kept me just busy enough, but my attention never strayed that far from drugs.

First and foremost, I noted that more drugs, particularly heroin, seemed to be pouring into the country than ever. That trend was coupled with an inordinate number of heroin deaths as we moved into the mid part of the first decade of the new millennium. What was going on? What had changed?

The prescription opioid crisis caught everyone by surprise, not really resonating even with me until it hit home—literally. The DEA remained a huge monolithic structure that churned and changed slowly. DEA agents were geared, more or less programmed, to look at heroin, cocaine, and crystal meth—the worst of the Schedule One drugs. The opioid craze slipped under the radar. No one saw it coming and, even when the signs started to show up in deaths, hospitalizations, and increased incarcerations, very few saw it for the nationwide trend that it was. If we'd gotten wind of things earlier and dedicated ourselves to dealing with the problem, a shift in priorities could've been made and we might have stopped it.

The opioid crisis once and for all put to bed the mythology that drugs were an urban problem, an African American problem, a Latino problem. Not so anymore. Now the scourge I'd first witnessed sharing that holding cell back in Philadelphia with a bunch of junkies had moved into Middle America. I guess those metaphorical suburban moats hadn't been able to keep out all the alligators. It's even worked its way into America's rural heartland, from the dusty reservations of New Mexico to the farm country of Indiana to the hills of New Hampshire.

From my viewpoint, the response to this crisis, unfortunately, typified how we'd been fighting the war on drugs for too long—coming, inevitably, when it was already too late. We were leading from behind, which is no way to win any war, least of all one as complicated as this one. But there was another societal issue fueling this problem, a far more pressing one.

* * * * *

The fox really had been left to guard the henhouse.

A May 29, 2018, *New York Times* article, headlined "Origins of an Epidemic: Purdue Pharma Knew Its Opioids Were Widely Abused," aptly summarized the opioid crisis this way:

> *Purdue Pharma, the company that planted the seeds of the opioid epidemic through its aggressive marketing of OxyContin, has long claimed it was unaware of the powerful opioid painkiller's growing abuse until years after it went on the market.*
>
> *But a copy of a confidential Justice Department report shows that federal prosecutors investigating the company found that Purdue Pharma knew about "significant" abuse of OxyContin in the first years after the drug's introduction in 1996 and concealed that information.*
>
> *Company officials had received reports that the pills were being crushed and snorted; stolen from pharmacies; and that some doctors were being charged with selling prescriptions, according to dozens of previously undisclosed documents that offer a detailed look inside Purdue Pharma. But the drug maker continued "in the face of this knowledge" to market OxyContin as less prone to abuse and addiction than other prescription opioids, prosecutors wrote in 2006.*
>
> *Based on their findings after a four-year investigation, the prosecutors recommended that three top Purdue Pharma executives be indicted on felony charges, including conspiracy to defraud the United States, that could have sent the men to prison if convicted.*
>
> *But top Justice Department officials in the George W. Bush administration did not support the move, said four lawyers who took part in those discussions or were briefed about them. Instead, the government settled the case in 2007.*

Prosecutors found that the company's sales representatives used the words "street value," "crush," or "snort" in 117 internal notes recording their visits to doctors or other medical professionals from 1997 through 1999.

Sounds crazy, right? Well, no crazier than tobacco companies covering up the fact that they were fully aware of the dangers of smoking for decades before it became common knowledge and accepted dogma. We can't blame Purdue or Big Pharma in general for all seventy thousand lives lost to the current crisis in 2017, but when you have an entire industry turning a blind eye to the ramifications of their actions, even ramping those actions up to increase their bottom line, you've found another enemy in the war on drugs. Add to that the fact the Justice Department didn't deem those actions criminal or serious enough to respond effectively, and it's hard to know who your allies really are in this war.

Big Tobacco had given way to Big Pharma, the similarities in how they went about their respective business strangely dissimilar. The major difference seemed to be that Big Pharma killed its comparable number of victims in much faster fashion.

And there's more. A May 2018 article in the *New York Times Magazine*, called "The Pain Hustlers," was subtitled, "Insys Therapeutics paid millions of dollars to doctors. The company called it a 'speaker program,' but prosecutors now call it something else: a kickback scheme."

The article went on to describe "a major vulnerability in policing the opioid crisis: Doctors have a great deal of power. The FDA regulates drug makers but not practitioners, who enjoy a wide latitude in prescribing that pharmaceutical companies can easily exploit. A respected doctor who advocated eloquently for wider prescribing can quickly become a key opinion leader, invited out on the lucrative lecture circuit. And any doctor who exercises a free hand with opioids can attract a flood of pain patients and income. Fellow doctors rarely blow the whistle, and some state medical boards exercise timid oversight, allowing unethical doctors to continue to operate. An assistant district attorney coping with opioids in upstate New York told me that it's easy to identify a pill-mill doctor, but 'it can take five years to get to that guy.' In the meantime, drug manufacturers are still seeing revenue, and that doctor is still seeing patients, one after another, day after day."

Insys had even figured out a way to manipulate the insurance companies, normally neither kind nor weak sisters when it comes to such things.

"According to a former employee and multiple court filings," the *New York Times Magazine* story continued, "including a manager's guilty plea, the company offered to relieve doctors' offices of insurance hassles and take on the task of getting prescriptions covered. Insys' 'prior authorization specialists'—workers who the company motivated with bonuses—would contact insurers or their contractors, giving the impression they were calling from the prescribing doctor's office. They used what managers called 'the spiel,' which led insurers to believe that patients had cancer when they did not. Sometimes they would falsify medical charts and outright lie, former staff members have acknowledged. [Michael] Babich, the chief executive, was involved in arranging for this unit's phone system to block Caller ID to disguise the fact that calls were not coming from the doctor's office, according to the Boston indictment. The initiative worked. By the following spring, a company estimate pegged the approval rate for commercial insurers at 87 percent."

To summarize the points raised in those two articles, doctors and pharmaceutical companies alike, to varying degrees, are in cahoots to line their pockets with blood money. It's not that they don't know that in 2018, as the upshot of their actions, people are going to die. You want to know why so many thousands of American families have been affected by the opioid crisis? Look no further than the people charged with looking after our health. Thank God we have our duly elected congressional representatives looking out for us.

Oops, maybe not. Take Tom Marino, for example, as the *Washington Post* reported on October 15, 2017:

> *Tom Marino is a four-term Republican member of the House who represents a district in northeastern Pennsylvania that has been hard-hit by the opioid crisis. Yet Marino also has been a friend on Capitol Hill of the giant drug companies that distribute the pain pills that have wreaked so much devastation around the nation.*
>
> *Marino was the chief advocate of the Ensuring Patient Access and Effective Drug Enforcement Act, which requires the government to meet a higher bar before taking certain enforcement actions.*
>
> *The Drug Enforcement Administration fought against the bill for years, but finally relented last year after a leadership change at the agency. The new law makes it virtually impossible for the DEA to freeze suspicious narcotic shipments from the companies, according to internal agency and Justice Department documents and an independent assessment by the DEA's chief administrative law judge in a soon-to-be-published law review article. That powerful tool had allowed the agency to immediately prevent drugs from reaching the street.*

Wait, it gets better. President Donald Trump wanted to *promote* Representative Marino and make him director of the Office of National Drug Control Policy, the nation's drug czar. Kind of like hiring a vampire to guard the blood bank.

Although action was immediately taken to repeal the absurdly named Ensuring Patient Access and Effective Drug Enforcement Act of 2016, and Marino ultimately withdrew his nomination, the damage had already been done.

"This law," Senator Claire McCaskill said at the time, "has significantly affected the government's ability to crack down on opioid distributors that are failing to meet their obligations and endangering our communities."

The *Washington Post* called it " the crowning achievement of a multifaceted campaign by the drug industry to weaken aggressive DEA enforcement efforts against drug distribution companies that were supplying corrupt doctors and pharmacists who peddled narcotics to the black market. The industry worked behind the scenes with lobbyists and key members of Congress, pouring more than $1 million into their election campaigns."

Sure, the DEA fought against passage of that absurd law. But a June 2018 report on *60 Minutes* revealed the staggering number of former agents now working for Big Pharma, using their knowledge of the territory to help the very drug manufacturers they were once paid to watch over map out a course for skirting the law to sell more pills.

It makes you wonder if the perpetual revolving door at the Drug Enforcement Administration headquarters was installed on purpose. Keep changing administrators through perpetual reorganizations, while replacing the best and most experienced chiefs and directors with political hacks and cronies…. Now that's a recipe for disaster.

When that new DEA administrator was named in 1982, I learned I'd been reassigned to New York via teletype; the guy didn't even have the courtesy to call or meet me. I guess he wanted to put his own stamp on the agency, but no one had any idea what his marching orders were or where they'd originated. I figured he must've had a mandate from somewhere and felt utterly disrespected, the sum total of my years of experience disregarded. I'd worked in some of the worst international hotbeds of crime and drug dealing across the globe and had never been treated like this in any of those cities and countries. And the end result didn't just include me and all my experience; plenty of other experienced veterans of the drug wars were summarily axed or reassigned, flushing our years of experience and knowledge down the toilet to serve a competing agenda.

And me thinking we had only one agenda: get the drugs off the streets. But thirty-five years later, in 2017, more than seventy thousand lives were lost to overdoses alone.

JOSEPH R. BIDEN, Jr., DELAWARE, CHAIRMAN

EDWARD M. KENNEDY MASSACHUSETTS   STROM THURMOND, SOUTH CAROLINA
HOWARD M. METZENBAUM, OHIO   ORRIN G. HATCH, UTAH
DENNIS DeCONCINI, ARIZONA   ALAN K. SIMPSON, WYOMING
PATRICK J. LEAHY VERMONT   CHARLES E. GRASSLEY IOWA
HOWELL HEFLIN, ALABAMA   ARLEN SPECTER, PENNSYLVANIA
PAUL SIMON, ILLINOIS   GORDON J. HUMPHREY NEW HAMPSHIRE
HERBERT KOHL, WISCONSIN

RONALD A. KLAIN, CHIEF COUNSEL
DIANA HUFFMAN, STAFF DIRECTOR
JEFFREY J. PECK, GENERAL COUNSEL
TERRY L. WOOTEN, MINORITY CHIEF COUNSEL
AND STAFF DIRECTOR

United States Senate

COMMITTEE ON THE JUDICIARY
WASHINGTON, DC 20510-6275

October 3, 1989

Mr. Daniel J. Addario
Addario and Associates
16 California Street, Suite 205
San Francisco, California 94111

Dear Mr. Addario:

    Thank you for your letter and for the enclosed articles regarding your efforts to fight the scourge of drugs. I appreciate your taking the time to contact me.

    I support wholeheartedly your desire to make the "Drug Czar" position as effective as possible, and I will certainly keep your ideas in mind as I continue my efforts to fight drug abuse.

    Again, thank you for your letter.

        Sincerely,

        Joseph R. Biden, Jr.
        Chairman

One of dozens of letters Dan received over the years from politicians in response to his unheeded suggestions on how to win the War on Drugs.

I didn't take the end of my professional career lying down. I figured I could still make a difference by writing elected officials and politicians to share my experience and suggestions. Some sent me polite boilerplate acknowledgments of receipt. Most sent me nothing. None asked for more details or the actual plans I was putting forth to reverse the tide in the war on drugs and actually start winning it. They didn't seem to care that my own son had been a casualty of that war, maybe because theirs hadn't.

Don't get me wrong: I think plenty of these politicos want to do something. Some have even tried. But their efforts are inevitably stymied by lobbyists and their fellow pols pursuing a different agenda. Many in Washington call that just the way business gets done.

I call it corruption.

I call it proof Washington isn't truly committed to winning the war on drugs. And if they were, they could turn this page and find out how.

SLAYING THE DRAGON

"The U.S. War on Drugs," the Cato Institute reported on April 12, 2017, "like the ill-fated war on alcohol of the early 20th century, is a prime example of disastrous policy, naked self-interest, and repeated ignorance on the part of elected officials and other policy makers. From its inception, the drug war has repeatedly led to waste, fraud, corruption, violence, and death."

There you have it, as they say. But that hasn't stopped me from fighting this war for as long as I have, and I suspect I'm still fighting it as you read this book. I've served for over a decade on the police commission under Mayor Dana Outlaw in my adopted hometown of New Bern, North Carolina. I do this to stay involved in law enforcement, even though I'm well into my eighties, and to keep my hand in the game. I've written letters to a slew of political officials over the past fifteen years—from Joe Biden, to Jeff Sessions, to Chris Christie, to Senator Thom Tillis, to Congressman Walter Jones, to Chuck Schumer, to Nancy Pelosi, to President Trump, just to name a few—and have never received anything back but lip service. If I'd gotten anything of substance in return, I'd tell them what I'm about to tell you:

Ten of the steps we need to take, and strategies we need to pursue, to win the war on drugs.

Reform the DEA

The top position of administrator needs to be filled by a person with the proper credentials that include prosecutorial or police command experience, as opposed to being a political appointee. Someone with a track record of managing law enforcement personnel instead of being a partisan hack. He or she needs to have the proper credentials and be informed about the issues going in. Beyond that, as I've alluded to before, he or she needs to be vetted by Congress, the way it is for the CIA and FBI, instead of just appointed to the position. And, like the FBI, future directors need to serve ten-year terms to insulate them and their efforts from the whims of administrations whose ever-changing policies, dynamics, and agendas blow in the wind. Right now, sadly, we have far higher standards for an entry-level DEA agent than the person running the entire DEA. And, thanks to those agents, a huge portion of drugs are kept off the streets and a lot of lives are saved. That doesn't make the problem any less in need of addressing, only to raise the issue of how much worse things would be if not for the dedicated agents who followed in the footsteps of me and others that were first to carry the DEA badge.

Similarly, to insulate the agency from outside interference and constant reorganization, we need leaders and administrators like Harry Anslinger, Henry L. Giordano, Nelson B. Coon, Charles Siragusa (a.k.a. "Charlie Cigars"), Jack Cusack, John Finlator, Bill Durkin, John Ingersoll, Henry Dogan, John Bartels, and George Belk. I worked with all of them during my tenure and consider myself much the better for it, as is the country.

Promote the Drug Czar

As mentioned above, every time a new president is sworn in, the effort fighting the war on drugs goes back to square one, lacking any sense of continuity whatsoever. Instead, the post of drug czar needs to be an official, recognized cabinet-level position that similarly serves in ten-year terms to provide consistent oversight of everyone involved in narcotics interdiction, from Customs, to the DEA, to the FBI, and even the CIA operating overseas. The czar needs to be a man or woman of sufficient stature to be able to go head-to-head with the directors of those other agencies in order to best proactively head off the kind of internecine conflicts that have crippled our efforts at fighting this scourge in the past. He or she needs a direct line of authority over all of these agencies when it comes to their efforts at drug enforcement.

Pay for Crop Substitution and Subsidies

Neither heroin nor cocaine is produced in this country to any degree whatsoever. We know where it comes from, the fields where the coca and poppies are grown across foreign countries from South America to Southeast Asia. The international nature of the problem means we need the United Nations to get involved and join the United States in aggressively pursuing a crop substitution initiative. But such things don't happen overnight and will require a lot of funding, most of which I suspect will have to originate in Washington. That funding would include subsidies to compensate foreign farmers for as long as the transition from coca or poppies to something like coffee takes place. A lot of money? Yes. As much as the over fifty billion dollars spent annually fighting this war, far more than that when the human costs of this scourge are added in, though? Not even close. Call it about the most worthwhile investment in our future we could possibly make.

Aggressively Pursue Eradication

We, or the host countries, know where the manufacturing plants that use the raw product to produce heroin and cocaine are located. We can't, of course, bomb them ourselves. But we can, as we did in the Golden Triangle during my tenure as regional director there, give the host governments the funding and ordnance they need to get the job done so the drugs never reach the streets of America. This model would be akin to that episode I described in Thailand, where our government supplied General Pao with the firepower he needed to wipe out the jungle-based drug manufacturing labs on the border with Burma. This is a relatively drastic move, but we've got to think out of the box to at least mitigate this scourge. And that means pressuring the host countries to follow the Thai example. Imagine shutting down the Panama Canal, for example, if Panama were to shirk its duties. Or to engage severe border restrictions with Mexico, of the kind President Nixon used to constrain the cartels, if the Mexican government refuses to get tough enough.

It's also vital to go after the precursors, the chemical ingredients and compounds, necessary to turn poppies into heroin and coca plants into cocaine. According to Recovery.org, "Coca plants are grown, refined, and processed in local areas, often in protected sites such as native reserves, national parks, and areas along the border, which are off limits to aerial spraying efforts to kill the crops."

Those limits should be lifted, and at the same time chemicals like potassium permanganate, required for the purification process, need to be treated with the severity of radioactive isotopes. Sure, the processors will ultimately find workarounds, but how many lives might the resulting setback save because fewer drugs would be reaching the streets?

Pressure Foreign Governments

Going after the source of drugs is equivalent to cutting the head off the dragon—that's the way to kill it. I say, if all else fails, deny the governments in question foreign aid, impose sanctions, and do anything else it takes to get them on board. In that respect, I think the carrot would be a lot more effective than the stick here in terms of creating policy that rewards countries that cooperate, while actively punishing countries that don't. The DEA maintains a very effective training division that can teach foreign countries how to get this done. And their buying into the program should result in an increase in general foreign aid. No, we're not going to get 100 percent cooperation, but you settle for the best you can get because 10 percent of something is better than 100 percent of nothing. The likes of dictators like Manuel Noriega can be either a relentless ally or prickly foe. The choice, really, is ours.

Legalize Marijuana

In *Takedown* (Forge Books, March 2016), an excellent study of a drug operation written by one of the foremost undercover cops in the country, Jeff Buck discusses a career spent making cases against a slew of marijuana dealers.

"The more marijuana use becomes socially acceptable," Buck writes, "the more money organized crime will make from it. Kind of like Prohibition when bars and speakeasies fattened the wallets of countless wise guys by buying booze from them. You end up with more people getting high and messing up their lives, while a different brand of wise guys fatten their bank accounts. People say it's a victimless crime, right? Well, in a word, wrong. Because the low-level dealer from whom a thirty or forty-year-old business and family man is probably buying kicks that money back up the food chain. All the way up to the Mexican cartels or Hell's Angels who use it to expand their empire deeper into other criminal pursuits like human trafficking, prostitution, gun running, even in some cases terrorism."

Buck is unintentionally making a case not only to declassify marijuana as a Schedule One drug, but also to legalize it. After all, right now the profits from all those illegal weed sales are going into the pockets of drug dealers. Legalize it and that same money will go toward buffering local, state, and even federal coffers to be dedicated, at least in part, to efforts aimed at fighting the drugs like prescription opiates and heroin that are actually killing people. Far too many resources are spent on efforts to interdict marijuana distribution when those resources would be far better spent elsewhere. Beyond that, according to a *Washington Post* article on January 10, 2018, a study by New Frontier Data estimated that "legalizing marijuana nationwide would create at least $132 billion in tax revenue." That's twenty-five times more than the entire budget submitted by the Trump administration in 2018 to fight the war on drugs.

Engage in Treatment Instead of Criminalization

More and more states and municipalities are opting for aggressive treatment strategies instead of jailing first-time drug users. Like drug courts, for example, dedicated exclusively to drug crimes to make sure the perpetrator's punishment is considered within the totality of that individual's plight, prison being a last resort instead of a first. Putting these people in jail accomplishes nothing other than making it more likely their drug use will resume once they're released, or even continue while they're incarcerated, given the successful drug smuggling efforts into penal institutions nationwide.

Of course, in the case of victims of the drug war like Dan, no one close to him, no one who loved him, had any clue he was addicted. So before we can treat addicts like my son, we need to be increasingly vigilant with our relatives and friends, keeping a close eye on any behavior that may suggest something could be awry. That's not an easy thing to do now and it never will be. But at the very least we can follow the modern-day maxim of terrorism: "If you see something, say something."

Hold Doctors and Big Pharma Accountable

This new, post-modern generation of dealers and distributors need to be held accountable in a way that harms them the most: in the pocketbook. Take what's happening in the state of Rhode Island, as the *Providence Journal* wrote on March 26, 2018:

> *Twenty-six Rhode Island cities and towns are suing major drug manufacturers, accusing them of conspiring to generate enormous profits while spurring the nationwide opioid epidemic.*
>
> *Warwick, Cranston, North Providence, Charlestown, Jamestown and a host of other towns filed suit this week in U.S. District Court arguing the AmerisourceBergen Drug Corp., Johnson & Johnson, and its subsidiary Janssen Pharmaceuticals, and other drug companies engaged in a racketeering conspiracy by manufacturing and marketing the powerful narcotics at devastating societal costs.*
>
> *The lawsuit asserts that the companies—the five largest producers of prescription narcotics and three largest wholesale drug distributors—engaged in deceptive marketing campaigns aimed at increasing opioid use. The cities and towns say they seek to "eliminate the hazard to public health and safety" and abate the nuisance caused by the companies. They are seeking unspecified damages.*

The smallest state in the union, essentially, is showing the rest of us the way, and neighboring Massachusetts was quick to take Rhode Island's response one step further by becoming the first state ever to actually target a drug company's executives, in this case "sixteen former executives and board members, including CEO Craig Landau and members of the Sackler family, which owns [Purdue Pharmaceuticals]," according to NBC News.

"I promised to find out what these companies knew and when they knew it and the extent to which they misled patients into think[ing] their drugs were actually safe," Attorney General Maura Healey said, as also reported by NBC. "We found that Purdue misled doctors, patients and the public about their dangerous opioids, including OxyContin."

The suit, according to Boston's NPR news station WBUR, was filed on behalf of over 670 Massachusetts residents who were victims of opioid overdoses.

The DEA has already significantly increased its efforts to review all narcotics prescriptions in search of those that reveal something amiss, anomalies that suggest the kind of overprescribing and manufacturing abuse that have turned the United States into a nation of addicts. Remember, my own experience on the streets of Philly in the 1950s included busting a string of pharmacies doing just that. If it could be done then, it can be done with far more effectiveness now. The drug pushers of today often wear Brooks Brothers suits or white lab coats, a fact we must acknowledge, even as we chop this head off the dragon too.

"Judge Dan Aaron Polster of the Northern District of Ohio," the *New York Times* reported on March 6, 2018, "has perhaps the most daunting legal challenge in the country: resolving more than 400 federal lawsuits brought by cities, counties and Native American tribes against central figures in the national opioid tragedy, including makers of the prescription painkillers, companies that distribute them, and pharmacy chains that sell them."

On an episode of *60 Minutes* that ran originally in 2017 entitled "The Whistleblower," former DEA assistant administrator Joe Rannazzisi labeled the drug industry as "out of control." He went on to say that "this is an industry that allowed millions of drugs to go into bad pharmacies and doctors' offices, that distributed them out to people who had no legitimate need for these drugs."

Rannazzisi and others point the finger at not just doctors and Big Pharma but also the three largest distribution companies responsible for getting prescription opiates into pharmacies. These distributors—AmerisourceBergen, Cardinal Health, and McKesson—are essentially, in Rannazzisi's and my mind, "creating one-stop shopping for illicit narcotics." In one example cited on that same *60 Minutes* episode, in a single year, eleven million prescription pain pills were shipped to Mingo County, West Virginia, which boasts a population of only 25,000 people in total. That's 440 pills per every resident in a single year! And as long as Congress continues to write laws crafted to a large extent by ex-DEA lawyers turned lobbyists, those distributors will be able to continue such actions with impunity. Winning the war on drugs requires both clamping down on such distributors and shutting off the spigot that allows former DEA officials to provide counsel to them on how best to game the system and avoid prosecution.

Strengthen the Borders

Mexico remains the primary port of entry for illicit drugs. And, no, building a wall isn't going to do anything to slow that traffic. It might do something to reduce illegal immigration, but not illegal drugs.

This isn't a Democratic or Republican problem, it's a societal problem, and we need a unified effort to encourage and aid Mexico's efforts to stem the flow rooted in the tremendous power and resources of the cartels. Remember, the flow of drugs shrunk demonstratively after Nixon closed the US-Mexican border for a brief stretch, suggesting that we need to mount more of an economic argument here whereby Mexico sees its vast array of imports into the United States curtailed if drugs remains one of them. The people in power who have the capacity to do something about the cartels must be provided with the motivation required to do so in both a carrot and a stick approach.

Of course, those cartels traffic almost exclusively in cash, American dollars. It's another powerful argument to change the color of the currency, on at least our largest bills, in order to render all their fifties, hundreds, and maybe even twenties worthless. Money makes up the head of the snake in this world. Cut the head off and it can still bite for a time, but ultimately the snake dies.

Go After Police and Prison Corruption

The August 16, 2017 issue of the *Atlanta Journal-Constitution* featured the headline "46 Georgia Prison Guards Sentenced for Transporting Drugs," followed by a story that included:

> *One by one, dozens of Georgia correctional officers have gone from being guards to being the guarded.*
>
> *The last of 46 one-time prison guards was sentenced Thursday for using their uniforms and badges to smuggle what they believed to be cocaine and methamphetamine for the inmate Ghost Face gang. They are now prisoners themselves, much like the men and women they were once paid to watch.*
>
> *The operation—much of it captured on video—is one of the biggest corruption scandals ever to hit Georgia's prison system.*
>
> *"We knew it was a problem but we didn't appreciate the severity," Kurt Erskine, first assistant U.S. attorney, said of the investigation.*
>
> *The arrests sprang from a broader 2014 probe into corruption at two state lockups in Gwinnett and Mitchell counties, where inmates were running scams using cell phones officers had smuggled in to them. It grew to involve 130 people at nine prisons around the state.*
>
> *Once federal and prison agents started looking, "one institution would lead to another institution," Erskine said. Federal authorities launched an elaborate sting operation in which an informant offered prison guards cash for moving what they believed to be drugs. Many took them up on it.*

To put it bluntly, putting more corrupt guards away, making an example of them as was done in Georgia, makes for the best deterrent to corrupt behavior.

A different brand of corruption continues to riddle various levels of law enforcement. It can be spotted in the form of expensive cars in the driveways of homes, often second or beach homes, of police officers not making a salary sufficient to afford either. So as drug testing has drastically curtailed the use of both recreational and performance-enhancing drugs in professional sports, I would advocate for comparably random financial audits of law enforcement officers. And I would add a provision that all law enforcement officers be subjected to a regular review every five years. Officers have signed off on drug testing in any number of states and municipalities, so why not sign off on financial audits as well? No law enforcement official should have a problem with that, unless he or she has something to hide. Under this scenario, when you take the job you'd know exactly what you are getting into. A financial review can only flag something, after all, if there's something to flag.

* * * * *

It's been a while since I've visited Dan's grave. It lies in a Northern California cemetery outside of San Francisco beneath a shady grove of elm and maple trees. The inscription on my son's grave marker tells so much of the story of the war on drugs that rages on today:

DANIEL ADDARIO 1959–1993

I once heard a wonderfully inspirational speech about how the real sum of a person's life lies in the dash between the date of their birth and the date of their death. That dash should contain so much more in my son's case, and in the case of countless other sons and daughters who've fallen as casualties to this war.

I keep fighting, but it's not always easy, and sometimes life gets in the way. My middle son Bobby, the great tennis player, died in

2013 of inflammatory bowel disease. My first wife, Joy, had passed away seven years earlier. We never lost touch with each other, even as distance came to increasingly divide us. Mark, a warrant officer in the US Army, still lives in Orinda when he's stateside in a condominium Joy purchased after selling our house in the hills.

All told, I've now chased the dragon for more than half a century. I've won some battles, lost some battles. Seen the dragon weakened, but never quite slain. And I don't intend to stop until it's taken its last breath and claimed its last victim.

ACKNOWLEDGMENTS

My deepest thanks to the friends, associates, and fellow agents who aided my efforts and steered me in the right direction, helping me fight the good fight. It's impossible to list every one of them, but this representative sampling is a testament to them all.

John Finlator, Congressman, Charles Rangel, Robert Mueller, Ed Guy, District Attorney Terence Hallinan, Nelson B. Coon, Bill Jennings, Harry Anslinger Henry Giordano, Paul Avery, Jack Ingersoll, Russ Coughlin, John Bartels, Rob Hasler, Jerry Jenson, Paul Rust, Chief Thomas McDermott, Herb Cain, the Honorable Frank Rizzo, Warren Hinkle, Captain Jack Kerrigan , Reno Rapagnani, Ray Smith, Billy Hunter, James Browning, San Francisco Chief of Police Fred Lau, Sonny Grasso, Eddie Egan, and Frank Waters (aka "Frankie Black"). Jim Beckner, Reynaldo Cantu, Fred Ford, Doris Fanning, Debra Hayes, Jean Devers, B Francis Lederer, Frank Macolini, Henry Dogan, Jim Richie, Arthur Lewis, Luciano Repeto, Tom Duffy.

And a special thanks to this novice author's Girl Friday #2, Peggy Barnes who knows her way around a computer the way I know mine around a drug bust.

ABOUT THE AUTHORS

As the highest-ranking field agent for the DEA under five presidents, **Dan Addario** fought against some of the world's biggest international drug rings, directing the war on drugs in South America and the Golden Triangle. Fueled by the death of his own son to an opiate overdose, he continues to fight that war today as a civilian.

Jon Land is the award-winning, *USA Today* bestselling author of forty-six books, including nine titles in the critically acclaimed Caitlin Strong series, the most recent of which, *Strong to the Bone*, won the 2018 International Book Award for Mystery and Thriller and the 2017 American Book Fest Award for Best Mystery. He is also the author of four acclaimed works of nonfiction that include *No Surrender*, which won the 2017 International Book Award and *1st and Forever* which won the 2018 American Book Fest Award. Both titles were also published by Post Hill Press. He lives in Providence, Rhode Island, and can be reached at jonlandbooks.com or on Twitter @jondland.

Lindsay Preston has written numerous nonfiction works for some of the most prominent figures in the world. She is the co-author of *Takedown* and *Not Even A Number*. She is also the creator of Writingroom.com, forging a community for writers. She lives in Chagrin Falls, Ohio with her young daughter.